The Journal of Human Sexuality

Executive Editor:
George A. Rekers, Ph.D.

Editor-in-Chief:
J. Stanley Oakes Jr.

Managing Editor:
John Gay

Publisher:
Lewis and Stanley

For ordering information for this publication, please call 972-713-7130,
Monday through Friday, 8 a.m. to 5 p.m. Central Standard Time.

The Journal of Human Sexuality is published by Lewis and Stanley. Please address your comments, suggestions, and requests concerning *The Journal of Human Sexuality* to: Lewis and Stanley, 3440 Sojourn Drive, Suite 200, Carrollton, TX 75006 Phone: (972) 713-7130 Fax: (972) 713-7670 E-Mail: lewisstanley@clm.org

In this age, in this country, public sentiment is everything. With it, nothing can fail; against it, nothing can succeed.
Whoever molds public sentiment goes deeper than he who enacts statutes, or pronounces judicial decisions.
—Abraham Lincoln

The Gay Gene?

by Jeffrey Satinover, M.D.

On July 15, 1993, National Public Radio (NPR) made a dramatic announcement on stations across the country: Was a team of scientists at the National Institutes of Health on the trail of a gene that causes homosexuality? Their report would be published the next day in *Science,* one of the two most prestigious scientific research journals in the world.[1]

The discussion that followed explained for the listening public the implications of these findings for social attitudes toward homosexuality and for public policy concerning it. Science was on the verge of proving what many had long argued: that homosexuality is innate, genetic and therefore unchangeable—a normal and commonplace variant of human nature. In the light of these findings, surely only the bigoted or ignorant could condemn it in any way.

Shortly after the announcement, amidst a well-orchestrated blizzard of press discussions, there ensued the watershed legal battle over "Proposition 2" in Colorado. (This popularly enacted legislation precluded making sexual orientation the basis of "privileged class" minority status, a status conferred previously only on the basis of immutable factors such as race.)

Among the many crucial issues raised by the legislation was the question as to whether homosexuality was indeed normal, innate and unchangeable. One prominent researcher testified to the court, "I am 99.5% certain that homosexuality is genetic." But this personal opinion was widely misunderstood as "homosexuality is 99.5% genetic," implying that research had demonstrated this. Certainly, that was the message promulgated by NPR's report on the recent research, and by all the discussions that followed. In a few weeks, *Newsweek* would emblazon across its cover the phrase that would stick in the public mind as the final truth about homosexuality: "Gay Gene?"

Of course, just near the end of the NPR discussion, certain necessary caveats were fleetingly added. But only an expert knew what they meant—that the research actually showed nothing whatever in the way of what was being discussed. The vast majority of listeners would think that homosexuality had been all but conclusively proven to be "genetic." But the real question is whether or not there is such a "gay gene."

In fact, there is not, and the research being promoted as proving that there is provides no supporting evidence. How can this be? In order to understand what is really going on, one needs to understand some little-known features of the emerging study of *behavioral genetics* (much subtler than the genetics of simple, "Mendelian" traits such as eye color).

When it comes to questions of the genetics of any behavior—homosexuality included—all of the following statements are likely to be at least roughly true:

1. Such and such a behavior "is genetic";
2. There are no genes that produce the behavior;
3. The genes associated with the behavior are found on such and such a chromosome;
4. The behavior is significantly heritable;
5. The behavior is not inherited.

The scientific distinctions that make these seeming contradictions perfectly reasonable and consistent seem completely misunderstood by the media who report on them.

For example, in response to the "gay gene" research, the *Wall Street Journal* headlined their report (which appeared the next day), "Research Points Toward a Gay Gene."[2] A subheading of the *Journal* article stated, "Normal Variation"—leaving the casual reader with the impression that the research led to this conclusion. It did not, nor could it have. The subhead alluded to nothing more than the chief researcher's personal, unsubstantiated *opinion* that homosexuality, as he put it, "is a normal variant of human behavior." Even the *New York Times,* in its more moderate front-page article, "Report Suggests Homosexuality is Linked to Genes," noted that other researchers warned against over-interpreting the work, "or taking it to mean anything as simplistic as that the 'gay gene' had been found."

At end of the *Wall Street Journal* article, at the bottom of the last paragraph on the last page deep within the paper, a prominent geneticist was quoted for his reactions to the research. He observed that "the gene...may be involved in something other than sexual behavior. *For example, it may be that the supposed gene is only 'associated' with homosexuality, rather than a 'cause' of it.*"

This rather cryptic comment would be most difficult to understand without the needed scientific background. Yet it is the most critical distinction in the entire article; indeed, it renders the findings almost entirely worthless. Why bury and fail to explain what it means? Perhaps the motives were innocent, but in fact, the belief that homosexuality is "biological" or "genetic" causes people to develop more positive attitudes toward it. They need not have the foggiest understanding of what "biological" or "genetic" really mean in order to change their view:

> 105 volunteer[s]...were exposed to one of three...conditions....[T]he experimental group read a summary...emphasizing a biological component of homosexual orientation....[O]ne control group read a summary...focusing on the absence of hormonal differences between homosexual and heterosexual men. [A]nother control group w[as] not exposed to either article....As predicted, subjects in the experimental group had significantly lower[3] scores [more positive attitudes toward homosexuals] than subjects in the control groups.[4]

And:

> Analysis indicated that subjects who believed that homosexuals are "born that way" held significantly more positive attitudes toward homosexuals than subjects who believed that homosexuals "choose to be that way" and/or "learn to be that way."[5]

What was actually going in the study the media was trumpeting? Dean Hamer and his colleagues had performed a kind of behavioral genetics study now becoming widespread—the so-called "linkage study." Researchers identify a behavioral trait that runs in a family and then look to see whether there is a chromosomal variant in the genetic material of that family, and if that variant is more frequent in the family members who have the trait.

To the uninitiated, a positive finding ("correlation" or "association" of a genetic structure with a behavioral trait) is taken to mean that the trait "is genetic"—that is, *inherited.*

In fact, it means absolutely nothing of the sort, and it should be emphasized that there is virtually no human trait without innumerable such correlations. We will see shortly just how this is can be so. The most important take-home messages will be these:

(1) All the research that has been done on homosexuality has been selectively trumpeted through the press in carefully crafted form in order to shape public opinion—hence public policy—in predictable ways. The research itself means almost nothing.

(2) The research projects that would *truly* mean something are scarcely being done because they would all explicitly or tacitly lead to but one end highly undesirable to activists: a method or methods for preventing homosexuality or changing it with ever-increasing efficacy; and to one conclusion: homosexuality *per se* is not inherited.

(3) Most of the research has been hastily and often sloppily done—but this point is a distraction. Even were it superb, the findings would still mean almost nothing.

(4) To whatever extent this research has been good enough to generate valid conclusions at all, these conclusions are precisely the opposite of what is claimed in the press.

Before we talk about specifics, here is what serious scientists think about the recent behavior-caused-by-genes research. From *Science,* 1994:

> Time and time again, scientists have claimed that particular genes or chromosomal regions are associated with behavioral traits, only to withdraw their findings when they were not replicated. "Unfortunately," says Yale's [Dr. Joel] Gelernter, "it's hard to come up with many" findings linking specific genes to complex human behaviors that have been replicated. "...All were announced with great fanfare; all were greeted unskeptically in the popular press; all are now in disrepute."[6]

A scientist at Washington University School of Medicine calculated what would be required for such a replication. He:

> ...projected that if the trait [in question] was 50% heritable...detecting [just] one of [its] genes would require studying 175 families—that is, almost 2000 people.[7] Replicati[on] would require studying 781 families—another 8000 people.... [E]ach additional gene (for a polygenic trait), researchers would need...the whole business again. "Suddenly you're talking about tens of thousands of people and years of work and millions of dollars."[8]

Nothing even remotely close to this has been done with respect to homosexuality.

Using arguable-at-best methods, two American activists recently published studies showing that if one of a pair of identical twins is homosexual, the odds that the other one is, too, are less than 50% (the study examined a few dozens of pairs). On this basis, they argue that "homosexuality is genetic." British researchers generated comparable results in a similar study. Their conclusion? The surprisingly low odds that both twins were homosexual:

> ...confirmed that genetic factors are insufficient explanation for the development of sexual orientation.[9]

Two Columbia University researchers (who have published the most comprehensive research summary on the subject to date) note the unexpectedly:

> ...large proportion of monozygotic twins who [did not share] homosexuality despite sharing not only their genes but also their prenatal and familial environments.[10] The...[50% odds]...for homosexuality among the identical twins could be entirely accounted for by the increased similarity of their developmental experiences. In our opinion, the major finding of that study is that 48 percent of identical twins who were reared together [and where at least one was homosexual] were discordant for sexual orientation.[11]

Two other genetics researchers (one heads one of the largest genetics departments in the country, the other is at Harvard) comment:

> ...recent studies seeking a genetic basis for homosexuality suggest that...we may be in for a new molecular phrenology, rather than true scientific progress and insight into behavior.

> While the authors interpreted their findings as evidence for a genetic basis for homosexuality, we think that the data in fact provide strong evidence for the influence of the environment.[12]

The author of the lead article on genes and behavior in a special issue of *Science* notes:

> ...the growing understanding that the interaction of genes and environment is much more complicated than the simple "violence genes" and "intelligence genes" touted in the popular press. Indeed, *renewed appreciation of environmental factors is one of the chief effects of the increased belief in genetics' effects on behavior* [my emphasis]. The same data that show the effects of genes also point to the enormous influence of non-genetic factors.[13]

The director of the Center for Developmental and Health Genetics at Pennsylvania State University comments:

> Research into heritability is the best demonstration I know of the importance of the environment.

(Note the term "heritability;" we will be returning to it in detail as it lies at the heart of much confusion).

With regard to the work announced by NPR, genetics researchers from Yale, Columbia and Louisiana State Universities noted that:

> Much of the discussion of this finding [of a purported gene locus for homosexuality] has focused on its social and political ramifications. [But] inconsistencies...suggest that this finding should be interpreted cautiously....
>
> The results are not consistent with any genetic model....neither of these differences [between homosexuality in maternal versus paternal uncles or cousins] is statistically significant....small sample sizes make these data compatible with a range of...hypotheses.
>
> [T]he...data...present no consistent support for the...results.[14]

By contrast to their public policy statements, the researchers responded carefully as follows:

> We did not say that [the chromosome segment under study] "underlies" sexuality, only that it contributes to it in some families. Nor have we said that [it] represents a "major" gene, only that its influence is statistically detectable in the population that we studied.[15]

Ignoring possible flaws in the research, have the researchers actually pointed to this more modest claim with any degree of certainty? In fact, they have not—as they themselves acknowledge, but in language that will surely evade general understanding—and that will continue to be avoided by the press:

> ...the question of the appropriate significance level to apply to a non-Mendelian trait such as sexual orientation is problematic.[16]

English translation: "It is not possible to know what the findings mean, if anything, since sexual orientation cannot possibly be inherited the way eye-color is." Thus, to their fellow scientists, the researchers properly acknowledge what every serious researcher knows, but the public does not.

Complex behavioral traits are the product of multiple genetic and environmental antecedents, with 'environment' meaning not only the social environment but also such factors as the 'flux of hormones during development, whether you were lying on your right or left side in the womb and a whole parade of other things'...the relationships among genes and environment probably have a somewhat different effect on someone in Salt lake City than if that person were growing up in New York City.[17]

English translation: "You're more likely to become gay growing up in Manhattan than in Utah among Mormons and Christian fundamentalists, even if everything else is the same, including genes."

Unfortunately, anyone who is so disposed can readily offer the public partial truths which are seriously misleading. This is so only in part because of an easily led or poorly educated press. The major reason is really that the ideas being cooked beyond recognition once they leave the labs are inherently complex, even if originally formulated and presented properly. There are no "lite," soundbite versions of behavioral genetics that are not fundamentally in error in one way or another.

Nonetheless, if one grasps at least some of the basics, in simple form, it will be possible to see exactly why the current research into homosexuality means so little—and will continue to mean little even should the quality of the research methods improve—so long as it remains driven by political, rather than scientific objectives.

There are really only two major principles that need to be carefully assimilated in order to see through public relations distortions to the actual meaning of recent research. They are as follows:

1. *Heritable* does not mean *inherited*.
2. Meaningful genetics research identifies and then focuses on traits that *are* directly *inherited*. One prominent genetics researcher (discussing a matter unrelated to homosexuality, but equally frustrated with the bad science reporting) flatly calls the question of heritability "trivial."

Heritable Does Not Mean Inherited

Heritability studies can be done on almost any human trait—physical, behavioral, emotional, etc.—and will show positive results. That is, almost every human characteristic you can think of is in significant measure *heritable* (thus discussing it is "trivial"). But few human behavioral traits are directly inherited the way simple physiological traits are (e.g., eye color). *Inherited* means "determined directly by genes," with little or no way of changing the trait by choice, or by preventing it, or by modifying the environment in which the trait has emerged (or is more likely to emerge).

Here is a simple hypothetical example, but it is 100% plausible. It tracks the kinds of studies that have been done with innumerable other traits, including homosexuality. (But only in the area of homosexuality has the meaning of such studies been so badly distorted).

Suppose that for political reasons you want to demonstrate that there is a "basketball gene" that "makes" people become basketball players ("BBPs"). (Please suspend your immediate, correct understanding that the idea is absurd.) To make your case you would use the same methods as with homosexuality. These methods fall into three categories, and represent important forms of preliminary research when investigating any trait: (1) twin studies; (2) brain dissections; (3) gene "linkage" studies.

Twin Studies

The basic idea in twin studies is to show that the more genetically similar are two people, the more likely it is that they will share the trait you are studying. So, you create a study set of pairs of people, divided into categories according to how genetically similar they are, as follows:

Pair Type	Degree of Similarity (% same genes)
Identical Twins	100%
Fraternal Twins	50%
Non-Twin Siblings	50%
Unrelated People	<5%

The most similar are identical twins, the next most similar are fraternal twins (who are on average as different as non-twin brothers or sisters, but no more so), the least similar are unrelated people.

Then you identify those pairs of twins in which at least one is a BBP. It will not be difficult to show that if one such identical twin is a BBP, his brother (or her sister) more frequently will be, too, than would a non-identical twin or a non-twin sibling or a non-sibling. You would create groups of such different kinds of pairs to make the comparison in a large number of cases. (One set of identical twin pairs, one set of non-identical twin pairs, one set of non-twin siblings, and so on.)

From the "concordance rate" in each set (the percentage of pairs in each set in which either both are BBPs or both are not. Pairs in which one was and the other was not would be called "discordant for BBP") you would calculate a "heritability" rate. (Perhaps you have an armchair guess as to how many identical twin-pairs either *both* play or *both* do not play basketball. Probably a good deal *more* than half, the concordance rate for homosexuality in such twin-pairs.)

You respond to the reporter from *Sports Illustrations* that, "Our research demonstrates that BBP is very strongly heritable," and you would be right. But the article that comes out that month reads something slightly different, but completely wrong. "…Recent research shows that BBP is probably inherited. A number of outside researchers examined the work and found it substantially accurate and well-performed. They cautioned against arriving at hasty conclusions, however." No one notices the difference.

Brain Dissections

Second, your colleagues perform a series of autopsies on the brains of some dead people who appear to have been BBPs. (Old jerseys, high-top sneakers and Knicks ticket-stubs were found among their possessions, for example.) They do the same with a group of dead non-players (no sneakers, jerseys or tickets.) They report that, on average, "certain parts of the brain long thought to be involved with BBP are much larger in the group of BBPs than in the controls." Certain nationally renowned newspapers in the Northeast pick up on the story and editorialize, "It will be very difficult for anyone except poorly educated yokels who believe in Santa Claus, the Tooth-Fairy and God to argue that BBP is not inborn. For not only has it been proven to run in families, even the *brains* of basketball players are different."[18]

In a pretense of balance, some of these papers interview diehard believers in the old view—yokels who still think that one must decide to play basketball, and play it for a long time, before you really can be considered "a BBP." One of them is quoted as claiming that, "maybe if you do something long enough your brain changes as you get better at it, and that part of the brain gets bigger." (Remarkably enough, this surmise seems obvious to the old-time believer.) The reporter does not merely report the comment, however, he also hints that it is especially idiotic—typical of diehards and yokels—since everyone knows the brain does not change.

Of course, you yourself are well aware that among neuroscientists it is extremely old news that the brain indeed changes, quite dramatically, in just the way the old diehard guessed: those parts responsible for an activity get much bigger over time (and there are definitely parts that are more utilized in BBP). You will not lie about it if asked (since you will not be), but neither will you go out of your way to confirm the truth.

Gene "Linkage" Studies

Now for the coup de grâce. You find a couple of families of BBPs and compare them to some families of non-BBPs. You have a hunch that of innumerable genes of every imaginable sort likely to be "associated" or "linked" to BBP (you never use the word "causing" because you do not need to—no one knows the difference), there are some genes on, say, the X-Chromosome. After a few false starts, sure enough, you find what you are looking for: among the BBP families one particular chromosomal variant (cluster of genes) is more commonly found (though not always) than among the non-players.

Now, sympathizers at National People's Radio were long ago quietly informed of your research, since they want people to come around to certain beliefs, too. So, as soon as your work hits the press, they are on the air: "Researchers are hot on the trail of the 'Basketball Gene!' In an article to be published tomorrow in *Sports Science*…" Learned-sounding commentators pontificate in soft, accentless, perfectly articulated and faintly condescending tones about the enormous public policy implications of this superb piece of science-in-the-service-of-humankind. Two weeks later, there it is again, at a jaunty angle across the cover of the major national newsweekly: "Basketball Gene."

Now what is wrong with this scenario? It is simple: of course BBP is *heritable* ("has a non-zero *heritability*" to use the words of homosexuality researchers). That is because many physiological traits—muscle strength, speed, agility, reflex speed, height, etc.—are themselves directly *inherited*, and they make it more or less likely that one can, and will want to, and will successfully, and will therefore continue to want to, and will in fact continue to, play basketball. In short, because of intermediate *inherited* traits *associated* with BBP (none of which *are* BBP), it shows significant *heritability*. (The genetic *association*, of course, is in no way necessary or predetermined, and is highly culturally conditioned: there were no BBPs at all in, say, ancient Greece, yet the same genes were there.)

BBP also shows a strong *biological representation in the brain*, both at birth (e.g., nervous system factors contributing to reflex speed) and especially later (e.g., the parts of the cortex that are cultivated and become responsible for the movements of basketball, as in the huge increases in finger-related brain tissue among blind people who learn Braille).

And the specific genes that run in families that are responsible for height, athleticism, etc. can surely be found and they will be statistically *linked* to BBP. And if one identical twin decides to play basketball, the unusually strong emotional bond between such siblings will make it even more likely that his twin will, too. (The fact of their genetic *identity*, not their specific genes, are here influencing an outcome above and beyond the indirect contributions from any specific genes.)

The basic problem is this: BBP is "influenced" (made more or less an easy and enjoyable thing to do) by the presence or absence of other associated traits. For BBP we can readily guess what they are and so immediately see that the "genetic" component of BBP has nothing to do with the game itself but with these associated (facilitating) traits. What are these traits? Height, athleticism, bone structure, reflexes, muscle refresh rate, and so on. So evident are the specifics of this association that no serious researcher will waste his time looking into the genetics of BBP proper; he will concentrate on the obvious intermediate traits—height, athleticism and so on.

The same is true for homosexuality, except (a) the more important, intermediate traits with which it is associated are mostly unknown and suspected ones are harder to confirm, and (b) the research agenda is being distorted by the political requirement that no such associated traits be discovered and that homosexuality be falsely presented as directly inherited.

Meaningful Genetics Research Identifies and Focuses on Traits That Are Directly Inherited

Research into merely *heritable* traits is useful only in generating hypotheses about what the directly inherited traits might be. Here is what this means: Let us imagine that it was not immediately evident to us that the heritable aspects of BBP were intermediate traits such as height. A good researcher would not be at all tempted to conclude from the studies we described that BBP itself was inherited. He would conclude however that, indeed, there must be some inherited traits that facilitate BBP, and it would be these as-yet-unknown traits that were producing the "non-zero heritability" results. If he could identify the traits correctly, *he would find that the heritability results, when he redirected his genetics research, would increase dramatically.*

In other words, studying the genetics of BBP is really a crude way of unwittingly studying the genetics of height and athleticism, etc. If he selects his population on the basis of the indirect trait (BBP), when it is other traits that are really inherited, the researcher's results will be "fuzzed up" by the inevitable proportion of BBP's who lack these traits, or have them in lesser degree (e.g., a small number of shortish BBPs). But if he correctly identifies the traits in question, his next round of studies will "divide the herd" more efficiently, corralling his subjects not by BBP (or "sexual orientation"), but by height. Of course, there will be more BBPs among the tall subjects than among the short, but that is incidental. He will seek out other tall people who are not BBPs, and in his new study, the heritability factor (height) will be even more concentrated.

How might he guess at what the most important traits are, and then try to confirm his guess, so he could investigate the genetics of these traits? Very simply: he looks, does the best he can to name what he sees, and tries not to run afoul of the currently fashionable taboos enforced by the thought-police! He will probably have no trouble studying height, but he might run into difficulties should he suspect that athleticism (or even height) has a racial association. (More people of Nordic stock, being taller, become basketball players than do people of Appenzeller Swiss stock, being short. Perhaps other such groupings might occur to a researcher.)

In the case of homosexuality, the *inherited* traits that are more common among homosexuals (and that produce "non-zero *heritability*" in studies) might include such qualities as greater than average tendency to anxiety, shyness, sensitivity, intelligence, aesthetic abilities and so on. (Of course, these traits may themselves be further reducible to a variety of mutually influencing, associated genetic and non-genetic factors.) The brain changes that are more prevalent among homosexuals, the tendency of homosexuality to run in families (and to vary with degree of genetic similarity within families) and the presence of associated chromosomal markings are all certainly due to as yet unresearched and therefore not-yet-identified intermediate traits. There is *no* evidence that homosexuality itself is inherited.

Like height and BBP, these traits—intelligence, say, or anxiety—are surely widely distributed in the population at large and densely present therefore in groups that are properly selected to have them. If researchers had divided their populations by shyness or aesthetic sensibility, and ignored the homosexual/non-homosexual division, they might well have found even stronger chromosomal linkages as well as brain changes and twin concordance rates.

Conclusion

Here, then is a final summary, in the form of a dialogue.

Isn't homosexuality heritable?
Yes, significantly.

So it is inherited?
No, it is not.

I'm confused. Isn't there is a "genetic component" to homosexuality?
Yes, but "component" is just a loose way of indicating genetic associations and linkages. This will not make sense unless you understand what, and how little, "linkage" and "association" really means.

What about all the evidence that shows that homosexuality "is genetic"?
There is not any, and none of the research itself claims there is; only the press and, sadly, certain researchers do—when speaking in sound bites to the public.

But isn't homosexuality "biologically in the brain"?
Of course it is. So is just about everything else. I'll

bet people who pray regularly have certain enlarged portions of their brains!

So doesn't that mean that homosexuality is "innate"?

No more than prayer is. The brain changes with use or nonuse as much as muscles do—a good deal more, in fact. We just do not usually see it happening.

But doesn't homosexuality run in families?

Yes.

So you get it from your parents, right?

You get viruses from your parents, too, and some bad habits. Not everything that is familial is innate or genetic.

But it just seems to make sense. From the people I know there's a type—it's got to be inherited—that runs in families and a lot of these people are gay, right?

That is what associated traits are—but what exactly is the associated trait—or traits—you are detecting? If there is one thing the research confirms, it is that it is not "gayness" itself. That is why these traits are sometimes in evidence at a very early age, long before sexuality is shaped.

So what are these traits?

An important question, indeed. Science is being seriously obstructed in its effort to answer that question. If we were allowed—encouraged—to answer it, we would soon develop better ideas on what homosexuality is and how to change, or better, prevent it. We would know who was at greater risk for becoming homosexual and what environments—family or societal—foster it. As one prominent gay activist researcher implied, all genetic things being equal, it is a whole lot easier to become "gay" in New York than in Utah. So who do you think would benefit most from *that* kind of research?

Well, what traits do you guess are "associated," as you put it, with homosexuality?

May I speculate, perhaps wildly? That is how scientific hypotheses are first generated. The important thing is not to avoid ideas that prove wrong, just not to cling to them if they do.

Okay, go ahead, speculate.

Intelligence, anxiety, sensitivity, aesthetic abilities, taste. You know, all the stereotypes.

But where do these traits come from? Aren't they inherited?

We do not know yet. Some may be. Or rather, we do not know how much is inherited, and which elements are direct and which merely further associated and linked with other yet more fundamental traits. But you are getting the picture. That is how the research ought to proceed. It

is not necessarily that the traits that facilitate homosexuality are themselves bad; perhaps many are gifts. Athleticism is a generally good thing, and we think highly of people who satisfy their athletic impulses as, say, outstanding BBPs. Not so the fellow who merely becomes a thug.

Jeffrey B. Satinover, M.D. has practiced psychoanalysis for more than nineteen years, and psychiatry for more than ten. He is a former Fellow in Psychiatry and Child Psychiatry at Yale University, a past president of the C.G. Jung Foundation, and a former William James Lecturer in Psychology and Religion at Harvard University. He holds degrees from MIT, the University of Texas, and Harvard University. He is the author of *Homosexuality and the Politics of Truth* (Baker Books, 1996).

Endnotes:

[1] D. H. Hamer et al, "A Linkage Between DNA Markers on the X-chromosome and Male Sexual Orientation," *Science* (1993), 261, no. 5119, pp. 321–27.

[2] "Research Points Toward a Gay Gene," *Wall Street Journal*, 16 July 1993.

[3] A lower score on this scale means a less negative attitude toward homosexuality.

[4] Piskur and Degelman, "Attitudes Toward Homosexuals," *Psychological Reports* 71 (1992); my emphasis, pp. 1219-25 (part 2 of 3). See also K. E. Ernulf, "Cross-National Analysis."

[5] K. E. Ernulf, S. M. Innala, and F. L. Whitam, "Biological Explanation, Psychological Explanation, and Tolerance of Homosexuals: A Cross-National Analysis of Beliefs and Attitudes," *Psychological Reports* 65 (1989), pp. 1003–10 (1 of *3).*

[6] Mann C. Genes and behavior. *Science* 264:1687 (1994).

[7] None of the studies of the genetics of homosexuality (all of which are initial; none are replicatory) have come even remotely close to studying this many subjects.

[8] Mann C. *op. cit.* p. 1688.

[9] King, M and McDonald, E. Homosexuals who are twins: a study of 46 probands. British Journal of Psychiatry 160:407-409 (1992)

[10] Byne W and Parsons B. Human sexual orientation: the biologic theories reappraised. *Archives of General Psychiatry.* 50, 3:230 (1993).

[11] Quoted by Horgan, J., *Scientific American*: Eugenics Revisited. June 1993, p. 123.

[12] Billings, P. and Beckwith, J. *Technology Review*, July, 1993. p. 60.

[13] Mann C. *op. cit.* pp. 1686-1689.

[14] Risch N., Squires-Wheeler E., and Bronya J.B.K., "Male Sexual Orientation and Genetic Evidence," *Science* 262 (1993), pp. 2063-65.

[15] Hamer DH et al. Response to Risch N et al. *ibid.* p. 2065

[16] Hamer DH et al. Response to Risch N et al. *loc. cit.*

[17] Mann C., *op. cit.* p. 1687.

[18] Readers may recall Simon LeVay's much touted discovery that the certain parts of the brains of (supposedly) homosexual men were larger than among (supposedly) heterosexual men. But even if the research is valid—its quality has been strongly criticized—the discovery of brain differences per se is on a par with the discovery that athletes have bigger muscles than non-athletes. For though a genetic tendency toward larger muscles may make it easier to—and therefore more likely that one will—become an athlete, becoming an athlete will certainly give one bigger muscles.

When this particular critique was raised, the press quickly took its accustomed potshot at the usual "poorly educated and easily led" religious groups for the suggestion's politically incorrect implications: "Some religious fundamentalists even suggested that homosexual activity somehow could have caused the structural differences [that LeVay claimed to have discovered]."

But as the editor of Nature—an equally prestigious publication—wrote, commenting on the LeVay research: "Plainly, the neural correlates of genetically determined gender are plastic at a sufficiently early stage....Plastic structures in the hypothalamus allowing the consequences of early sexual arousal to be made permanent might suit [those who claim an environmental origin to homosexuality] well." This editor is not, to anyone's knowledge, a religious fundamentalist.

Gender Identity Disorder

by George A. Rekers, Ph.D.

The past three decades have witnessed a well-publicized trend for certain vocal elements in education and the media in American culture to sharply question the legitimacy of many, if not all, sex role distinctions in the socialization of children. Television programs and textbook revisions have been used by these social forces in the attempt to normalize father-absent families as well as household of various combinations of unmarried adults as simply *alternate family forms* with no inherent adverse social consequences.

Paradoxically, during these same recent decades, two developments emerged in the mental health and behavioral science disciplines. First, a mass of research data accumulated which led to a recognition of the often detrimental effects of father absence on several critical aspects of child development, including normal sex role development and sexual adjustment (see reviews by Biller, 1974; Hamilton, 1977; Hetherington, Cox & Cox, 1979; Lamb, 1976; Mead and Rekers, 1979; and Rekers, 1986b, 1992, for example). Secondly, clinical and research data accumulated to a sufficient degree to enable the mental health professions to officially identify a newly recognized form of psycopathology—"Gender Identity Disorder of Childhood" (American Psychiatric Association, 1980).

Recent years witnessed the swing of the pendulum of public attention to the social advocates of "eliminating all distinctions based on sex." However, an objective consideration of the whole scope of findings in human development research and clinical studies yields an appreciation and recognition of appropriate sex roles in the family and their critical importance to the normal gender identity development of children.

Normal Versus Abnormal Sex Role Development

As part of the process of normal gender identity in the family, young children will often try out a variety of sex role behaviors as they learn to make the fine distinctions between masculine and feminine roles. Some young boys occasionally perform behaviors that our culture traditionally has recognized as feminine, such as wearing a dress, using cosmetics or play acting the roles of bearing and nursing infants. Similarly, many young girls will occasionally assume a masculine role—pretending to be "daddy" while playing house, or temporarily adopting a cluster of masculine behaviors which leads to the social designation of "tomboy." This type of temporary and episodic exploration of cross-sex-typed behaviors is typical of many boys and girls and usually constitutes a learning experience in the process of normal sex role socialization (Maccoby & Jacklin, 1974, Mischel, 1970; Serbin, 1980).

In pathological cases, however, children deviate from the normal pattern of exploring masculine and feminine behaviors and develop an inflexible, compulsive, persistent and rigidly stereotyped pattern (Zucker, 1985). On one extreme is the distorted supermasculinity of boys who are belligerent, destructive, interpersonally violent, and uncontrolled and simultaneously lacking gentle and socially sensitive behaviors (Harrington, 1970). Professional intervention is required for these exaggeratedly "hypermasculine" boys who actually have adopted a maladaptive caricature of masculinity. The opposite extreme is observed in effeminate boys who reject their masculinity to the extent of rigidly insisting that they are a girl or that they want to become a mother and bear children (Rekers, 1981; Rekers & Milner, 1978; Rekers & Kilgus, 1997). Such a boy frequently avoids play with boys, dresses in girls' clothing, plays predominantly with girls, tries on cosmetics and wigs, and displays stereotypically feminine arm movements, gait, and body gestures. This boyhood femininity goes beyond normal transitory, curiosity induced exploration of feminine behavior to constitute a serious clinical problem (Rekers, 1985d, 1985e) Although little research exists on female childhood gender disorders, it is possible to identify the parallel conditions of maladaptive hyperfemininity and hypermasculinity in girls (Rekers & Mead, 1979, 1980).

One of the clinician's tasks is to differentiate normal adjustment phases in psychosexual development from gender disturbances that require specific treatment intervention (Rekers & Kilgus, 1995; Rekers, 1995a). To illustrate this task, let me describe a boy to you.

Carl (a pseudonym) was referred to me for treatment at the age of 8 years, 8 months (Rekers, Lovaas & Low, 1974). The referring physician had found Carl to be physically normal in terms of currently available methods of biomedical testing. Prior to referral to me, Carl had been evaluated by two separate psychiatric agencies as having a severe cross gender identity problem. In one clinic, Carl had been treated in family therapy for a period of 8 months in a largely unsuccessful attempt to alleviate his personal problems and his major difficulties in peer and family relationships.

He came from a broken family in which his mother had had four marriages in Carl's lifetime. Carl had a brother seven years old and a sister six years old.

Since the age of our years, Carl had pronounced feminine voice inflection and feminine speech content. He was extremely verbal, and his conversations were dominated by topics such as dresses, cosmetics, maternal roles, female impersonators, delivering babies, and female underclothing. He had several recurring exclamatory feminine sounding remarks, such as "goodness gracious," and "oh, dear me."

His feminine gestures were exaggerations of an effeminate, swishy gait and arm movements. He would typically sit with his legs crossed very effeminately and his arms folded like a female model. At home, he would frequently use towels after a bath to simulate female garments and long hair.

In his peer relationships, Carl passively allowed boys to lease him without asserting himself in return. He preferred girls in play, assuming the female role himself with great....played house with his sister frequently. Carl was ostracized by his male peers who labeled him "sissy" and "queer." He harbored a strong fear of "getting hurt" and feigned illnesses and injuries to avoid play with boys. Not only was Carl labeled by his peers as effeminate, but also he referred to himself as a "sissy" and "fag," and his speech regularly implied that he preferred to be considered a girl.

Carl's feminine behavior was increasingly leading him to social isolation, ridicule, and chronic unhappiness. His mother, who had found his feminine gestures to be amusing before he was age four, was very alarmed when they persisted to the age of eight years. She strongly wanted him to receive professional help, and she requested help herself to solve the related problems in her family.

Disorder Created by Incongruity Across Dimensions

Physically, Carl's physician had determined that his sexual status was normal prepubertal male with a normal 46XY male karyotype. His sex of assignment had been male, and his mother had raised him as a boy.

His gender identity was that of a girl. In other words, he had a cross gender identity. He called himself a "sissy" and a "fag," and this constituted an aspect of his sex role identity. His gender role behavior was predominantly feminine.

Because of his age, his sexual object orientation and genital interpersonal behavior were not assessed at the time of his initial evaluation. He was not involved in sexual behavior.

Carl's case illustrates how any incongruity across any two of these psychosexual dimensions can create psychological conflict and associated maladjustment problems (Rekers, 1981b; Rosen & Rekers, 1980). This brings us to a distinction between Gender Role Behavior Disturbance and Cross Gender Identification in boys.

Gender Role Behavior Disturbance

A Gender Role Behavior Disturbance may be present in a boy as young as three years old who has normal male physical sex status. Typically, the sex assignment has been male, although cases have been reported where family members have given incongruent or ambiguous messages to a young child regarding his physical sex status. Gender identity is typically male and not female, although sex role identity may range from male gender role, to self-labeling as "fag" or "queer" across settings. For this reason, our case of Carl is not a classic example of Gender Role Behavior Disturbance. In this developmental disorder, sexual orientation may be absent, unreported, or varied—including sexual arousal tom feminine clothing. At the sexual behavior level, the boy may or may not have a documented history of deviant sexual behavior or masturbation patterns associated with feminine clothing or articles.

The distinguishing features of Gender Role Behavior Disturbance exist at the interpersonal dimension where any of the following behavior are observed over an extended period of time; Cross dressing; play with cosmetic articles; "feminine" appearing gestures; avoidance of masculine sex-typed activities; avoidance of male peers; predominant ratio of play with female peers; high "feminine" like voice inflection; predominant ratio of feminine speech content over masculine; and taking predominately female roles in play.

Of course, Gender Role Behavior Disturbance may occur in either boys or girls, although it is detected more frequently in boys. And there are two major extremes that can be manifested in terms of role inflexibility in either the masculine or feminine direction, in either boys or girls. The two possible chromic patterns in boys are (1) excessive feminine behavioral rigidity, and (2) pathological hypermasculinity. The two possible chronic patterns in girls are (1) excessive masculine behavioral rigidity, and (2) pathological hyperfemininity.

Gender Identity Disorder of Childhood

In addition to the behavioral manifestations of a Gender Role Behavior Disturbance, a boy with a Gender Identity Disorder also manifests one or more of these features: (1) And expressed desire to be a girl or a woman, (2) expressed fantasies of bearing children and breast-feeding infants or assuming a female identity, or (3) a request to have his penis removed.

Carl illustrates the potentially more serious disorder of Cross Gender Identification. This condition in boys involves gender identification as a female, including requests to change one's physical sex status.

I have observed and reported in the literature (Rosen & Rekers, 1980) this distinction between the Gender Role Behavior Disturbance and the Cross Gender Identification Disturbance. Theoretically, Gender Role Behavior Disturbance in child development may parallel the adulthood conditions of transvestism, while the problem of Cross Gender Identification in children may parallel the adulthood condition of transsexualism. But this remains a question for empirical research into the life span development of these individuals.

Cross Gender Identification in boys is only one potential type of Gender Identity Disorder because a parallel condition can be found in some girls.

Prognosis for Child Gender Disorders

In terms of atypical gender development in children, the literature deals almost exclusively with the cases of deficit masculine development in boys, including cross gender identity disturbance, gender role behavior disturbance and homosexual behavior development. This state of the research literature is, in part, a function of the frequently replicated finding that problems of sexual dysphoria and deviation occur more frequently in males than females and may be a function of the relatively greater concern by American parents over feminine sex role behavior in their sons.

The feminine sex-typed behaviors which are used as the initial screening criteria for assessment of gender disturbed boys can exist in many different developmental contexts. Theoretically speaking, it is probable that the prognosis and treatment of gender role behavior disturbance and cross gender identity disturbance are not the same; but research on this question has not yet been conducted. The developmental histories of all these types of gender deviant boys parallels the retrospective reports of adult male transsexuals, transvestites, and some homosexuals; and the prospective longitudinal studies of children as they grow up to adolescence and adulthood indicate that most of these effeminate boys became homosexual in orientation and some are transvestite or transsexual (Green, 1982; Zucker, 1985; Zuger, 1966, 1978, 1984).

There are no base rate data on the occurrence of these various types of sex role disturbance.

Medical Examination for Research Subjects

Over the past 12 years, over 100 boys have been referred to my N.I.M.H. supported Gender Research Project for evaluation and potential treatment for a gender disturbance. My research team completed comprehensive psychological evaluations of approximately 70 of these children, and we required a complete physical examination and medical history report from the child's pediatrician. In addition, a pediatric geneticist joined us to conduct a more complete medical examination for a subset of consecutive referrals to our project. According to our geneticist, baseline endocrinological studies were considered unnecessary unless abnormalities were detected in the physical examination. The following medical examination was given to the subset of research subject referrals: Medical history; physical examination, including external genitalia; chromosome analysis, including two cells karyotyped and 15 counted; and sex chromatin studies.

All 70 of the gender disturbed boys were found to be normal physically and the more completely evaluated boys were found to be normal physically, with the single exception of one boy with one undescended testicle (Rekers, Crandall, Rosen & Bentler, 1979). No evidence was found for maternal hormone treatment during pregnancy nor were there any histories of hormonal imbalance in the mothers. Our findings were consistent with the literature on adulthood gender disturbances such as transsexualism and transvestism—namely, occur in individuals without detectable or measurable abnormalities in any of the five physical variables of sex.

The Importance of Family Variables

In these cases, therefore, the social environment of child-rearing is primarily implicated in the etiology of the psychosexual disturbance. I investigated the family variables correlated with the degree of gender disturbances in the sample of subjects that I have accumulated.

Why should the families of gender disturbed children be studied? I believe that much has been learned about normal life span development by investigations of deviant cases which shed light upon critical processes relevant to normal social development.

My first step in the analysis for the families of these boys was to focus upon the fathers, the father substitutes, and the male models available to these boys with inadequate masculine role development. The research literature of the psychosexual development of normal children has revealed that the father is the parent whose role behaviors are most likely to generate sex appropriate behaviors in the children in a family unit (Mead & Rekers,

1979). The characteristics that have been reported to foster the establishment of normal gender identity in children include the father's nurturance and dominance. In contrast, literature on the effects of paternal deprivation indicates that the sex role learning process is adversely affected when fathers are either physically or psychologically absent from the home (Biller, 1974; Hamilton, 1977).

The impact of paternal deprivation on psychosexual development is most conspicuous in the retrospective clinical studies of homosexual and transsexual men. But direct studies of the families of gender disturbed children have been few.

Family Problems Associated with Gender Disturbance

My own study of the family variables associated with childhood gender disturbance was based upon a subset of the boys we evaluated for gender disturbance, for whom we completed three independent psychological evaluations, each of which took into account these factors: Identity statements, cross dressing history and frequency, cross gender role play behavior, parent-child relationships, parental attitude toward gender behaviors, peer relationships, social and academic adjustment, emotional adjustment, and congruence of diagnoses by independent psychologists.

Two other clinical psychologists, in addition to myself, completed independent diagnostic evaluations of each subject, and rated each subject on two scales one scale for gender role behavior and another for gender identity. Each of these scales constituted a five-point continuum from "normal" to "profound" disturbance (Bentler, Rekers & Rosen, 1979; Rekers, 1988a; Rekers & Morey, 1989a, 1989b, 1989c, 1990).

One of the most striking findings in the families of these boys I studied was the incidence of *psychiatric* problems. Eighty percent of the mothers and 45% of the fathers had a history of mental health problems and/or psychiatric treatment. It may be possible that these figures are somewhat inflated compared to the larger population of gender disturbed boys in that parents who have sought treatment for themselves may be more likely to seek treatment for their children. However, these findings suggest that the parents of gender disturbed boys have an unusual degree of psychological maladjustment.

Our findings with regard to paternal deprivation in these boys parallels much of the literature on the detrimental effects of father absence on normal psychosexual development.

In the boys who were classified as the most profoundly disturbed, father absence was observed for *all* cases. In the remaining *less* disturbed cases, father absence was found in 54% of the cases. Using the nonparametric Fisher's exact probability test, this difference was found to be statistically significant.

For the entire group of 46 subjects, 37% had no adult male role model (either biological father or father substitute) present in the home. According to the 1977 U.S. Census figures (which are comparable to this sample) only 12% of all white children lived with their mother only, therefore without the benefit of a father or a father surrogate. Of the 36 boys in this study who received a diagnostic rating, 75% of the most severely disturbed boys and 21% of the less severely disturbed had neither the biological father nor a father substitute living in the home—a statistically significant difference (p = .01, Fishers).

Eighty percent of the boys whose fathers left their family were five years or under at the time of that separation—the mean age at separation from the father was 3.55 years. Figure 2 shows that the most common cause for father absence was marital separation or divorce.

For all the gender disturbed boys, if the biological father or a father substitute were present, he was described in 60% of the cases as being psychologically distant or remote by the other family members.

A consistent picture is beginning to emerge from these findings and from other small sample studies. The young males with the most pronounced gender disturbances tend to be less likely to have a male role model in the home, as compared to less severely gender disturbed boys (Rekers, Mead, Rosen & Brigham, 1983; Rekers & Swihart, 1989).

In general, the picture of the fathers of gender disturbed children found in these data is in sharp contrast to the image of the idealized father who promotes masculinity in his sons through his psychological and physical presence, his active involvement with his children and with the family decision making, his leadership, his dominance and his nurturance (Mead & Rekers, 1979).

In a large number of instances, no male role model existed during early childhood developmental years in the home, whether it be father, father substitute or older male sibling. This absence of male role models with whom to identify was even more characteristic of the most severely disturbed effeminate boys. In cases where the father or a father surrogate was present in the home, he was typically described as psychologically remote from the family.

These various sources of clinical evidence suggest that fathering variables are correlated with male sex role disturbance, even though the direction of causality between these variables is inferred, not established, by scientific observation. An ideal future study in this area would be a longitudinal investigation of a large enough sample of boys selected at random at birth that would contain a sufficient number of male role disturbed boys to provide definite causal evidence. Two comparison groups would be in order—a normal control group and a group of boys with other types of psychological disturbance.

Child and Family Treatment Interventions

There are numerous interrelated reasons for intervening in the life of a boy diagnosed with a gender disturbance. The first reason for treatment is the psychological maladjustment of gender disturbed children. The second reason for intervention is to prevent severe sexual problems of adulthood such as transsexualism and homosexuality (Rekers, 1985b; Rekers & Kilgus, 1995) that are highly resistant to treatment in later phases of development. The third reason is to prevent the serious emotional, social and economic maladjustments secondary to severe adulthood sexual problems. And the fourth main reason is to cooperate with appropriate parental concern over gender deviance. I have published several detailed articles developing this rationale with reference to the clinical data (Rekers, 1977, 1984; Rekers, Bentler, Rosen & Lovaas, 1977; Rekers & Mead, 1980; Rekers, Rosen, Lovaas & Bentler, 1978; Rosen, Rekers & Bentler, 1978).

I have developed and validated several child and family treatment interventions with *intrasubject* research studies on gender disturbed children (Rekers, 1995b). The mother-child and father-child interventions in the clinic have focused upon behavioral counseling and behavioral rehearsal with *in vivo* training sessions. The most effective therapeutic techniques for the therapist to use in the clinic pertain to instructions regarding the performance of feminine speech and gesture/mannerism behaviors, coupled with videotape feedback and behavior shaping sessions. Family interventions in the home and consultation with school personnel have involved social learning approaches. We have developed father-son interaction programs, including athletic skill training. We have provided male role models if fathers are not available to young boys, and we have insured that the child received appropriate sex education in either the home or in counseling sessions. I have also published some intrasubject studies on the efficacy of various self-monitoring and self-reinforcement interventions with the children. I have evaluated these approaches with intrasubject designs, and published long-term followup outcome studies (Rekers, Kilgus & Rosen, 1990; Rosen, Rekers & Brigham, 1982).

Let me illustrate this program of treatment strategies by returning to the case of the young boy, Carl, whom I described earlier. With a multiple baseline intrasubject design across stimulus environments and across behaviors, Carl was treated in one setting at a time in order to assess the generalization of behavioral treatment effects.

Both before and during the brief treatment in the clinic, Carl's gender role behaviors were recorded in the home by the mother and a research assistant using time sampling procedures. The major portion of Carl's treatment took place in the home and school settings because Carl felt overly self-conscious in the clinic with its one way mirrors; and because our previous investigations had found no stimulus generalization of treatment effects from the clinic to the home environment.

Because Carl enjoyed telling elaborate fantasized stories while drawing pictures on a chalkboard, the brief clinic intervention procedure was designed to demonstrate simple reinforcement control over the sex-typed verbal behavior during the boy's story telling.

You will recall that Carl's conversations at the initial evaluation were dominated by topics such as dresses, cosmetics, maternal roles, female impersonators and female underwear. After obtaining a baseline measure of masculine and feminine speech content, a psychology intern introduced a differential social reinforcement contingency in which Carl's questions regarding masculine or neutral topics were answered by giving short, nonleading, direct answers, expressing positive interest. When Carl referred to a feminine topic, the psychology intern immediately withdrew social attention by looking away and by reading a magazine. If Carl persisted with direct questions regarding feminine topics, the intern expressed disinterest.

An ABA reversal design demonstrated reinforcement control over sex-typed speech; the therapeutic contingency resulted in a sharp decrease in feminine speech and an increase in masculine content. The data suggested, but did not confirm, a generalized suppression effect to feminine voice inflection as well, even though that behavior was not specifically treated.

Then Carl's mother was trained to administer a token and point economy reinforcement procedure in the home which successively increased Carl's masculine play with brother and decreased his feminine gestures, feminine speech content, feminine voice inflection and predominant play with his sister.

Because Carl's treatment in the clinic had not generalized to the home or to the school setting, his teacher was trained to apply a response cost procedure to what she called his "brat behaviors" and to his feminine/gesture mannerisms. The "brat behaviors" included: Creating a class disturbance, bossing another child, behaving rudely to teacher and teasing another child.

When the contingency was applied to the brat behaviors, they decreased immediately. The contingency for feminine gestures resulted in a gradual suppression of both gestures and feminine speech. These effects were found to be stimulus-specific to the classroom setting, necessitating a reintroduction of the contingencies into Carl's new classroom when he was promoted to the next grade level the following fall.

After a 15 month period, this treatment program in the clinic, home and school setting was completed. The social learning interventions for the boy had been combined with individual counseling for the mother and her marital problems and family relationship difficulties.

Carl and his mother were then referred for an independent evaluation by two clinical psychologists who administered tests, interviews and unobtrusive observations of the boy at school. They found no evidence of any feminine behavior or cross-gender identification in the boy after treatment. His mother, school teachers, and neighbors all agreed that he had changed in a comprehensive way from a feminine appearing to a masculine boy. Major improvements were found by those psychologists in Carl's overall social and emotional adjustment. However, Carl retained his previous social reputation as a "sissy" and "queer." We, therefore, assisted the mother in obtaining a transfer of Carl to a new school where he developed a normal social reputation and was well accepted by his peers.

However, Carl remained inept at most games and sports played by his male peers at school and in his home neighborhood. We, therefore, provided an additional 15 month program of behavior shaping procedures to overcome his deficits in throwing the ball, socking a playground ball, and in playing kickball. This training was combined with what are called "companionship therapy" in which a relationship was established between Carl and a male psychology student who modeled appropriate masculine behaviors and took Carl on numerous trips to the park, beach, and for tumbling lessons.

Twelve months after this additional program, another clinical evaluation was made of Carl's adjustment. Once again, no evidence of feminine behavior or cross gender identification were found. He was found to be normal in emotional and social adjustment.

Six years after the completion of therapy, we arranged another followup evaluation by an independent clinical psychologist. Carl was then 16 years and ten months of age. A comprehensive set of interviews, personality tests and observations were completed. This independent psychologist concluded: "This young man appears to be a normal gender appropriate adolescent boy with no salient evidences of difficulty in gender role or gender identity. He has some difficulty in feeling unsure of himself in social interactions and is generally, however, emotionally within the normal adolescent range."

Similar positive outcomes have been obtained with the other previously treated gender-disturbed children in my group (Rekers, 1979; Rekers & Lovaas, 1974; Rekers et al, 1974; Rekers & Mead, 1979a; Rekers & Milner, 1979, 1981; Rekers & Varni, 1977a; Rekers, Willis, Yates, Rosen & Low, 1977; Rekers, Yates, Willis, Rosen & Taubman, 1976) which we are following up into late adolescence now (Rosen, Rekers & Brigham, 1982). It was in the Third Edition of the Diagnostic and Statistical Manual of Mental Disorders (DSM-III) published in 1980 that the American Psychological Association included, for the first time, the diagnosis of "Gender Identity Disorder of Childhood" (pages 264-266). Reflecting on the results of longitudinal studies of untreated children with gender disorders (e.g., Green, 1982; Money & Russo, 1979; Zucker, 1985; Zuger, 1966, 1978, 1984), the Fourth Edition of DSM published in 1994 states, "By late adolescence or adulthood, about three-quarters of boys who had a childhood history of Gender Identity Disorder report a homosexual or bisexual orientation, but without concurrent Gender Identity Disorder. ...Some adolescents may develop a clearer cross-gender identification and request sex-reassignment surgery or may continue in a chronic course of gender confusion or dysphoria" (page 536). From the result of my research studies, it now appears that a preventive treatment for transvestism, transsexualism, and some forms of homosexuality may have been isolated in these techniques of early identification and early intervention in the childhood years (Rekers, 1978, 1980, 1981b, 1983, 1987).

If the psychopathology of "Gender Identity Disorder of Childhood" is one of the major etiological precursors to adulthood homosexual orientation disturbance (as the research indicates at present), it would now appear logical that homosexuality *per se* be re-examined as a mental disorder.

In the introduction to his political analysis of the psychiatric battle over homosexuality, Ronald Bayer described the subject of his book:

> In 1973, after several years of bitter dispute, the Board of Trustees of the American Psychiatric Association decided to remove homosexuality from the *Diagnostic and Statistical Manual...* Instead of being engaged in a sober consideration of data, psychiatrists were swept up in a political controversy. The American Psychiatric Association had fallen victim to the disorder of a tumultuous era, when disruptive conflicts threatened to politicize every aspect of American social life. A furious egalitarianism that challenged every instance of authority had compelled psychiatric experts to negotiate the pathological status of homosexuality with homosexuals themselves. The result was not a conclusion based on an approximation of the scientific truth as dictated by reason, but was instead an action demanded by the ideological temper of the times... (Bayer, 1981, pages 3-4).

It remains to be seen if the mental health professions will be able to readdress the issue of homosexuality from a logical and scientific perspective in the near future (Lundy & Rekers, 1995b, 1995c). The use (or abuse) of research may continue to be influenced by ideological factors in American culture (Lundy & Rekers, 1995a).

Suggestions for Future Research Study

1) Prior to my own series of studies, no treatment procedures for Gender Identity Disorder in Childhood had been experimentally demonstrated to be effective. We, therefore, intervened with labor intensive, multiple methods to achieve a positive therapeutic outcome. Future clinical research should investigate the most efficient set of treatment variables, for economically feasible treatment applied on a larger scale in routine clinical practice.

2) Preliminary findings have been published in the literature which report on the positive therapeutic effects of religious conversion for curing transsexualism (Barlow, Abel & Blanchard, 1977) and on the positive therapeutic effect of a church ministry to repentant homosexuals (Pattison & Pattison, 1980). Further research should be addressed to the relationship of spiritual conversion and spiritual well-being upon sexual identity development and sexual adjustment. The anecdotal reports of the healing effects of the social support of a local church should be followed up with systematic empirical study.

3) Research is needed to further understand the etiology and treatment of the other type of inadequate male role development in boys namely, those boys who are interpersonally violent, destructive and sexually promiscuous with girls sometimes to the extent of aggressive rape (Harrington, 1970; Rekers & Jurich, 1983; Rekers, 1992, 1996). This pattern, too, has been associated with father absence; but the paternal deprivation typically occurs after the age of six years (Mead & Rekers, 1979).

It is possible that our society has not yet fully reaped the full consequences of widespread breakdown of family units caused by divorce. Too often divorce of the parents results in a divorce of the father from the children. If research on the effects of divorce and separation on children can be better communicated to the general population of our culture, perhaps the American public will make greater efforts to achieve stable marriage and family life and be more highly motivated to seek genuine problem solving solutions to marital conflict rather than so quickly considering divorce, as though it were the only alternative (Rekers, 1985a).

4) As a matter of public policy, it appears now to be necessary for federal and local governments to direct funding not only to the remediation of categorical problems associated with family dysfunction (such as gender identity disorder of childhood, run away youth, or teenage pregnancy) but also toward evaluation research of community level demonstration projects using preventative educational approaches to teach fathers the value and importance of their active, warm emotional involvement with their children. Baseline measures of paternal involvement with children might be recorded before and after an intensive educational effort. Data should be gathered regarding the maintenance of the hoped for increase in paternal involvement over time.

5) Finally, in a generation confused by radical ideologies on male and female roles, we need solid research on men and women who are well adjusted examples of a secure male identity and a secure female identity. Such research could demonstrate what adaptive masculinity and femininity bring about for family life and the larger culture (Rekers, 1986a, 1991). Children with poor parental models need substitute male role and female role models. Such research could serve this need.

Figure 2
FAMILY CORRELATES TO MALE GENDER DISTURBANCE

Gender Distributed Boy Sample
46 boys with diagnoses by 3 independent clinicians aged 3 to 13 years, mean age 7 years.
Psychiatric History of Family Available on 30 of 46 Boys
80% of mothers with mental health problems/history
45% of fathers with mental health problems/history
Male Role Model Deprivation
67% of biological fathers physically absent from the home for all cases; 100%* fathers absent for **most** severely disturbed boys; 54%* fathers absent for **less** severely disturbed boys; * Significant at .02 level (Fisher's Exact Test)
3.55 Years = Mean Age of Boys at Time of Father's Separation
(80% of boys were aged 5 years or under at separation)
Reason for Separation from Father
82% due to marital separation or divorce
10% due to death of the father
8% due to birth out of wedlock
Presence of Stepfather or Surrogate Father Figure in
25% of most severely disturbed boys
60% of less severely disturbed boys
Presence of Older Male Sibling in
25% of most severely disturbed boys
48% of less severely disturbed boys

[This paper was presented at the First Annual Meeting of the North American Social Science Network, Washington, D.C., on June 15, 1985. The author's research presented herein was supported by major research grants from the National Institute of Mental Health, by a post-doctoral fellowship at Harvard University from the Foundations' Fund for Research in Psychiatry, and a predoctoral fellowship at U.C.L.A. from the National Science Foundation. This article was taken from *The Journal of Family and Culture*, Vol. II, No. 3., 1986, The Free Congress Research and Education Foundation, and updated by the author. Used by permission.]

George A. Rekers, Ph.D., is Professor of Neuropsychiatry and Behavioral Science, Research Director for Child and Adolescent Psychiatry, and Chairman of Faculty in Psychology at the University of South Carolina School of Medicine in Columbia, S.C. He has authored nine books, over 120 academic journal articles, and numerous book chapters. He is the editor of the *Handbook of Child and Adolescent Sexual Problems* (Lexington/Jossey-Bass/Simon & Schuster, 1995) which can be ordered by calling 1-800-956-7739.

References:

American Psychiatric Association. *Diagnostic and Statistical Manual of Mental Disorders, Third Edition.* Washington, D.C.: A.P.A., 1980, pages 264-266.

American Psychiatric Association. *Diagnostic and Statistical Manual of Mental Disorders, Fourth Edition.* Washington, D.C.: A.P.A., 1994, pages 532-538.

Barlow, D.H., Abel, G.G. & Blanchard, E.B. Gender identity change in transsexuals: An exorcism. Archives of Sexual Behavior, 1977, 6, 387-395.

Bayer, R. *Homosexuality and American Psychiatry: The Politics of Diagnosis.* New York: Basic Books, 1981.

Bentler, P.M., Rekers, G.A. & Rosen, A.C. Congruence of childhood sex-role identity and behaviour disturbances. *Child: Care, Health and Development,* 1979, 5(4), 267-284.

Biller, H.B. *Paternal Deprivation.* Lexington, Mass: D.C. Heath, 1974.

Green, R. Relationship between "feminine" and "masculine" behavior during boyhood and sexual orientation during manhood. In Z. Hoch & H.I. Lief (Eds.), *Sexology: Sexual Biology, Behavior, and Therapy.* Amsterdam: Excerptica Medica, 1982.

Hamilton, M.L. *Father's Influence on Children.* Chicago: Nelson-Hall, 1977.

Harrington, C.C. *Errors in Sex-role Behavior in Teen-age Boys.* New York: Teachers College Press, 1970.

Hetherington, E.M., Cox, M. & Cox, R. The development of children in motherheaded families. In D. Reiss & H.A. Hoffman, *The American Family: Dying or Developing?* New York: Plenum, 1979.

Lamb, M.E. (Editor). *The Role of the Father in Child Development.* New York: Wiley, 1976.

Lundy, M., & Rekers, G.A. Homosexuality: Development, risks, parental values, and controversies. Chapter 14 in G.A. Rekers (Ed.), *Handbook of Child and Adolescent Sexual Problems.* New York, NY: Lexington Books of Macmillan/Simon & Schuster, 1995, pages 290-312. (a)

Lundy, M., & Rekers, G.A. Homosexuality: Presentation, evaluation, and clinical decision-making. Chapter 15 in G.A. Rekers (Ed.), *Handbook of Child and Adolescent Sexual Problems.* New York, NY: Lexington Books of Macmillan/Simon & Schuster, 1995, pages 313-340. (b)

Lundy, M., & Rekers, G.A. Homosexuality in adolescence: Interventions. Chapter 16 in G.A. Rekers (Ed.), *Handbook of Child and Adolescent Sexual Problems.* New York, NY: Lexington Books of Macmillan/Simon & Schuster, 1995, pages 341-377. (c)

Maccoby, E.E. & Jacklin, C.N. *The Psychology of Sex Differences.* Stanford: Stanford University Press, 1974.

Mead, S.L. & Rekers, G.A. The role of the father in normal psychosexual development. *Psychological Reports,* 1979, 45, 923-931.

Mischel, W. Sex-typing and socialization. In P.H. Mussen (Ed.), *Carmichael's Manual of Child Psychology, Third Edition, Vol. 11.* New York: Wiley, 1970, pages 3-72.

Money, J. & Russo, A.J. Homosexual outcome of discordant gender identity/ role: Longitudinal follow-up. *Journal of Pediatric Psychology,* 1979, 4, 29-41.

Pattison, E. M. & Pattison, M.L. Ex-Gays: Religiously mediated change in homosexuals. *American Journal of Psychiatry,* 1980, 137(12), 1553-62.

Rekers, G.A. *Pathological sex-role development in boys: Behavioral treatment and assessment.* Ph.D. dissertation in psychology, University of California, Los Angeles. Ann Arbor, Michigan: University Microfilms, 1972. No. 7233, 978.

Rekers, G.A. Stimulus control over sex-typed play in cross-gender identified boys. *Journal of Experimental Child Psychology,* 1975, 20, 136-148.

Rekers, G.A. Assessment and treatment of childhood gender problems. Chapter 7 in B.B. Lahey and A.E. Kazdin (Eds.), *Advances in Clinical Child Psychology, Volume 1,* New York: Plenum, 1977, pages 267-306.

Rekers, G.A. Atypical gender development and psychosocial adjustment. *Journal of Applied Behavior Analysis,* 1977, 10, 559-571.

Rekers, G.A. Sexual problems: Behavior modification. Chapter 17 in B.B. Wolman (Ed.), *Handbook of Treatment of Mental Disorders in Childhood and Adolescence.* Englewood Cliffs, New Jersey: Prentice Hall, 1978, pages 268-296.

Rekers, G.A. Sex-role behavior change: Intrasubject studies of boyhood gender disturbance. *Journal of Psychology,* 1979, 103, 255-269.

Rekers, G.A. Therapies dealing with the child's sexual difficulties. In Jean Marc-Samson (Ed.), *Enfance et Sexualité / Childhood and Sexuality.* Montreal & Paris: Les Editions Etudes Vivantes, Inc., 1980, pages 525-538.

Rekers, G. A. Childhood sexual identity disorders. *Medical Aspects of Human Sexuality,* 1981, 15(3), 141-142.

Rekers, G.A. Psychosexual and gender problems. In E.J. Mash & L.G. Terdal (Eds.), *Behavioral Assessment of Childhood Disorders.* New York: Guilford Press, 1981, pages 483-526.

Rekers, G.A. Play therapy with cross-gender identified children. Chapter 20 in Charles E. Schaefer and Kevin J. O'Connor (Eds.), *Handbook of Play Therapy.* New York: John Wiley and Sons, 1983, pages 369-385.

Rekers, G.A. Ethical issues in Child assessment. Chapter 12 in Thomas H. Ollendick and Michael Hersen (Eds.), *Child Behavioral Assessment: Principles and Procedures.* New York: Pergamon Press, 1984, pages 244-262.

Rekers, G.A. (Editor) *Family Building: Six Qualities of a Strong Family.* Ventura, CA: Regal Books, 1985. (a)

Rekers, G.A. Gender identity disorder of childhood. In David G. Benner (Ed.), *Baker's Encyclopedia of Psychology.* Grand Rapids, Michigan: Baker Book House, 1985, pages 446-448. (b)

Rekers, G.A. Transsexualism. In David G. Benner (Ed.), *Baker's Encyclopedia of Psychology.* Grand Rapids, Michigan: Baker Book House, 1985, pages 1178-1179. (c)

Rekers, G.A. Transvestism. In David G. Benner (Ed.), *Baker's Encyclopedia of Psychology.* Grand Rapids, Michigan: Baker Book House, 1985, pages 1179-1181. (d)

Rekers, G.A. Gender identity problems. In Philip H. Borstein & Alan E. Kazdin (Eds.), *Handbook of Clinical Behavior Therapy with Children.* Dorsey Press, 1985, pages 658-699. (e)

Rekers, G.A. Inadequate sex role differentiation in childhood: The family and gender identity disorders. *Journal of Family and Culture.* 1986, 2(3) 8-37. (a)

Rekers, G.A. Fathers at home: Why the intact family is important to children and the Nation. *Persuasion at Work.* C.V. Mosby Publishing Company, 1986, 9(4):1-7. (b)

Rekers, G.A. Cross-sex Behavior. In Sheridan Phillips, Chapter 26, "Behavioral and Developmental Problems in Childhood" in R.A. Hoekelman, S. Blatman, S.B. Friedman, N.M. Nelson & and H.M. Seidel (Eds.), *Principles of Pediatrics: Health Care of the Young, Second Edition.* C.V. Mosby Publishing Company, 1987, pages 719-721

Rekers, G.A. Psychosexual assessment of gender identity disorders. In R.J. Prinz (Ed.), *Advances in Behavioral Assessment of Children and Families*, Volume 4, Greenwich, CN: JAI Press, Inc., 1988, pages 33-71. (a)

Rekers, G.A. The formation of homosexual orientation. In P.F. Fagan (Ed.), *Homosexuality*. Washington, D.C.: The Center for Child and Family Policy, 1988, pages 1-27. (b)

Rekers, G.A. Psychological foundations for rearing masculine boys and feminine girls. Chapter 17 in Piper and W. Grudem (Eds.), *Recovering Biblical Manhood and Womanhood*, Wheaton, IL: Crossway Books, 1991, pages 292-311, and endnotes pages 510-523.

Rekers, G.A. Development of problems in puberty and sex roles in adolescence. Invited chapter in C.E. Walker & M.C. Roberts (Eds.), *Handbook of clinical child psychology: Second edition*, New York: John Wiley and Sons, 1992, pages 606-622.

Rekers, G.A. Early detection and treatment of sexual problems: An introductory overview. Chapter 1 in G.A. Rekers (Ed.), *Handbook of Child and Adolescent Sexual Problems*. New York, NY: Lexington Books of Macmillan/Simon & Schuster, 1995, pages 3-13. (a)

Rekers, G.A. Assessment and treatment methods for gender identity disorder and transvestism. Chapter 13 in G.A. Rekers (Ed.), *Handbook of Child and Adolescent Sexual Problems*. New York, NY: Lexington Books of Macmillan/Simon & Schuster, 1995, pages 272-289. (b)

Rekers, G.A., Amaro-Plotkin, H., & Low, B.P. Sex-typed mannerisms in normal boys and girls as a function of sex and age. *Child Development*, 1977, 48, 275-278.

Rekers, G.A., Bentler, P.M., Rosen, A.C., & Lovaas, O.I. Child gender disturbances: A clinical rationale for intervention. *Psychotherapy: Theory, Research and Practice*, 1977, 14, 2-11.

Rekers, G.A., Crandall, B.F., Rosen, A.C. & Bentler, P.M. Genetic and physical studies of male children with psychological gender disturbances. *Psychological Medicine*, 1979, 9, 373-375.

Rekers, G.A., & Hohn, R. Sex education. In J. Sears & J. Carper (Eds.), *Public Education and Religion: Conversations for Enlarging the Public Square*. New York: Teachers College Press, 1996, in press.

Rekers, G.A. & Jurich, A.P. Development of problems of puberty and sex-roles in adolescence. Chapter 33 in C. Eugene Walker and Michael C. Roberts (Eds.), *Handbook of Clinical Child Psychology*. New York: John Wiley and Sons, 1983, pages 785-812.

Rekers, G.A., Kilgus, M. & Rosen, A.C. Long-term effects of treatment for childhood gender disturbance. *Journal of Psychology and Human Sexuality*, 1990, 3(2), 121-153.

Rekers, G.A., & Kilgus, M.D. Differential diagnosis and rationale for treatment of gender identity disorders and transvestism. Chapter 12 in G.A. Rekers (Ed.), *Handbook of Child and Adolescent Sexual Problems*. New York, NY: Lexington Books of Macmillan/Simon & Schuster, 1995, pages 255-271.

Rekers, G.A., & Kilgus, M.D. Cross-sex behavior problems. Chapter in R.A. Hoekelman, S. Blatman, S.B. Friedman, N.M. Nelson & H.M. Seidel (Eds.), *Primary pediatric care: Third edition*. St. Louis, MO: C.V. Mosby Publishing Company, 1997, in press.

Rekers, G.A., & Lovaas, O.I. Behavioral treatment of deviant sex-role behaviors in a male child. *Journal of Applied Behavior Analysis*, 1974, 7, 173-190.

Rekers, G.A., Lovaas, O.I., & Low, B.P. The behavioral treatment of a "transsexual" preadolescent boy. *Journal of Abnormal Child Psychology*, 1974, 2, 99-116.

Rekers, G.A. & Mead, S. Early intervention for female sexual identity disturbance: Self-monitoring of play behavior. *Journal of Abnormal Child Psychology*, 1979, 7(4), 405-423.

Rekers, G.A. & Mead, S. Human sex differences in carrying behaviors: A replication and extension. *Perceptual and Motor Skills*, 1979, 48, 625-626.

Rekers, G.A. & Mead, S. Female sex-role deviance: Early identifica-

tion and developmental intervention. *Journal of Clinical Child Psychology*, 1980, 9(3), 199-203.

Rekers, G.A., Mead, S.L., Rosen A.C. & Brigham, S.L. Family correlates of male childhood gender disturbance. *Journal of Genetic Psychology*, 1983, 142, 31-42.

Rekers, G.A. & Milner, G.C. Sexual identity disorders in childhood and adolescence. *Journal of the Florida Medical Association*, 1978, 65, 962-964.

Rekers, G.A. & Milner, G.C. How to diagnose and manage childhood sexual disorders. *Behavioral Medicine*, 1979, 6(4), 18-21.

Rekers, G.A. & Milner, G.C. Early detection of sexual identity disorders. *Medical Aspects of Human Sexuality*, 1981, 15(11) 32EE-32FF.

Rekers, G.A. & Moray, S.M. Relationship of maternal report of feminine behavior and extraversion to the severity of gender disturbance. *Perceptual and Motor Skills*, 1989, pages 387-394. (a)

Rekers, G.A. & Moray, S.M. Sex-typed body movements as a function of severity of gender disturbance in boys. *Journal of Psychology and Human Sexuality*, 1989, pages 183-196. (b)

Rekers, G.A. & Moray, S.M. Personality problems associated with childhood gender disturbance. *Italian Journal of Clinical and Cultural Psychology*, 1989, 1, 85-90. (c)

Rekers, G.A. & Moray, S.M. The relationship of sex-typed play with clinician ratings on degree of gender disturbance. *Journal of Clinical Psychology*, 1990, 46, 28-34.

Rekers, G.A., Rosen A.C., Lovaas, O.I. & Bentler, P.M. Sex-role stereotype and professional intervention for childhood gender disturbances. *Professional Psychology*, 1978, 9, 127-136.

Rekers, G.A. & Rudy, J.P. Differentiation of childhood body gestures. *Perceptual and Motor Skills*, 1978, 46, 839-845.

Rekers, G.A., Sanders, J.A., Strauss, C.C., Rasbury, W.C. & Mead, S.L. Differentiation of adolescent activity participation. *Journal of Genetic Psychology*, 1989, 150(3), pages 323-335.

Rekers, G.A., Swihart, J.J. The association of parental separation with gender disturbance in male children. *Psychological Reports*, 1989, 65, 1272-1274.

Rekers, G.A. & Varni, J.W. Self-monitoring and self-reinforcement processes in a pre-transsexual boy. *Behavior Research and Therapy*, 1977, 15, 177-180.

Rekers, G. A. & Varni, J.W. Self-regulation and gender-role behaviors: A case study. *Journal of Behavior Therapy and Experimental Psychiatry*, 1977, 8, 427-432.

Rekers, G.A., Willis, T.J., Yates, C.E., Rosen, A.C., & Low, B.P. Assessment of childhood gender behavior change. *Journal of Child Psychology and Psychiatry*, 1977, 18, 53-65.

Rekers, G.A. & Yates, C.E. Sex-typed play in feminoid boys vs. normal boys and girls. *Journal of Abnormal Child Psychology*, 1976, 4, 1-8.

Rekers, G.A., Yates, C.E., Willis, T.J., Rosen, A.C., & Taubman, M. Childhood gender identity change: Operant control over sex-typed play and mannerisms. *Journal of Behavior Therapy and Experimental Psychiatry*, 1976, 7, 51-57.

Rosen, A. C. & Rekers, G.A. Toward a taxonomic framework for variables of sex and gender. *Genetic Psychology Monographs*, 1980, 102, 191-218.

Rosen, A.C. & Rekers, G.A. & Bentler, P.M. Ethical issues in the treatment of children. *Journal of Social Issues*, 1978, 34(2), 122-136.

Rosen, A. C., Rekers, G.A. & Brigham, S.L. Gender stereotypy in gender-dysphoric young boys. *Psychological Reports*, 1982, 51, 371-374.

Rosen, A.C. & Rekers, G.A. & Friar, L.R. Theoretical and diagnostic issues in child gender disturbances. *Journal of Sex Research*, 1977, 13(2), 89-103.

Rosen, A.C. & Rekers, G.A. & Moray, S.M. Projective test findings for boys with gender disturbance. *Perceptual and Motor Skills*, 1990, 71, 771-779.

Serbin, L.A. Sex-role socialization: A field in transition. In B.B. Lahey and A.E. Kazdin (Eds.), *Advances in Clinical Child Psychology, Volume Three*. New York: Plenum Publishing Corp., 1980, pages 41-96.

Zucker, K.J. Cross-gender-identified children. Chapter 4 in B.W. Steiner (Ed.), *Gender Dysphoria: Development, Research, Management*. New York: Plenum Publishing Corp., 1985, pages 75-174.

Zuger, B. Effeminate behavior present in boys from early childhood. I. The clinical syndrome and follow-up studies. *Journal of Pediatrics*, 1966, 69, 1098-1107.

Zuger, B. Effeminate behavior present in boys from childhood: Ten additional years of follow-up. *Comprehensive Psychiatry*, 1978, 19, 363-369.

Zuger, B. Early effeminate behavior in boys: Outcome and significance for homosexuality. *Journal of Nervous and Mental Disease*, 1984, 172, 90-97.

Kinsey and the
Homosexual Revolution

by Judith Reisman, Ph.D.[1]

Americans bestow authority—and billions of tax dollars—upon science in the belief that scientists will make important contributions to society. There is the further belief that scientists, in their responsibility and trust, will behave ethically, especially in research that involves human subjects.[2] While the former is certainly historically accurate, such trust in the class "scientists" as honest, humane persons who deserve unquestioned public faith is sustained neither by cross-cultural or American science history.

Under scrutiny is the role of Dr. Alfred C. Kinsey and his contention that Americans are 10% to 47%, more or less, homosexual. Kinsey's percentage was seized upon by Harry Hay, the father of the homosexual "civil rights" movement, when Hay formed the Mattachine Society, urging that homosexuality be seen no longer as an act of sodomy but as a 10% minority class. Today, scores of homosexual activists cite Kinsey as the man who made the homosexual movement possible.[3]

But what if all of Kinsey's work was fraudulent, or worse? What if it reflects unethical scientists conducting unprosecuted criminal acts? For example, is it possible that scientists have conducted sexual experiments on children? Or that they could allow or encourage child abusers to conduct such experiments? The possibility that this actually occurred—and indeed that the claimed results of such experiments have played a critical and sustained role in our law and public policy—has led Congress to submit legislation which calls for an examination of the relevant facts. The legislation focuses on the research and publications of Dr. Alfred Kinsey and his colleagues ("The Kinsey Institute") conducted at Indiana University in Bloomington, Indiana from the late 1930s to the early 1950s. The legislation is known as H.R. 2749, "The Child Protection and Ethics in Education Act."

The Science Crime & Fraud Context

Imperial Japan, Nazi Germany and Communist Rus-

sia are modern cross-cultural examples of totalitarian regimes which produced highly educated scientists who served their leaders without question—but with frightening and disastrous results. As cruel as were the actions of key scientific brutes like Dr. Joseph Mengele, just as instructive is the evidence of wholesale collusion by colleagues, universities, colleges and higher order think tanks. Thousands of state and private professional and pedagogical clubs and agencies were aware of the inhuman and unethical scientific activity, but rarely was there a protest made. Instead, their educated colleagues obsequiously bowed and jealously coveted association with the chosen scientific barbarians.

But, it has not only been totalitarian governments which have produced unethical scientists. Our own nation—a government designed to be of and by and for the people—was betrayed by our fantasy of non-judgmental, objective science. (It is only the trust in scientists as a "special" moral population that permits our nation to approve of fetal and DNA experimentation, as well as other forms of God-like tampering.) For example, consider the Willowbrook school scandal:

Pappworth published *Human Guinea Pigs*, a detailed recitation of experiments reported in reputable journals in which subjects were exposed to a variety of risky procedures not intended to benefit them. In chapter after chapter, he described the insertion of catheters and biopsy needles into important organs of the body (bladder, kidney, heart, liver) and resulting meningitis, shock, liver damage and cardiac arrest. The subjects of these procedures were newborns, infants and children (both healthy and diseased), pregnant women, prisoners, patients undergoing surgery, the mentally disabled, the aged, the critically ill, and the dying...[revealing] little concern on the part of investigators for their subjects ....experiments which involved injecting hepatitis virus into mentally retarded children at the Willowbrook State School in New York.[4]

Part of the problem is that the establishment press remains amazingly silent in the face of the most vile domestic scientific barbarisms. The Willowbrook school scandal and similar inhumane scientific abuses reflect but a few of the unprosecuted science felonies to reach the public. For example, examine some cites from *Harry S. Truman and the War Scare of 1948* by Frank Kofsky (1995):

Beginning in the late 1940s, under programs authorized by Truman, the U.S. government deliberately dropped radioactive material from planes or released it on the ground in a dozen experiments after World War II....Eight of the tests occurred in Tennessee and Utah in an effort to create a battlefield radiation weapon. In four other tests, radiation was released into the air in New Mexico....In at least four of these 12 experiments, radiation spread beyond the planned boundaries of the test....[5]

[And] All the tests were conducted between 1948 and 1952. The implication is clear: so vile were these "experiments" that even the Eisenhower administration could not stomach their continuation.... Nineteen mentally retarded boys who thought they were participating in a science club in the 1940s and 1950s were actually fed radioactive milk by scientists who wanted to learn about the digestive system, the *Boston Sunday Globe* reported." The "scientists" in question were affiliated with such ruling-class institutions as Harvard University and the Massachusetts Institute of Technology; their too-trusting subjects came from the Fernald State School....

[On radiating expectant mothers to see what the results would be] The figures in the *Boston Globe's* initial stories, however, proved to be far short of the mark, for the number of expectant women actually dosed with radioactive materials during these "experiments" probably numbered in the thousands. . . .several of the children exposed to the radioactive iron during their mother's pregnancy died....Army spokesmen acknowledged that 239 populated areas from coast to coast had been blanketed with bacteria between 1949 and 1969. Tests involved covering areas of Alaska and Hawaii and the cities of San Francisco, Washington, D.C., Key West, and Panama City in Florida. Some tests were more focused, such as those in which bacteria were sprayed onto the Pennsylvania Turnpike or into the New York City subway system.

"Distinguished scientists," writes Leonard A. Cole, "testified at the hearings that the tests were inappropriate and dangerous....the incidence of illnesses suddenly increased in some areas near the tests.[6]

The other part of the problem is, without an informed public directing its own community affairs, science historically serves its funders. Scientific patrons tend to be a small, powerful elite, which is necessarily subversive of a self-governing republic. If the medical, or the harder science experiments cited here are difficult for Americans to come to terms with, these aberrant experiments at least adhere to scientific form and are possible to replicate and validate or repudiate. However, the public does not understand (nor do scientists seem to understand) that the softer social sciences are largely not science, but rather what Professor Hobbs termed, "scientism." Human behavioral experiments without the limits of scientific protocol are easily manipulated and have frequently been misused by those in positions of trust to undermine the American way of life in the second half of the twentieth century.

Who, by now, has not heard of the Tuskegee syphilis experiments? If some American scientists could knowingly allow men to die slowly of syphilis, if others could infect pregnant women and endanger the lives of their unborn children, if still other unethical scientists could inject healthy and mentally retarded children with hepatitis, could not some American scientists teach pederasts and pedophiles techniques for sexually abusing children for "science"? Looking candidly at the facts of American scientific felons and the commonality of collegial collusion through silence or support, could scientists—who often feel unconstrained by Biblical standards or fears—not deceive a plebeian public about the percentage of men engaging in illicit sex, and those who are homosexual? Could scientists, together with philanthropic, pedagogical and legal colleagues of like mind and sexual proclivity, now strategize to use their considerable influence in the latter half century to change America's attitudes and sex crime laws to favor their own personal interests?

The Historical Context

Truman took office in 1945 and shortly thereafter released the atomic bomb. Kofsky's documentation suggests that Kinsey's revolutionary report was a welcome public diversion for Truman's administration. However, while the A-bomb took the lives of thousands and did untold damage to Japan for generations, "Kinsey's Bomb" has taken the lives of millions and is fomenting the disintegration of the local school, university, and public control, nationwide.

The 1945 A-Bomb: World War II ended in 1945 after America, under scientists headed by Dr. J. Robert Oppenheimer, and like a modern Prometheus, dropped the atomic bomb on Hiroshima and Nagasaki. In an instant, all of America was reeling, as both joy and anguish hit the nation with the force of that nuclear blast. Emotion rode high, for along with the immense relief that "it worked" and the brutal war was ended, came the quaking realization that while God had created the earth, science could now destroy it.

On the one hand, Americans were awed by Oppenheimer's ability to end the worldwide threat of war. On the other hand, our faith in ourselves as the world's savior was shattered by both the nuclear scare and ensuing newsreels of burning Japanese children, subverting our sense of moral integrity and who we really were as Americans. Aided by an army that now dispensed condoms, Yankee soldier-saviors of Europe and Asia broke the promises of their Puritan homeland. GIs returned home to wives and sweethearts in 1946 with the highest rate of venereal disease since the original VD epidemics of World War I. Yet, the overwhelming VD epidemic which raged overseas was quenched in the U.S. as young lads overflowing with penicillin waited for the marriage bed to carnally embrace the "girl next door."

The 1948 A-Bomb: Three years later, after decades of clandestine preparation and a relentless publicity campaign, Dr. Kinsey launched what was then called "The Kinsey A-Bomb" on America's now fragile sense of moral virtue. Wrapped in Oppenheimer's flag of science as the final authority, Kinsey's fraudulent sex science statistics seemed to "prove" middle America to be a nation of sexual hypocrites, liars, cowards and closet deviates, despite the fact that all of Kinsey's data were repudiated by the then current public health data. While the Armed Services found skyrocketing VD and illegitimacy rates abroad, we found no such domestic rates for these disorders or for abortion, rape and other sex crimes and sexual disorders. Wrong or right, the fighting men might be misbehaving overseas but by and large they *were not doing over here, what they were doing over there.*

Despite the common sense fact of low rates of illegitimacy and VD, despite personal knowledge of faithful and virtuous family and friends, mainstream America was dramatically shaken by Kinsey's data. The popular press hawked Kinsey as a diversion from Truman's ominous cold-war warnings, heralding the astonishing scientific findings—that 98% of men and roughly half of women had premarital sex, 95% of American men were legally sex offenders and 10% or more of men were largely homosexual. And, while *no one noted* that 317 infants and children were "tested" for Kinsey's child sex data, educators repeated his conclusions—that children were sexual from birth, hence school sex education, Kinsey style,

should be mandated.

The question anyone should be asking is: How did Kinsey get the statistics on childhood sexuality…that were to revolutionize the schoolroom, courtroom, pressroom, and bedroom? More succinctly put, did the Kinsey team participate in the pedophile abuse of 317 infants and children?

Kinsey's Research on Child Orgasm

Dr. Alfred Kinsey's research on child orgasm is described in Chapter 5 of his book *Sexual Behavior in the Human Male* (1948).[7] Some of the observations are summarized in Tables 30-34 of the book. The numbers of the children in the five tables were, respectively, 214, 317, 188, 182, and 28. The minimum ages were, respectively, one year, two months, five months, (ages of children not recorded for Table 33), and five months. The tables identify sex experiments; for example, Table 32 speaks of: "Speed of pre-adolescent orgasm; Duration of stimulation before climax; Observations timed with

Below is a reproduction of… "**Table 34. Examples of multiple orgasm in pre-adolescent males. Some instances of higher frequencies**" (*Sexual Behavior in the Human Male*, 1948). How were these figures gleaned?

AGE	NO. OF ORGASMS	TIME INVOLVED
5 mon.	3	?
11 mon.	10	1 hr.
11 mon.	{ 14	38 min.
	7	9 min.
2 yr.	11	65 min.
2.5 yr.	4	2 min.
4 yr.	6	5 min.
4 yr.	17	10 hr.
4 yr.	26	24 hr.
7 yr.	7	3 hr.
8 yr.	8	2 hr.
9 yr.	7	68 min.
10 yr.	9	52 min.
10 yr.	14	24 hr.
11 yr.	11	1 hr.
11 yr.	19	1 hr.
12 yr.	7	3 hr.
12 yr.	{ 3	3 min.
	9	2 hr.
12 yr.	12	2 hr.
12 yr.	15	1 hr.
13 yr.	7	24 min.
13 yr.	8	2.5 hr.
13 yr.	9	8 hr.
13 yr.	{ 3	70 sec.
	11	8 hr.
	26	24 hr.
14 yr.	11	4 hr.

second hand or stop watch."

Did Kinsey instigate or encourage these practices? And did he actually use pedophiles to obtain the data for Tables 30-34? In his book, acting as the on-site reporter, Kinsey did not clearly describe his own role. However, Kinsey's close colleague, C. A. Tripp, made a revealing statement in a 1991 televised interview by Phil Donahue:

[Reisman is] talking about data that came from pedophiles, that he [Kinsey] would listen only to pedophiles who were very careful, used stopwatches, knew how to record their thing, did careful surveys....[T]hey were trained observers.[8]

Two questions cry out for an answer: What was the nature of the training given to these "trained observers"? And, who "trained" them? Perhaps Dr. Tripp or others can answer these questions. A 1991 book review in the respected British medical journal, *The Lancet*, noted:

[T]he important allegations from the scientific viewpoint are the imperfections in the [Kinsey] sample and unethical, *possibly criminal observations on children*....Kinsey...has left his former co-workers some explaining to do.[9]

Tripp is not the only former Kinsey colleague to admit that actual pedophiles were involved in the Kinsey Institute's child sexuality studies. A taped telephone interview with Dr. Paul Gebhard, former head of the Kinsey Institute and Kinsey co-author, also confirms this fact:

Interviewer: "So, do pedophiles normally go around with stopwatches?"

Dr. Paul Gebhard: "Ah, they do if we tell them we're interested in it!"

* * *

Interviewer: "And clearly, [the orgasms of] at least 188 children were timed with a stopwatch, according to...."

Dr. Gebhard: "So, second hand or stopwatch. OK, well, that's, ah, you refreshed my memory. I had no idea that there were that many."

* * *

Interviewer: "These experiments by pedophiles on children were presumably illegal."

Dr. Gebhard: "Oh yes."[10]

Molesting Children in the Name of Science

In *Sexual Behavior in the Human Male*, Dr. Kinsey reported that the data on the 317 children came from "9 of our adult male subjects."[11] However, Dr. John Bancroft, current Director of the Kinsey Institute, contradicted this claim. After examining the data, Dr. Bancroft indicated that the data for Table 31 came from a single adult male subject.[12] There are a number of other instances where Kinsey's published claims about numerical or factual data—claims with important implications if true—are now believed to be misleading or false.[13,14,15] A review of Kinsey's original data, claims and possible involvement is long overdue.[16,17]

Kinsey's "trained observers" tested babies "5 months in age," for repeated orgasms via:

...empirical study and statistical procedures... which resulted in...reported observations on such specifically sexual activities as erection, pelvic thrust and several other characteristics of true orgasm in a list of 317 pre-adolescent boys, ranging between infants of 5 months and adolescence age.[18]

Orgasm was defined as follows:

Extreme tension with violent convulsions: ...sudden heaving and jerking of the whole body... gasping... hands grasping, mouth distorted, sometimes with tongue protruding; whole body or parts of it spasmodically twitching...violent jerking of the penis...groaning, sobbing, or more violent cries, sometimes with an abundance of tears (especially among younger children).... hysterical laughing, talking, sadistic or masochistic reactions... extreme trembling, collapse, loss of color, and sometimes fainting of subject.... some...suffer excruciating pain and may scream ...if the penis is even touched....some...before the arrival of orgasm, will fight away from the partner and may make violent attempts to avoid climax although they derive definite pleasure from the situation.[19]

Lester Caplan, M.D., Diplomate, the American Board of Pediatrics, reviewing Kinsey's Chapter 5 (as above) said, "One person could not do this to so many children—these children had to be held down or subject to strapping down, otherwise they would not respond willingly,"[20] especially if, as Dr. Gebhard notes, a cinema record was being made.[21]

Child interviews were unusually long. Kinsey said after two hours, "the [adult] becomes fatigued and the quality of the record drops."[22] Still, Kinsey reported 24-hour orgasm "interviews" of a four-, a 10- and a 13-year-old;[23] a four-year-old for 10 hours; a nine and 13-year-old for eight hours; and so on.[24] Dr. Gebhard's taped phone interview further details some of these techniques.[25]

Dr. Kinsey even reported that some observers "induced...erections [in the children]...over periods of months or years,"[26] but that the Kinsey team interviewed no "psychotics who were handicapped with poor memories, hallucination, or fantasies that distorted the fact."[27] What kind of men were they, this Kinsey team? The question remains: Who did these experiments? As noted, the Kinsey team reported on a cadre of "trained observers." In Kinsey's own words…

Better data came from adult males *who have had sexual contacts with younger boys* and who, with their adult backgrounds, are able to recognize and interpret the boys' experiences. Unfortunately ....[only] 9 of our adult male subjects have observed such orgasm. Some of these adults are technically trained persons who have kept diaries or other records which have been put at our disposal....on 317 pre-adolescents who were either observed in self-masturbation or....with other boys or older adults.[28]

There are serious questions which must be answered by the Kinsey Institute directors—*for Kinsey's is arguably the most influential model for scientific sex taught to the nations' schoolchildren today.* The proposed Congressional investigation is critical for that reason alone. How did the Kinsey team know that an 11-month-old had 10 orgasms in one hour? (See Table this article.) How did they verify these data? Where were the children's parents? Have attempts been made to locate the children? Who were the subjects of Table 34?[29,30] Certainly these were not the children pictured in the publicity photographs which were distributed to the press and the gullible academic world, such as the little, braided girl of roughly four years, sitting with "Uncle Prock" in innocent play.

Further, Dr. Gebhard claimed in a letter to me, that they did *no* follow-up on these children since it was "impossible or too expensive."[31] Later Gebhard said Kinsey was correct, some children were followed up and *"we do have some names"* of the children.[32] There is still no answer to the question, "Where are the children of Table 34?" It is finally in the hands of Congress to determine what really happened at the Kinsey Institute.

H.R. 2749, the Child Protection and Ethics in Education Act of 1995, is a bill to determine if Kinsey's two principal books on human sexual behavior "are the result of any fraud or criminal wrongdoing." Clearly a useful step would be the gathering of facts on the work of Kinsey and his colleagues and a public disclosure of these facts in a responsible fashion. The U.S. Congress is in a strong position to carry out this kind of fact-finding as a precursor to legislation. An attempt should be made to answer certain questions that bear directly or indirectly on H.R. 2749:

- Did Kinsey and his colleagues behave in an ethical fashion in the way they collected and published data from human subjects, especially children?

- Apart from the ethical considerations, did they analyze and publish their data correctly from the scientific point of view?

- Were federal funds solicited, used, and accounted for appropriately?

- Do the answers to the preceding three questions indicate any violations of federal law?

If the information collected and published by Kinsey proves, on examination, to be badly flawed or to involve fraud or criminal wrongdoing, what are the implications for the use of this information in science, education, law and public policy? Specifically, to what extent should the federal government[33] fund or recall the dissemination and use of this information?

Kinsey's Figures on Homosexuality

With the above in mind, it is shocking that, almost overnight, following release of Kinsey's *Sexual Behavior in the Human Male* (and a succession of earlier private, public relations briefings at the Kinsey Institute for favorable interviewers), books, articles, films, news clips, cartoons, radio, TV, and front-page stories appeared coast to coast as part of a publicity campaign to institutionalize Kinsey's claims. Americans believed "the most famous man for ten years" that primitive, sexually permissive cultures were happier than were Mr. and Mrs. Jones.

However, without question, any "scientists" who reprint and encourage production of data on child sexuality which have been taken from child sex offenders engaged in "manual or oral" sex with babies and children, are not scientists but propagandists—indeed guilty of admitted criminal sexual conduct, by the descriptions in their publications, whether the sexual offender(s) were identified and prosecuted or not. To trust anything these men or their disciples produce is to put one's faith in those who use the language of science to accomplish personal, criminal, and/or sexual interests. Hence, whatever Kinsey's claims of homosexual percentages and normality were, these become, pragmatically, as invalid as his child sexuality data.

Kinsey fathered not only the sexual revolution, as Hugh Hefner and others have said, but the homosexual revolution as well. Harry Hay gave Kinsey that credit when Hay read in 1948 that Kinsey found "10%" of the male population homosexual. Following the successful path of the Black Civil Rights movement, Hay, a long-time communist organizer, said 10% was a political force which could be melded into a "sexual minority" only seeking "minority rights." With Kinsey as the wind in his sails, Hay formed the Mattachine Society.

But 26% (1,400) of Kinsey's alleged 5,300 white male subjects were already "sex offenders."[34] As far as the data can be established, an additional 25% were incarcerated prisoners; some numbers were big city "pimps," "hold-up men," "thieves;" roughly 4% were male prostitutes as well as sundry other criminals; and some hundreds of homosexual activists at various "gay bars" and other haunts from coast to coast.[35] This group of social outcasts and deviants were then redefined by the Kinsey team as representing your average "Joe College." With adequate press and university publicity, the people believed what they were told by our respectable scientists, that mass sexual perversion was common nationwide—so our sex education and our laws must be changed to reflect Kinsey's "reality."

Following the release of *Kinsey, Sex and Fraud*,[36] the then Kinsey Institute Director, Dr. June Reinisch, initiated a "CONFIDENTIAL," international, 87-page mass-mailing of accusatory materials calling upon recipients to repudiate "Judith Reisman's accusations." One of the accusations Reinisch wanted repudiated was the fact that Kinsey's 10% to 47% or more homosexual data were fraudulently generalized to the "general public." (Kinsey's homosexual figures were exposed as wholly false in 1948 by Albert Hobbs et al, as well as by several other scientists then and since.) In her letter to past Kinsey Director and Kinsey co-author Dr. Paul Gebhard, Reinisch denies the Kinsey team's culpability for the child sex abuse data and states that the Kinsey team never did "conduct experiments." She asks Gebhard's aid in discrediting me. She adds:

> Further, with regard to sampling and the generalizability of the findings to a broader portion of Americans, throughout both volumes Kinsey very clearly identifies exactly which data from which groups he is referring to when drawing conclusions. He *never* used data from the special samples, derived from such populations as the gay community or prisons, to generalize to the general public.[37]

Unfortunately, Dr. Gebhard wrote back to Reinisch on December 6, 1990 that she was wrong and that Kinsey did use "the gay community," pedophiles and prisoners to generalize to the population at large. Gebhard writes:

In your recent letter of December 3, which I gather was sent to a number of individuals as well as me, you refuted Judith Reisman's allegations about Kinsey and the Institute. However, I fear that your final paragraph on page 1 may embarrass you and the university if it comes to Reisman's attention. Hence I want to warn you and relevant university officials so that some damage control might be devised. The paragraph ends with this sentence: "He *never* used data from the special samples, derived from such populations as the gay community or prisons, to generalize to the general public." This statement is incorrect. Kinsey did mix male prison inmates in with his sample used in *Sexual Behavior in the Human Male....*

As to generalizing to a wider population, in his first volume Kinsey did generalize to the entire U.S. population. See, for one example, the tables on page 188 and 220 where he clearly extrapolates to the U.S.....

I am distressed that neither you nor your staff seem to be familiar with Kinsey's first book nor with *The Kinsey Data* and consequently produced the erroneous statement in your letter.[38]

Conclusion

Kinsey is a powerful example of one's personal orientation affecting one's science and the moral shape of society. What could be the motive of Kinsey's fraudulent data, which often found up to even half of average American males homosexual? Quite possibly, it amounts to Kinsey's wishful thinking, which he quantified in order to recreate others in his own distorted image. Was Kinsey himself a closet homosexual, pedophile or pederast?

In the past, science fraud has taken place for economic and political reasons—but with Kinsey, was his "science" rather the outgrowth of personal morality and sexual proclivity? If that were true, he has certainly not been the last. In recent years, the world has seen other "men of science" (Hamer, LeVay, Pillard et al) whose work lacks objectivity and who seem to be justifying their own lives with their [questionable] findings. Were these scientists making claims about beetles, fauna or supernovae, there would be less cause for alarm; however, the travesty is that—in a culture in which science is the preferred religion (a no-fault religion) and scientists its high priests— these men's words are being received as "gospel" (no matter how little factual basis they have) on a subject as important and wide-sweeping as human sexuality. Unfortunately, the scientific world and the western world at large has all too eagerly embraced Kinsey's work.

No matter what Kinsey's own sexual orientation, scientists and laypersons alike must acknowledge that he engineered a study of child sexuality which was unthinkable. The Kinsey Institute's data on child orgasms are, at best, a human concoction or, at worst, the results of child molestation. In either case, the Kinsey Institute is guilty of criminal activity and their findings on all subjects are suspect and misleading. Too, science must be re-evaluated, for Kinsey's work has hijacked an entire body of science for almost half a century, leaving behind untold damage to families, relationships and human souls.

The control of sexuality information has for too long been in the hands of the Kinsey elite—unethical scientists, men without moral conscience or honor, who fathered a bastard sexual revolution. It should come as no surprise then to those on our campuses and in the halls of legislative, judicial and educational power, that as our nation has followed Kinsey and his disciples, we too have become increasingly coarsened to conscience and honor. It is clear that sexual aggression, brutality and hedonism have greater sway in our society post-Kinsey than was the case pre-Kinsey.

No matter what Kinsey's own sexual proclivities and biases, after WWII Kinsey began to move in concert with a cadre of revisionist educators, lawyers and other professionals who determined with their sponsors to forever alter the American way of life through its educational system (the future) and the legal system (the standard of judgment). Prior to the Kinsey Reports, American law held that not only were sodomy, adultery, fornication and the like transgressions, those who committed such acts were themselves unacceptable. Post-Kinsey, these once-criminal acts and their actors began moving toward acceptability. The new law system used Kinsey as its primary and only scientific authority, and pointed America in a downward direction, promoting today's entire panoply of sexual deviances more common to the Pre-Christian era.

In the upheaval of the post-World War II period, Kinsey, for his part, refashioned the way humankind looked upon sexuality and separated this most powerful of human acts from its labor-intensive *procreational* function, pronouncing true human sexuality in the new human nature to be free, self-fulfilling and *recreational*.

Kinsey lives and reigns today in classrooms across America. The Ten Commandments may be out of our classrooms, but the Kinseyan-based "One in Ten" project is in, and "prima nocte"—the medieval practice of an overreaching government taking a young person's innocence, modesty and virtue (as depicted in the film *Braveheart*)—is a pervasive and accepted practice today in the schools of our American village.

Kinsey sold his soul to win his place in time, but now is the time to take back America's soul which has been led astray by fraudulent and criminal science. It is soon fifty years since Kinsey foisted his hoax upon a trusting and moral American people. The American standard was right all along. Let's pull the curtain back and call for a proper investigation of Kinsey's fraudulent investigation into human sexuality. Write and call your political representatives now to begin the debunking and defunding of Kinsey and truth will restore social virtue once again to our nation.

Author's note: Since the establishment media has largely censored this information, if you have or desire any information on Kinsey, the use of his materials, or his role in your life or the lives of others, kindly call the 800 number listed. *Kinsey, Sex and Fraud, The Children of Table 34*—a Family Research Council video of the Kinsey fraud (30 min.), and the *Reisman & Johnson Report* (comparing homosexual and heterosexual personals or "In Search Of" ads) can be obtained via First Principals Press, 1-800-837-0544.

Judith Reisman, Ph.D., President of The Institute For Media Education, received her doctorate in Communication from Case Western Reserve University. She authored the Department of Justice/Juvenile Justice and Delinquency Prevention report, *"Images of Children, Crime and Violence"* (1989), *Kinsey, Sex and Fraud* (Reisman & Eichel, 1990) and *Soft Porn Plays Hardball* (1991). She has appeared in scientific journals *Ethology and Sociobiology, The New Universities Quarterly* (England), *The New York University Review of Law and Social Change,* and has chapters and citations in numerous academic texts, scholarly books and lay books.

Endnotes:

[1] The Institute For Media Education, Box 7404, Arlington, Virginia, 22207.

[2] *Science* Magazine editorial, January 9, 1987.

[3] See *Long Road to Freedom: The Advocate History of the Gay and Lesbian Movement,* ed. Mark Thompson, Stonewall Inn Edition, New York: St. Martin's Press, 1994, pp. 22, 59-60, 102, 164.

[4] *The Lancet* (April 1971), as taken from the Department of Health and Human Services' "Protection of Human Subjects" report, FR 52880, November 23, 1982.

[5] Frank Kofsky, *Harry S. Truman and the War Scare of 1948*, New York: St. Maritn's Press (1995), p. xvii.

[6] Ibid., p. xix.

[7] Key pages from Kinsey's 1948 *Male* volume, pp. 157-192, "Early Sexual Growth and Activity."

[8] "The Donahue Show," transcript, December 5, 1990.

[9] *The Lancet*, March 2, 1991, p. 547. Emphasis added.

[10] Audiotaped phone discussion between J. Gordon Muir, editor of *Kinsey, Sex and Fraud*, and Paul Gebhard on November 2, 1992.

[11] *Male* volume, p. 177: The nine men "have observed such orgasm. Some of these adults are technically trained persons who have kept diaries or other records which have been put at our disposal; and from them we have secured information on 317 pre-adolescents who

were either engaged in self masturbation, or who were observed in contacts with other boys or older adults." *The Washington Post* (December 8, 1995, p. F1, F4) reports Dr. Bancroft saying, "Kinsey gives the impression that the data came from three or four men, but it was just the one." He speculates that Kinsey "kept that bit to himself because he thought the public might not react well to his use of data from a sex criminal." Elsewhere Bancroft is reported saying, "I have looked at the data on which these tables appear to be based, and I am fairly confident that the data for all 317 cases came from the one old man..." (September 19, 1995, *Indianapolis Star*, A1, A4), etc.

[12] *The Indianapolis Star*, September 19, 1995, p. 4, col. 1, "an elderly scientist."

[13] Activities such as "forcing" correct answers from subjects and suggesting that investigators might find some way to treat the data should they find these answers unacceptable is not science, Male volume, Op. cit., p. 55.

[14] Ibid., p. 58.

[15] Pomeroy, Wardell, *Dr. Kinsey and The Institute For Sex Research.* Harper & Row, New York (1972), pp. 208-209. "By 1946, he, Gebhard and I had interviewed about 1,400 convicted sex offenders in penal institutions scattered over a dozen states." (On this page Pomeroy notes Kinsey's explanation that all American males are really sex offenders, by law, hence the need to largely eliminate sex offender laws). Kinsey's data included these deviants and prisoners as average American men. In court documents, former Kinsey Institute Director, Dr. June Reinisch writes that Kinsey "never used data from the special samples, derived from such populations as the gay community or prisons, to generalize to the general public" and Dr. Gebhard replied, "I fear that your final paragraph will embarrass you and the university if it comes to Reisman's attention.... This statement is incorrect. Kinsey did mix male prison inmates in with his sample used in the Male volume."

[16] See Maslow and Sakoda, "Volunteer Error in the Kinsey Study," *Journal of Abnormal and Social Psychology*, 47, 1952 (pp. 259-262).

[17] Writing in *Our Sexuality*, (2nd edition), Menlo Park, California: The Benjamin/Cummings Publishing Co. sexologists, Crooks & Baur, offer a sexological view of the term "direct observation:" A third method for studying human sexual behavior is *direct observation*. [Original emphasis.] This type of research may vary greatly in form and setting, ranging from laboratory studies that observe and record sexual responses to participant observation where the researchers join their subjects in sexual activity," (p. 64).

[18] Kinsey, *Male* volume, p. 181.

[19] Ibid., pp. 160-161.

[20] Letter to Judith Reisman from Lester Caplan M.D. (Baltimore, Maryland), Diplomate, the American Board of Pediatrics, reviewing the child data.

[21] See exhibit E, Pomeroy's letter to Reisman, para 2, "Some of these sources have added to their written or verbal reports photographs, and, in a few instances, cinema." The Kinsey Institute is on record as possessing a selection of child pornography films and photographs.

[22] Kinsey, *Male* volume, p. 181.

[23] Ibid., p. 180.

[24] "Was Kinsey a Fake and a Pervert?," *The Village Voice*, December 11, 1990, p. 41.

[25] Op. cit. fn #9.

[26] Kinsey, *Male* volume, p. 177. Moreover, as Lewis Terman pointed out in his critique of Kinsey, "The author lists (p. 39) "many hundred" persons who brought in "delinquent groups: male prostitutes, female prostitutes, bootleggers, gamblers, pimps, prison inmates, thieves and hold-up men. These, presumably, would have brought in others of their kind, but in what numbers they did so we are not told." Terman also notes "a dozen prison populations" included "a state school for feeble-minded, two children's homes, and two homes for unmarried mothers....plus "more than 1,200 persons who have been con-

victed of sex offenses." (Kinsey's "Sexual Behavior in the Human Male: Some Comments and Criticisms," Lewis Terman, *Sexual Behavior in American Society:* An Appraisal of the First Two Kinsey Reports, NYC: W.W. Norton & Co., 1955, p. 447).

[27] Ibid., p. 37.

[28] Ibid., p. 177. Emphasis added.

[29] After I asked these questions in 1981, the Kinsey Institute launched a 12-year-long national campaign to undermine my investigation. The 87-page Kinsey Institute "confidential" package mailed worldwide, and especially to those who might interview Reisman on the issue are available.

[30] Beyond *Kinsey, Sex and Fraud* (1990), the recently released video, *The Children of Table 34,* narrated by Ephrem Zimbalist Jr., is a very important tool for understanding the way in which the Kinsey data have been used to mislead the nation. This half-hour video documents the history of the Kinsey fraud and establishes Kinsey as the foundation of current homosexual advocacy and classroom sex education and AIDS Prevention.

[31] Gebhard letter to me, March 11, 1981.

[32] In the *Male* volume, Kinsey describes the children's trauma (which he saw as orgasmic), claiming to also have data on "a smaller percentage of older boys and adults which continues these reactions throughout life," p. 161. Gebhard also says they have the names, Op. cit. fn #9.

[33] In most of their recent news releases, Indiana University denied they received any federal money which served to support Dr. Kinsey's research efforts.

However, in addition to other grants, in 1957 the National Institute of Mental Health granted approximately $50,000 per year for three years to the Institute, several years before Kinsey's sex study concluded. Furthermore, many millions of dollars from tax-free institutions were diverted to Dr. Kinsey's research during his lifetime, and millions of federal, state and tax-free funds continue to be funneled into the Kinsey Institute.

"[I]n 1957, under Gebhard's leadership, new sources of federal and private funding were found....During the 1970s, with funding from the National Institute of Mental Health, the Kinsey Institute was able to develop an information service," SIECUS Report, September 1985, 6-7.

The Official Brochure, *Institute for Sex Research, Indiana University* (1970) reads, "News of Kinsey's efforts reached the National Research Council's Committee for Research on Problems of Sex when he applied for a grant....in late 1940 [and was awarded] $1,600, the monies being provided by the Medical Division of the Rockefeller Foundation....increased to $7,500....by 1946, reached $35,000....the National Institute of Mental Health awarded the Institute the first in a series of grants which were destined to continue for years and to constitute the major financial support of the [Kinsey] research. In the Customs case a federal district course ruled in favor of the Institute, empowering it to import for research purpose any sort of erotic material and allowing such materials to be sent through the mails...*regarded as a landmark in the history of the relationship between science and law.*" pp. 3, 6. (Emphasis added.).

[34] Wardell Pomeroy, *Dr. Kinsey and the Institute for Sex Research*, New York: Harper and Row (1972), p. 208.

[35] Ibid. Also see British Broadcasting Company's biography of Kinsey, released on Arts and Entertainment, August 7, 1996.

[36] Judith Reisman, *Kinsey, Sex and Fraud* (Lafayette, Louisiana: Huntington House, 1990). The British medical journal, *The Lancet*, said: "*In Kinsey Sex and Fraud*, Dr. Judith Reisman and her colleagues demolish the foundations of the two [Kinsey] reports."

[37] Letter to Paul Gebhard, December 3, 1990.

[38] Letter from Paul Gebhard, December 6, 1990. Both letters are official deposition exhibits.

How America Went Gay

by Charles W. Socarides, M.D.

For more than 20 years, I and a few of my colleagues in the field of psychoanalysis have felt like an embattled minority, because we have continued to insist, against today's conventional wisdom, that gays aren't born that way. We know that obligatory homosexuals are caught up in unconscious adaptations to early childhood abuse and neglect and that, with insight into their earliest beginnings, they can change. This "adaptation" I speak of is a polite term for men going through the motions of mating not the with opposite sex but with one another.

For most of this century, most of us in the helping professions considered this behavior aberrant. Not only was it "off the track"; the people caught up in it were suffering, which is why we called it a pathology. We had patients, early in their therapy, who would seek out one sex partner after another—total strangers—on a single night, then come limping into our offices the next day to tell us how they were hurting themselves. Since we were in the business of helping people learn how not to keep hurting themselves, many of us though we were quietly doing God's work.

Now, in the opinion of those who make up the so-called cultural elite, our view is "out of date." The elite say we hurt people more than we help them, and that we belong in one of the century's dustbins. They have managed to sell this idea to a great many Americans, thereby making homosexuality fashionable and raising formerly aberrant behavior to the status of an "alternate lifestyle."

You see this view expressed in some places you would least expect. The Pope says same-sex sex is wrong, but a good many of his own priests in this country (some of whom are gay themselves) say the Pope is wrong. Indeed, in much of academe and in many secondary school classrooms gays are said to lead a new vanguard, the wave of the future in a world that will be more demographically secure when it has fewer "breeders" (which is what some gay activists call heterosexuals these days).

How did this change come about? Well, the revolution did not just happen. It has been orchestrated by a small band of very bright men and women—most of them gays and lesbians—in a cultural campaign that has been going on since a few intellectuals laid down the ideological underpinnings for the entire tie-dyed, try-anything-sexual Woodstock generation. In various ways, Theodore Reich, Alfred Kinsey, Fritz Perls, Norman O. Brown, Herbert Marcuse and Paul Goodman preached a new countercultural gospel: "If it feels good, do it."

It was all part of a plan, as one gay publication put it, "to make the whole world gay." I am not making this up. You can read an account of the campaign in Dennis Altman's *The Homosexualization of America.* In 1982 Altman, himself gay, reported with an air of elation that more and more Americans were thinking like gays and acting like gays. There were engaged, that is, "in numbers of short-lived sexual adventures either in place of or alongside long-term relationships." Altman cited the heterosexual equivalents of gay saunas and the emergence of the swinging singles scene as proofs that "promiscuity and 'impersonal sex' are determined more by social possibilities than by inherent differences between homosexuals and heterosexuals, or even between men and women."

Heady stuff. Gays said they could "reinvent human nature, reinvent themselves." To do this, these reinventors had to clear away one major obstacle. No, they didn't go after the nation's clergy. They targeted the members of a worldly priesthood, the psychiatric community, and neutralized them with a radical redefinition of homosexuality itself. In 1972 and 1973 they co-opted the leadership of the American Psychiatric Association and, through a series of political maneuvers, lies and outright flim-flams, they "cured" homosexuality overnight—by fiat. They got the A.P.A. to say that same-sex sex was "not a disorder." It was merely "a condition"—as neutral as lefthandedness.

This amounted to a full approval of homosexuality. Those of us who did not go along with the political redefinition were soon silenced at our own professional meetings. Our lectures were canceled inside academe and our research papers turned down in the learned journals. Worse things followed in the culture at large. Television and movie producers began to do stories promoting homosexuality as a legitimate lifestyle. A gay review board told Hollywood how it should deal or not deal with homosexuality. Mainstream publishers turned down books that objected to the gay revolution. Gays and lesbians influenced sex education in our nation's schools, and gay and lesbian libbers seized wide control of faculty committees in our nations' colleges. State legislatures nullified laws against sodomy.

If the print media paid any attention at all, they tended to hail the gay revolution, possibly because many of the reporters on gay issues were themselves gay and open advocates for the movement. And those reporters who were not gay seemed too intimidated by groupthink to expose what was going on in their own newsrooms.

And now, what happens to those of us who stand up and object? Gay activists have already anticipated that. They have created a kind of conventional wisdom: that we suffer from homophobia, a disease that has actually been invented by gays projecting their own fear on society. And we are bigots besides, because, they say, we fail to deal with gays compassionately. Gays are now no different than people born black or Hispanic or physically challenged. Since gays are born that way and have no choice about their sexual orientation, anyone who calls same-sex sex an aberration is now a bigot. Un-American, too. Astoundingly now, college freshmen come home for their first Thanksgiving to announce, "Hey, Mom! Hey, Dad! We've taken the high moral ground. We've joined the gay revolution."

My wife, Clare, who has an unerring aptitude for getting to the heart of things, said one day recently in passing, "I think everybody's being brainwashed." That gave me a start. I know "brainwashing" is a term that has been used and overused. But my wife's casual observation only reminded me of a brilliant tract I had read several years ago and then forgotten. It was called *After the Ball: How American Will Conquer its Fear and Hatred of Gays in the 1990's*, by Marshall Kirk and Hunter Madsen.

That book turned out to be the blueprint gay activists would use in their campaign to normalize the abnormal through a variety of brainwashing techniques once catalogued by Robert Jay Lifton in his seminal work, *Thought Reform and the Psychology of Totalism: A Study of Brainwashing in China.*

In their book Kirk and Madsen urged that gay activists adopt the very strategies that helped change the political face of the largest nation on earth. The authors knew the techniques had worked in China. All they needed was enough media—and enough money—to put them to work in the United States. And they did. These activists got the media and the money to radicalize America—by processes known as *desensitization, jamming* and *conversion.*

They would *desensitize* the public by selling the no-

tion that gays were "just like everyone else." This would make the engine of prejudice run out of steam, i.e., lull straights into an attitude of indifference.

They would *jam* the public by shaming them into a kind of guilt at their own "bigotry." Kirk and Madsen wrote:

> All normal persons feel shame when they perceive that they are not thinking, feeling, or acting like one of the pack....The trick is to get the bigot into the position of feeling a conflicting twinge of shame...when his homohatred surfaces. Thus, propagandistic advertisement can depict homophobic and homohating bigots as crude loudmouths....It can show them being criticized, hated, shunned. It can depict gays experiencing horrific suffering as the direct result of homohatred—suffering of which even most bigots would be ashamed to be the cause.

The best thing about this technique, according to Kirk and Madsen: The bigot did not even have to believe he was a loathsome creature:

> Rather, our effect is achieved without reference to facts, logic, or proof. Just as the bigot became such, without any say in the matter, through repeated infralogical emotional conditioning, his bigotry can be alloyed in exactly the same way, whether he is conscious of the attack or not. In short, jamming succeeds insofar as it inserts even a slight frisson of doubt and shame into the previously unalloyed, self-righteous pleasure. The approach can be quite useful and effective—if our message can get the massive exposure upon which all else depends.

Finally—this was the process they called conversion—Kirk and Madsen predicted a mass public change of heart would follow, even among bigots, "if we can actually make them like us." They wrote, "Conversion aims at just this...conversion of the average American's emotions, mind, and will, through a planned psychological attack, in the form of propaganda fed to the nation via the media."

In the movie "Philadelphia" we see the shaming technique and the conversion process working at the highest media level. We saw Tom Hank's character suffering (because he was gay and had AIDS) at the hands of bigots in his Philadelphia law firm. Not only were we ashamed of the homophobic behavior of the villainous straight lawyers in the firm; we felt nothing but sympathy for the suffering Hanks. (Members of the Motion Picture Academy felt so much sympathy they gave Hanks an Oscar.) Our feelings helped fulfill Kirk and Madsen's strategy:

"to make Americans hold us in warm regard, whether they like it or not."

Few dared speak out against "Philadelphia" as an example of the kind of propaganda Kirk and Madsen had called for. By then, four years after the publication of the Kirk-Madsen blueprint, the American public had already been programmed. Homosexuality was now simply "an alternate lifestyle." Best of all, because of the persuaders embedded in thousands of media messages, society's acceptance of homosexuality seemed one of those spontaneous, historic turnings in time—yes, a kind of conversion. Nobody quite knew how it happened, but the nation had changed. We had become more sophisticated, more loving toward all, even toward those "afflicted" with the malady—excuse me, condition.

By 1992 the President of the United States said it was time that people who were openly gay and lesbian should not be ousted from the nation's armed forces. In 1993 the nation's media celebrated a huge outpouring of gay pride in Washington, D.C. Television viewers chanted along with half a million marchers, "Two, four, six, eight! Being gay is really great." We felt good about ourselves. We were patriotic Americans. We had abolished one more form of discrimination, wiped out one of society's most enduring afflictions: homophobia. Best of all, we knew now that gay was good, gay was free.

Excuse me. Gay is not good. Gay is not decidedly free. How do I know this? For more than 40 years, I have been in solidarity with hundreds of homosexuals, my patients, and I have spent most of my professional life engaged in exercising a kind of "pastoral care" on their behalf. But I do not help them by telling them they are O.K. when they are not O.K. Nor do I endorse their "new claim to self-definition and self-respect." Tell me: Have we dumped the idea that a man's self-esteem comes from something inside himself (sometimes called character) and from having a good education, a good job and a good family—and replaced that notion with this, that he has an affinity to love (and have sex with) other men?

In point of fact, many of my patients had character; they had an education; they were respected ad men and actuaries and actors. But they were still in pain—for one reason and one reason alone. They were caught up in this mysterious compulsion to have sex with other men. They were not free. They were not happy. And they wanted to see if they could change.

Over the years, I found that those of my patients who really wanted to change could do so, by attaining the insight that comes with a good psychoanalysis. Others found other therapies that helped them get to the bottom of their compulsions, all of which involved high motivation and hard work. Difficult as their therapeutic trips were, hundreds and thousands of homosexuals changed their ways. Many of my own formerly homosexual patients—

about a third of them—are married today and happily so, with children. One-third may not sound like a very good average. But it is just about the same success rate you will find at the best treatment centers for alcoholics, like Hazelden in Minnesota and the Betty Ford Clinic in California.

Another third of my patients remain homosexual but not part of the gay scene. Now, after therapy, they still have same-sex sex, but they have more control over their impulses because now they understand the roots of their need for same-sex sex. Some of these are even beginning to turn on to the opposite sex. I add this third to my own success rate—so that I can tell people in all honesty that my batting average is .667 out of more than a thousand "at bats."

Of course, I could bat .997 if I told all my patients in pain that their homosexuality was "a special call" and "a liberation." That would endear me to everyone, but it would not help them. It would be a lie—despite recent pieces of pseudo-science bolstering the fantasy that gays are "born that way." The media put its immediate blessing on this "research," but we were oversold. Now we are getting reports, even in such gay publications as *The Journal of Homosexuality*, that the gay-gene studies and the gay-brain studies do not stand up to critical analysis. (The author of one so-called "gay-gene theory" is under investigation by the National Institutes of Health for scientific fraud.)

I was not surprised to hear this. My long clinical experience and a sizable body of psychoanalysis research dating all the way back to Freud tell me that most men caught up in same-sex sex are reacting, at an unconscious level, to something amiss with their earliest upbringing—overcontrolling mothers and abdicating fathers. Through long observation I have also learned that the supposedly liberated homosexual is never really free. In his multiple, same-sex adventures, even the most effeminate gay was looking to incorporate the manhood of others, because he was in a compulsive, never-ending search for the masculinity that was never allowed to build and grow in early childhood.

When I tried to explain these dynamics to the writer who helped me put together a kind of popular catechism on homosexuality, I found he had a hard time understanding what this "incorporation" meant. He said, "Your patient would be more manly if he took in the penis of another man? Sounds a little dumb. Would I run faster if I ate the flesh of a deer?"

I told him, "You have to understand that we are talking about feelings that come from deep in the unconscious mind. They are very primitive. In fact, if you have ever read any Indian lore, you may remember that Indians would, in fact, eat the flesh of a deer in order to become faster afoot. To us, that is a very primitive idea. But it had a mythic significance for a young Iroquois brave. And Madison Avenue still makes use of such mythic meanings. The ad people sell us things based on the notion that we will become what we eat or drink or possess." The point I was making was this: We do not understand same-sex sex until we realize that the dynamics involved are unconscious.

This is one reason why psychoanalysis is the tool that gets us to the heart of everything. Once my patients have achieved an insight into these dynamics—*and realized there is no moral fault involved in their longtime and mysterious need*—they have moved rather quickly on the road to recovery. Their consequent gratitude to me is overwhelming. And why shouldn't it be? They were formerly caught up in compulsions they could not understand, compulsions they could not control. Now they are in charge of their own lives.

Their former promiscuity may have looked a lot like "liberation." But it was not true freedom. It was a kind of slavery. And it was not a lifestyle. With the onset of AIDS, as the playwright and gay militant Larry Kramer said in a 1993 interview, it turned out to be a death style. I have had some patients tell me, "Doctor, if I weren't in therapy, I'd be dead."

Testimonials from my recovered patients make me feel my work is worthwhile—despite regular demands from the gay rights community for my silence. What would they have me do? Pack my bags, find a new profession, lock up a lifetime of research and analysis, hide my truth under a bushel? It is not my psychoanalytic duty to tell people they are marvelous when they are out of control, much less ask disingenuous rhetorical questions like, "What kind of God would afflict people with an 'objective disorder' in the disposition of their hearts?"

Giving God the credit for their gayness is a persistent refrain in much gay literature today, and I am saddened to see people of evident good will become unwitting parties to the blasphemy. Gays ascribe their condition to God, but he should not have to take that rap, any more than he should be blamed for the existence of other man-made maladies—like war, for instance, which has proven to be very unhealthy for humans and for all other living things. God does not make war. Men do.

And, when homosexuality takes on all the aspects of a political movement, it, too, becomes a war, the kind of war in which the first casualty is truth, and the spoils turn out to be our own children. An exaggeration? Well, what are we to think when militant homosexuals seek to lower the age of consensual sexual intercourse between homosexual men and young boys to the age of 14 (as they did in Hawaii in 1993) or 16 (as they tried to do in England in 1994)? In the Washington March for Gay Pride in 1993, they chanted, "We're here. We're queer. And we're coming after your children."

What more do we need to know?

[This article first appeared in *America* (November 18, 1995). Used by permission of the author.]

Charles W. Socarides, M.D., is clinical professor of psychiatry at Albert Einstein College of Medicine/Montefiore Medical Center in New York. He is president of the National Association for Research and Therapy of Homosexuality, and author of *Homosexuality: A Freedom Too Far* (Adam Margrave Books, Phoenix, Arizona).

Homosexuality and the Nazi Party

by Scott Lively

The pink triangle, symbol of the "gay rights" movement, is familiar to many Americans. As the badge used by the Nazis to designate homosexuals in the concentration camps, the pink triangle perfectly expresses the message of "gay rights." That message is that homosexuals are currently and historically victims of irrational prejudice and that those who oppose homosexuality are hateful bigots. This all-important victim status engenders sympathy for the homosexual "cause" among well-meaning heterosexuals. Thus, millions of otherwise rational Americans support a movement whose sole unifying characteristic is a sexual lifestyle they personally find repugnant.

When homosexuals display the pink triangle, they are equating all opposition to homosexuality with Nazism and themselves with the Jewish victims of the Holocaust. As pro-homosexual Rabbi Bernard Mehlman puts it, "Homophobia and Anti-Semitism are part of the same disease." This quote appeared in an advertisement in a homosexual newspaper. It announced the dedication ceremony of the New England Holocaust Memorial in Boston last year. An accompanying article reported that New England homosexuals had pledged $1 million to help build the memorial, including $50,000 for an initial monument consisting of six steel and glass towers. Alongside the monument is an inscription honoring homosexual victims of the Nazis. Another Holocaust memorial being prepared in New York City is expected to similarly honor homosexuals. Washington, D.C. is home to the official U.S. Holocaust Museum which not only maintains a pro-homosexual display, but also employs noted homosexual activist Klaus Mueller as a staff researcher. Other Holocaust related projects, such as the Anne Frank Exhibit now touring the United States, incorporate a similar message in their programs.

While some homosexuals were interned in Nazi work camps, the role of homosexuals in Nazi history cannot be accurately represented solely by a pink triangle. Our review of more than 200 history texts written since the 1930s suggests that a pink *swastika* is equally representative, if not more so. For, ironically, while many homosexuals were persecuted by the Nazi party, there is no doubt that the Nazi party itself had many homosexuals within its own ranks, even among its highest leadership.

The Homosexual Roots of the Nazi Party

The "gay rights" movement often portrays itself as an American phenomenon which arose from the civil rights movement of the 1950s. It is not uncommon to hear homosexualists (those both "gay" and "straight" who promote the legitimization of homosexuality) characterize "gay rights" as the natural third wave of civil rights activism (following blacks and women). In reality, however, Germany was the birthplace of "gay rights," and its legacy in that nation is truly alarming.

The "grandfather of gay rights" was a homosexual German lawyer named Karl Heinrich Ulrichs. Ulrichs had been molested at age 14 by his male riding instructor. Instead of attributing his adult homosexuality to the molestation, however, Ulrich devised in the 1860s what became known as the "third sex" theory of homosexuality. Ulrichs' model holds that male homosexuals are actually female souls trapped within male bodies. The reverse phenomenon supposedly explains lesbianism. Since homosexuality was an innate condition, reasoned Ulrichs, homosexual behavior should be decriminalized. An early follower of Ulrichs coined the term "homosexual" in an open letter to the Prussian Minister of Justice in 1869.

By the time Ulrichs died in 1895, the "gay rights" movement in Germany had gained considerable strength. Frederich Engels noted this in a letter to Karl Marx regarding Ulrich's efforts: "The pederasts start counting their numbers and discover they are a powerful group in our state. The only thing missing is an organization, but it seems to exist already, but it is hidden." After Ulrichs' death, the movement split into two separate and opposed factions. One faction followed Ulrichs' successor, Magnus Hirschfeld, who formed the Scientific Humanitarian Committee in 1897 and later opened the Institute for Sex Research in Berlin. The other faction was organized by Adolf Brand, publisher of the first homosexual magazine, *Der Eigene* (The Special). Brand, Benedict Friedlander and Wilhelm Janzen formed the *Gemeinschaft der Eigenen* (The Community of the Special) in 1902. What divided these groups was their concepts of masculinity. Ulrichs' theory embraced a feminine identity. His, and later Hirschfeld's, followers literally believed they were women trapped in men's bodies.

The followers of Brand, however, were deeply insulted by Ulrichs' theory. They perceived themselves not merely as masculine, but as a breed of men superior in masculine qualities even to heterosexuals. The Community of the Special (CS) asserted that male homosexuality was the foundation of all nation-states and that male homosexuals represented an elite strata of human society. The CS fashioned itself as a modern incarnation of the warrior cults of ancient Greece. Modeling themselves after the military heroes of Sparta, Thebes and Crete, the members of the CS were ultra-masculine, male-supremacist and pederastic (devoted to man/boy sex). Brand said in *Der Eigene* that he wanted men who "thirst for a revival of Greek times and Hellenic standards of beauty after centuries of Christian barbarism."

One of the keys to understanding both the rise of Nazism and the later persecution of some homosexuals by the Nazis is found in this early history of the German "gay rights" movement. For it was the CS which created and shaped what would become the Nazi persona, and it was the loathing which these "Butches" held for effeminate homosexuals ("Femmes") which led to the internment of some of the latter in slave labor camps in the Third Reich.

From Boy Scouts to Brownshirts

The "Butch" homosexuals of the CS transformed Germany. Their primary vehicle was the German youth movement, known as the Wandervogel (Rovers or Wandering Youth). "In Central Europe," writes homosexual historian Parker Rossman, "there was another effort to revive the Greek ideal of pedagogic pederasty in the movement of 'Wandering Youth'...Ultimately, Hitler used and transformed the movement...expanding and building upon its romanticism as a basis for the Nazi Party" (Rossman:103).

Rising spontaneously in the 1890s as an informal hiking and camping society, the Wandervogel became an official organization at the turn of the century, similar to the Boy Scouts. From early on, however, the Wandervogel was dominated and controlled by the pederasts of the CS. CS co-founder Wilhelm Janzen was its chief benefactor, and its leadership was rife with homosexuality. In 1912, CS theorist Hans Blueher wrote *The German Wandervogel Movement as an Erotic Phenomenon* which told how the

organization was used to recruit young boys into homosexuality.

Wandervogel youths were indoctrinated with Greek paganism and taught to reject the Christian values of their parents (mostly Catholics and Lutherans). The CS belief in a homosexual elite took shape within the Wandervogel in the concept of "der Fuehrer" (The Leader). E.Y. Hartshorne, in *German Youth and the Nazi Dream of Victory*, records the recollections of a former Wandervogel member in this regard: "We little suspected then what power we had in our hands. We played with the fire that had set a world in flames, and it made our hearts hot...It was in our ranks that the word Fuehrer originated, with its meaning of blind obedience and devotion...And I shall never forget how in those early days we pronounced the word Gemeinschaft ["community"] with a trembling throaty note of excitement, as though it hid a deep secret" (Hartshorne:12). Louis Snyder notes in the *Encyclopedia of the Third Reich* that, "The Fuehrer Principle became identical with the elite principle. The Fuehrer elite were regarded as independent of the will of the masses" (Snyder:104). Snyder was not writing about the Gemeinschaft der Eigenen or of the Wandervogel, but of the upper ranks of the Nazi party some thirty years later. Another Nazi custom from the Wandervogel was the "Seig Heil" salute, which was an early form of greeting popular among the wandering youth. During World War I, the greatest hero of the German youth movement was Gerhard Rossbach. Described by historian Robert G. L. Waite as a "sadist, murderer and homosexual," Rossbach was "the most important single contributor of the pre-Hitler youth movement" (Waite,1969:210). More importantly, Rossbach was the bridge between the Wandervogel and the Nazi Party.

In the turbulent days following Germany's defeat in World War I, Gerhard Rossbach was one of many former army officers placed in command of Freikorps (Free Corps) units. These unofficial auxilary military units were designed to circumvent limitations imposed on German troop strength by the Allies. Rossbach organized a Freikorps called Rossbach's Sturmabteilung (Rossbach's Storm Troopers). Rossbach also built the largest post-war youth organization in Germany, named the *Schilljugend* (Schill Youth) in honor of a famous Prussian soldier. In *The Black Corps*, historian Robert Lewis Koehl notes that both Rossbach's Storm Troopers and the Schilljugend "were notorious for wearing brown shirts which had been prepared for German colonial troops, acquired from the old Imperial army stores" (Koehl:19). These Storm Troopers would soon become known as Nazi Brownshirts. Konrad Heiden, a contemporary of Hitler and a leading authority on Nazi history, wrote that the Freikorps "were breeding places of perversion" and that "Rossbach's troop...was especially proud" of being homosexual

(Heiden:295). Rossbach's adjutant was Edmund Heines, noted for his ability to procure boys for sexual orgies. Ernst Roehm, recruited by Rossbach into homosexuality, later commanded the Storm Troopers for the Nazis, where they were more commonly known as the SA (an acronym for Sturmabteilung).

The Power Behind the Throne

While Adolf Hitler is today recognized as the central figure of Nazism, he was a less important player when the Nazi machine was first assembled. Its first leader was Ernst Roehm. Homosexual historian Frank Rector writes that "Hitler was, to a substantial extent, Roehm's protegé" (Rector:80). Roehm had been a captain in the German army. Hitler had been a mere corporal. After World War I, Roehm was highly placed in the underground nationalist movement that plotted to overthrow the Weimar government and worked to subvert it through assassinations and terrorism. In *The Order of the Death's Head*, author Heinz Hohne writes that Roehm met Hitler at a meeting of a socialist terrorist group called the Iron Fist and "saw in Hitler the demagogue he required to mobilize mass support for his secret army" (Hohne:20). Roehm, who had joined the German Worker's Party before Hitler, worked with him to take over the fledgling organization. With Roehm's backing, Hitler became the first president of the party in 1921 (ibid.:21) and changed its name to the National Socialist German Worker's Party. Soon after, Rossbach's Storm Troopers, the SA, became its military arm. In his classic Nazi history, *The Rise and Fall of the Third Reich*, author William Shirer describes Roehm as "a stocky, bull-necked, piggish-eyed, scar-faced professional soldier...[and] like so many of the early Nazis, a homosexual" (Shirer:64). Rector writes:

> Was not the most outstanding, most notorious, of all homosexuals the celebrated Nazi leader Ernst Ro[e]hm, the virile and manly chief of the SA, the *du* buddy of Adolf Hitler from the beginning of his political career? Hitler's rise had in fact depended upon Ro[e]hm and everyone knew it. Ro[e]hm's gay fun and games were certainly no secret; his amorous forays to gay bars and gay Turkish baths were riotous. Whatever anti-homosexual sentiments may have been expressed by straight Nazis were more than offset by the reality of highly visible, spectacular, gay-loving Ro[e]hm. If there were occasional ominous rumblings and grumblings about "all those queers" in the SA and Movement, and some anti-gay flare-ups, homosexual Nazis felt more-or-less secure in the lap of the Party. After all, the National Socialist Party member who wielded the greatest power aside from Hitler was Ro[e]hm (Rector:50f).

Betraying his roots in the "Butch" faction of the German "gay rights" movement, Roehm viewed homosexuality as the basis for a new society. Louis Snyder writes that Roehm "projected a social order in which homosexuality would be regarded as a human behavior pattern of high repute...he flaunted his homosexuality in public and insisted that his cronies do the same. What was needed, Roehm believed, was a proud and arrogant lot who could brawl, carouse, smash windows, kill and slaughter for the hell of it. Straights, in his eyes, were not as adept in such behavior as practicing homosexuals" (Snyder:55). "The principle function of this army-like organization," writes historian Thomas Fuchs, "was beating up anyone who opposed the Nazis, and Hitler believed this was a job best undertaken by homosexuals" (Fuchs:48f).

The favorite meeting place of the SA was a "gay" bar in Munich called the Bratwurstglockl where Roehm kept a reserved table (Hohne:82). This was the same tavern where some of the earliest formative meetings of the Nazi Party had been held (Rector:69). At the Bratwurstglockl, Roehm and associates—Edmund Heines, Karl Ernst, Ernst's partner Captain Rohrbein, Captain Petersdorf, Count Ernst Helldorf and the rest—would meet to plan and strategize. These were the men who orchestrated the Nazi campaign of intimidation and terror. All of them were homosexual (Heiden:371).

Indeed, homosexuality was all that qualified many of these men for their positions in the SA. Heinrich Himmler would later complain of this: "Does it not constitute a danger to the Nazi movement if it can be said that Nazi leaders are chosen for sexual reasons?" (Gallo:57). Himmler was not so much opposed to homosexuality itself as to the fact that non-qualified people were given high rank based on their homosexual relations with Roehm and others. For example, SA Obergruppenfuhrer (Lieutenant General) Karl Ernst, a militant homosexual, had been a hotel doorman and a waiter before joining the SA. "Karl Ernst is not yet 35," writes Gallo, "he commands 250,000 men...he is simply a sadist, a common thug, transformed into a responsible official" (ibid.:50f).

This strange brand of nepotism was a hallmark of the SA. By 1933 the SA had grown far larger than the German army, yet the Vikingkorps (Officers' Corps) remained almost exclusively homosexual. "Roehm, as the head of 2,500,000 Storm Troops," writes historian H.R. Knickerbocker, "had surrounded himself with a staff of perverts. His chiefs, men of rank of Gruppenfuhrer or Obergruppenfuhrer, commanding units of several hundred thousand Storm Troopers, were almost without exception homosexuals. Indeed, unless a Storm Troop officer were homosexual he had no chance of advancement" (Knickerbocker:55).

In the SA, the Community of the Special's Hellenic

ideal of masculine homosexual supremacy and militarism was fully realized. "Theirs was a very masculine brand of homosexuality," writes homosexualist historian Alfred Rowse, "they lived in a male world, without women, a world of camps and marching, rallies and sports. They had their own relaxations, and the Munich SA became notorious on account of them" (Rowse:214). The similarity of the SA to Freidlander and Brand's dream of Hellenic revival is not coincidental. In *Gay American History*, Jonathan Katz writes that Roehm was a prominent member of the Society for Human Rights (SHR), an offshoot of the CS (J.Katz:632).

The "relaxations" to which Rowse refers were, of course, the homosexual activities (many of them pederastic) for which the SA and the CS were both famous. Hohne writes that Roehm "used the SA for ends other than the purely political...Peter Granninger, who had been one of Roehm's partners...and was now given cover in the SA Intelligence Section. For a monthly salary of 200 marks he kept Roehm supplied with new friends, his main hunting ground being Geisela High School Munich; from this school he recruited no fewer than eleven boys, whom he first tried out and then took to Roehm" (Hohne:82).

Hitler's "Gay" Roots

In 1945 a Jewish historian by the name of Samuel Igra published *Germany's National Vice*, which called homosexuality the "poisoned stream" that ran through the heart of Nazism. (In the 1920s and 30s, homosexuality was known as "the German vice" across Europe because of the debaucheries of the Weimar period.) Igra, who escaped Germany in 1939, claims that Hitler "had been a male prostitute in Vienna at the time of his sojourn there, from 1907 to 1912, and that he practiced the same calling in Munich from 1912 to 1914" (Igra:67). Desmond Seward, in *Napoleon and Hitler*, says Hitler is listed as a homosexual in Viennese police records (Seward:299). Lending credence to this is the fact, noted by Walter Langer, that during several of those years Hitler "chose to live in a Vienna flophouse known to be inhabited by many homosexuals" (Langer:192). Rector writes that, as a young man, Hitler was often called "der Schoen Adolf" (the handsome Adolf) and that later his looks "were also to some extent helpful in gaining big-money support from Ernst Ro[e]hm's circle of wealthy gay friends" (Rector:52).

Langer, a psychiatrist, was commissioned by the Allies in 1943 to prepare a thorough psychological study of Hitler. His report, kept under wraps for 29 years, was published in book form in 1972 as *The Mind of Adolf Hitler*. Langer writes that Hitler was certainly a coprophile (a person who is sexually aroused by human excrement) and may have practiced homosexuality as an adult. He cites the testimony of Hermann Rauschning, a former Hitler confidante who "reports that he has met two boys who claimed that they were Hitler's homosexual partners, but their testimony can hardly be taken at face value. More condemning," adds Langer, "would be the remarks dropped by [Albert] Foerster, the Danzig gauleiter, in conversation with Rauschning. Even here, however, the remarks deal only with Hitler's impotence as far as heterosexual relationships go, without actually implying that he indulges in homosexuality. It is probably true that Hitler calls Foerster 'Bubi,' which is a common nickname employed by homosexuals in addressing their partners. This alone is not adequate proof that he has actually indulged in homosexual practices with Foerster, who is known to be a homosexual" (Langer:178). However, writes Langer, "Even today, Hitler derives sexual pleasure from looking at men's bodies and associating with homosexuals" (Langer:179). Too, Hitler's greatest hero was Frederick the Great, a well-known homosexual (Garde:44).

Like Langer, Waite also hesitates to label Hitler a homosexual but cites substantial circumstantial evidence that he was.

It is true that Hitler was closely associated with Ernst Ro[e]hm and Rudolf Hess, two homosexuals who were among the very few people with whom he used the familiar du. But one cannot conclude that he therefore shared his friend's sexual tastes. Still, during the months he was with Hess in Landsberg, their relationship must have become very close. When Hitler left the prison he fretted about his friend who languished there, and spoke of him tenderly, using Austrian diminutives: 'Ach mein Rudy, mein Hesserl, isn't it appalling to think that he's still there.' One of Hitler's valets, Schneider, made no explicit statement about the relationship, but he did find it strange that whenever Hitler got a present he liked or drew an architectural sketch that particularly pleased him, he would run to Hess—who was known in homosexual circles as "Fraulein Anna"—as a little boy would run to his mother to show his prize to her...Finally there is the nonconclusive but interesting fact that one of Hitler's prized possessions was a handwritten love letter which King Ludwig II had written to a manservant" (Waite, 1977:283f).

Hitler, if homosexual, was certainly not exclusively so. There are at least four women, including his own niece, with whom Hitler had sexual relationships, although these relationships were not normal. Both Waite and Langer suggest that his sexual encounters with women included expressions of his coprophilic perversion as well as other extremely degrading forms of masochism. It is interesting to note that all four women attempted suicide after becoming sexually involved with Hitler. Two succeeded (Langer:175f).

The Homoerotic Brotherhood

Whether or not Hitler was personally involved in homosexual relationships, the evidence is clear that he knowingly and intentionally surrounded himself with practicing homosexuals from his youth. Like Roehm, Hitler seemed to prefer homosexual companions and co-workers. In addition to Roehm and Hess, two of his closest friends, Hitler filled key positions with known or suspected homosexuals. Rector, himself a "gay Holocaust" revisionist, attempts to dismiss sources that attribute homosexuality to leading Nazis, but nevertheless writes that...

Reportedly, Hitler Youth leader, Baldur von Schirach was bisexual; Hitler's private attorney, Reich Legal Director, Minister of Justice, butcher Governor-General of Poland, and public gay-hater Hans Frank was said to be a homosexual; Hitler's adjutant Wilhelm Bruckner was said to be bisexual;...Walter Funk, Reich Minister of Economics [and Hitler's personal financial advisor] has frequently been called a "notorious" homosexual ...or as a jealous predecessor in Funk's post, Hjalmar Schacht, contemptuously claimed, Funk was a "harmless homosexual and alcoholic;" ...[Hitler's second in command] Hermann Goering liked to dress up in drag and wear campy make-up; and so on and so forth (Rector:57).

Igra, who confidently asserts that the above men were homosexuals, cites still other Hitler aides and close friends who were known homosexuals as well. He states that Hitler's chauffeur and one-time personal secretary, Emile Maurice, for example, was homosexual, as well as the pornographer Julius Streicher, who "was originally a school teacher, but was dismissed by the Nuremberg School Authorities, following numerous charges of pederasty brought against him" (Igra:72f). SS Chief Heinrich Himmler's "pederastic proclivities [were] captured on film" by Nazi filmmaker Walter Frenz (Washington City Paper, April 4, 1995). Reinhard Heydrich, mastermind of the first pogrom, Kristallnacht, and of the death camps, was homosexual (Calic:64). In *The Twelve Year Reich*, Richard Grunberger tells of a party given by Nazi propagandist, Joseph Goebbels, which degenerated into a homosexual orgy (Grunberger:70). A recent biography of Albert Speer by Gitta Sereny speaks of a "homo-erotic (not sexual) relationship" between Speer and Hitler (Newsweek, Oct. 30, 1995). Langer notes that Hitler's personal bodyguards were "almost always 100 percent homosexuals" (Langer:179). Hitler's later public pronouncements against homosexuality never quite fit with the lifelong intimacy—sexual or otherwise—which he maintained with men he knew and accepted as homosexuals.

In light of the above it is not surprising that many of those whose ideas influenced Hitler were also homosexual. Chief among those were occultists Jorg Lanz Von Liebenfels and Guido von List. In 1958, Austrian psychologist Wilhelm Daim published *Der Mann der Hitler die Ideen gab* ("The Man Who Gave Hitler His Ideas") in which he called Lanz the true "father" of National Socialism. Lanz was a former Cistercian monk who had been excommunicated for homosexuality (Sklar:19). After being expelled from the monastery, Lanz formed an occultic order called the Ordo Novi Templi or The Order of the New Temple (ONT). The ONT was an offshoot of the Ordo Templi Orientis which practiced tantric sex rituals (Howard:91).

On Christmas day, 1907, many years before it would become the symbol of the Third Reich, Lanz and other members of the ONT raised the swastika flag over the castle which Lanz had purchased to house the order (Goodrick-Clarke:109). Lanz chose the swastika, he said, because it was the ancient pagan symbol of Wotan, the god of storms (Cavendish:1983). (Wotan, the inspiration for "Storm Troopers," was the Teutonic equivalent of Baal in the Old Testament and Zeus in Greek culture). Waite notes that it was through Lanz that Hitler would learn that most of his heroes of history were also "practicing homosexuals" (Waite, 1977:94f).

Refuting "Gay Holocaust" Revisionism

"Gay Holocaust" revisionists assert that Hitler's ascension to the Chancellorship marked the beginning of a homosexual Holocaust in Germany. For example, in *The Pink Triangle*, Richard Plant writes, "After years of frustration...Hitler's storm troopers now had the opportunity to smash their enemies: the lame, the mute, the feebleminded, the epileptic, the homosexual, the Jew, the Gypsy, the communist. These were the scapegoats singled out for persecution. These were the 'contragenics' who were to be ruthlessly eliminated to ensure the purity of the 'Aryan race.'" (Plant:51). Rector, another revisionist, makes a similar statement: "Hitler's homophobia did not surface until 1933-1934, when gays had come to affect adversely his New Order designs—out of which grew the simple solution of murdering them en masse" (Rector:24). The fact is that homosexuals were never murdered "en masse" or "ruthlessly eliminated" by the Nazis. Yet many homosexuals *were* persecuted and some did die in Nazi work camps. What is the truth about Nazi persecution of homosexuals? There are several incidents in Nazi history which are most often cited as evidence of a "gay Holocaust." This list includes a series of increasingly harsh public pronouncements and policies against homosexuality by Hitler and Himmler, the sacking of the Sex Research Institute of Berlin, "the Roehm Purge" (also known as "the Night of the Long Knives"), and the internment of homosexuals in work camps.

The law against homosexual conduct had existed in Germany for many years prior to the Nazi regime as Paragraph 175 of the Reich Criminal Code, to wit: "A male who indulges in criminally indecent activity with another male, or who allows himself to participate in such activity, will be punished with imprisonment" (Burleigh and Wipperman:188). When Hitler came to power he used this law as a means of tracking down and punishing those homosexuals who, in the words of one victim, "had defended the Weimar Republic, and who had tried to forestall the Nazi threat" (ibid.:183). Later he expanded the law and used it as a convenient tool to detain other enemies of the regime.

In February of 1933, Hitler banned pornography, homosexual bars and bath-houses, and groups which promoted "gay rights" (Plant:50). Ostensibly, this decree was a blanket condemnation of all homosexual activity in Germany, but in practice it served as just another means to find and destroy anti-Nazi groups and individuals. "Hitler," admit Oosterhuis and Kennedy, "employed the charge of homosexuality primarily as a means to eliminate political opponents, both inside his party and out" (Oosterhuis and Kennedy: 248).

The masculine homosexuals in the Nazi leadership selectively enforced this policy only against their enemies and not against all homosexuals. Even Rector lends credence to this perspective, citing the fact that the decree "was not enforced in all cases" (Rector:66). Another indication is that the pro-Nazi Society for Human Rights (SHR) continued to participate in German society for several years after the decree. In *The Racial State*, Michael Burleigh and Wolfgang Wippermann remind us that Roehm was a leading member of the SHR; and we know from Anthony Read and David Fisher that the SHR was still active in Germany as late as 1940 (Read and Fisher:245). Furthermore, Oosterhuis and Kennedy write that "although he was well known as a gay-activist, [Adolf] Brand was not arrested by the Nazis" (Oosterhuis and Kennedy:7). Some of Brand's files were confiscated by the Nazis in their attempt to gather all potentially self-incriminating evidence.

In 1935, Paragraph 175 was amended with Paragraph 175a which criminalized any type of behavior that could be construed as indicating a homosexual inclination or desire (Burleigh and Wipperman: 190). (Interestingly, the new criminal code addressing homosexuality deleted the word "unnatural" from the definition—Reisman, 1994:3.) This new law provided the Nazis with an especially potent legal weapon against their enemies. It will never be known how many non-homosexuals were charged under this law, but it is indisputable that the Nazis used false accusations of homosexuality to justify the detainment and imprisonment of many of their opponents. "The law

was so loosely formulated," writes Steakley, "that it could be, and was, applied against heterosexuals that the Nazis wanted to eliminate...the law was also used repeatedly against Catholic clergymen" (Steakley:111). Kogon writes that "The Gestapo readily had recourse to the charge of homosexuality if it was unable to find any pretext for proceeding against Catholic priests or irksome critics" (Kogon:44).

The charge of homosexuality was convenient for the Nazis to use against their political enemies because it was so difficult to defend against and so easy to justify to the populace. Since long before the Nazis, homosexuals had generally lived clandestine lives, so it was not unusual for revelations of their conduct to come as a surprise to their communities when it became a police matter. This is not to say that actual homosexuals were not prosecuted under the law. Many were. But the law was used selectively against the "Femmes." And even when they were threatened, many effeminate homosexuals, especially those in the arts community, were given protection by certain Nazi leaders (Oosterhuis and Kennedy:248). Plant writes:

> The most famous example is that of the actor Gustaf Grundgens...Despite the fact that his homosexual affairs were as notorious as those of Roehm's, Goering appointed him director of the State Theater...[And] On October 29, 1937 ...Himmler advised that actors and other artists could be arrested for offenses against paragraph 175 only with his personal consent, unless the police caught them *in flagrante* (Plant:116).

There is one additional reason why the Nazis arrested homosexuals and raided even the homes of their supporters. They were looking for incriminating evidence against themselves (the Nazi leaders). Blackmail of homosexuals by estranged partners and prostitutes was a simple fact of life in Germany. "[H]omosexuals were particularly vulnerable to blackmailers, known as Chanteure on the homosexual scene," write Burleigh and Wippermann. "Blackmail, and the threat of public exposure, resulted in frequent suicides or suicide attempts" (Burleigh and Wipperman:184). The Nazi leaders were quite familiar with this phenomenon. Igra reports that Heinrich Hoffman, the official Nazi photographer, gained his position by using information about Hitler's perverse abuse of his (Hoffman's) daughter to blackmail the future Fuehrer (Igra:74). Heiden relates another story in which Hitler bought an entire collection of rare political writings to regain possession of a letter to his niece in which he openly revealed his "masochistic-coprophil inclinations" (Heiden:385). Once he was in power he had other ways to solve these kinds of problems.

Targeting "Femmes"

The Nazis' hunt for incriminating evidence, as well as the selectivity of the Nazi violence, was obvious in the attack on Magnus Hirschfeld's Sex Research Institute, May 6th, 1933. As noted previously, the Sex Research Institute of Berlin had been founded by Hirschfeld (in 1919) as a center for "study" of homosexuality and other sexual dysfunctions. For all intents and purposes, it served as the headquarters for the effeminate branch of the German "gay-rights" movement. For this reason alone, the "Butch" homosexuals of the Nazi Party might have destroyed the Institute. Indeed, throughout the preceding years the Nazis had increasingly harassed Hirschfeld personally. Victor Robinson, Hirschfeld's biographer, wrote in 1936:

> Although the Nazis themselves derived great profit from Hirschfeld's theories (and called on him personally for help), they continued his persecution relentlessly; they terrorized his meetings and closed his lecture halls, so that for the safety of his audiences and himself, Hirschfeld was no longer able to make public appearances (Haeberle:368).

Homosexualist James Steakley acknowledges the "Butch/Femme" aspect of the incident, saying that some German homosexuals "could conceivably have approved of the measure, particularly if they were Nazi sympathizers or male supremacists" (Steakley:105).

However, the attack against the Institute was not motivated solely by the Nazi enmity against effeminate homosexuals. It was an attempt to cover up the truth about rampant homosexuality and other perversions in the Nazi Party. Sklar writes that, "Hitler attempted to bury all his earlier influences and his origins, and he spent a great deal of energy hiding them...[In this campaign to erase his past] Hitler ordered the murder of Reinhold Hanish, a friend who had shared his down-and-out days in Vienna" (where Hitler is suspected of having been a homosexual prostitute) (Sklar:21). Hitler also knew that Hirschfeld's facility had extensive records that could be damaging to himself and his inner circle. This was the reason for the raid, according to Ludwig L. Lenz, the assistant director of the Sex Research Institute, who was in charge on the day of the raid. A part of the following quote was cited earlier:

> ...our Institute was used by all classes of the population and members of every political party...We thus had a great many Nazis under treatment at the Institute. Why was it then, since we were completely non-party, that our purely scientific Institute was the first victim which fell to the new re-

gime? The answer to this is simple...We knew too much. It would be against medical principles to provide a list of the Nazi leaders and their perversions [but]...not ten percent of the men who, in 1933, took the fate of Germany into their hands, were sexually normal...Many of these personages were known to us directly through consultations; we heard about others from their comrades in the party...and of others we saw the tragic results....Our knowledge of such intimate secrets regarding members of the Nazi Party and other documentary material—we possessed about forty thousand confessions and biographical letters—was the cause of the complete and utter destruction of the Institute of Sexology (Haberle:369).

Burleigh and Wipperman report that the ransackers had "lists" of materials they were looking for (Burleigh and Wipperman:189) and that they carted away two truckloads of books and files. The materials taken from the Institute were burned in a public ceremony, captured on film, on May 10th. The spectacular and oft replayed newsreel footage of this event has caused the burning of books to become synonymous with Nazism. What information went up in smoke on that day will never be known, but we can infer that the pile of burning paper contained many Nazi secrets. According to homosexual sources at the time, the Nazis destroyed twelve thousand books and thirty-five thousand photographs. The building itself was confiscated from the SHC and turned over to the Nazi Association of Jurists and Lawyers (Steakley:105).

The Roehm Purge

The event in history most frequently cited as evidence of Nazi persecution of homosexuals is known variously as the Blood Purge, the Night of the Long Knives, and the Roehm Purge. Steakley writes that "the indisputable beginning of Nazi terror against homosexuals was marked by the murder of Ernst Ro[e]hm on June 28, 1934, 'The Night of the Long Knives'" (Steakley:108). It was on that night (actually over an entire weekend) that Adolf Hitler's closest aides orchestrated the assassinations of hundreds of his political enemies in one bloody sweep. Among the victims of this purge were Roehm and several of the top officers of the SA.

We have emphasized that the leadership of the SA was mostly, if not entirely, homosexual. The fact that SA leaders were the primary targets in the massacre could therefore be construed as a sort of "moral cleansing" of the Nazi ranks, which, in fact, Hitler claimed it was. But Hitler lied. The Roehm Purge was driven by political, not moral concerns. Hitler feigned disgust and outrage about the homosexuality of the murdered SA leaders to justify himself to the German people; it was a tactic he had used previously to allay public suspicions about the sexual deviancy of his inner circle. The importance of this fact is asserted in many leading works by both mainstream and homosexualist historians. The following are excerpts from four different historians who have examined the issue:

> Hitler eliminated his closest friend Roehm and certain SA leaders as potential rivals. The strictly political motivation of this ruthless power play was initially too obvious to be entirely denied, but later it was conveniently obscured by charges of homosexual depravity (Haberle:369f).

> The formal accusations against Roehm and those arrested with him centered on their homosexual activities, which Hitler had of course known about for fifteen years and shrugged off, it being alleged that these activities disgraced the party. For those victims without any homosexual background, "the Great Blood Purge" continued all over Germany, as Nazi leaders got rid of all their most hated enemies, as well as the inevitable "mistakes" (Garde:726f).

> Ernst Roehm wasn't shot because the Nazi Party felt outraged by the abrupt discovery that he was "having" his storm troopers—that had been known for ages; but because his sway over the SA had become a menace to Hitler. In the Hitler Youth the "dear love of comrades" was evilly turned into a political end. And if the Nazi hierarchy was well larded with homosexuals, so was Wilhelm II's court and so was the Weimar Republic (Davidson:152).

> Hitler himself, of course, had been well aware of Roehm's sexual orientation from the earliest days of their long association....So strong was Roehm that the Wehrmacht [German Army High Command] was concerned that he might seize control of the army. In 1934, Hitler became fearful that the Wehrmacht was plotting a coup against him to prevent such a takeover. To forestall this danger, Hitler had Roehm and about one thousand other men murdered one weekend in June 1934, the famous "Night of the Long Knives" (Crompton:79f).

Igra provides us with a long and detailed account of the power struggle which led to the purge, beginning with a refutation of the idea that it represented a policy of extermination of homosexuals by Hitler:

> We shall find that, far from eliminating the sex perverts from his party, Hitler retained most of them, and that he moved against those whom he did eliminate only with the greatest reluctance and after he had been relentlessly pushed by outside forces and circumstances. On June 14 and 15 Hitler was in Venice to see Mussolini. It soon became common knowledge that the German Dictator and his entourage had made an unfavorable impression upon the Italians... Mussolini was never a stickler for puritan morality, to say the least, but there was one vice which the Italians particularly loathe; they call it *il visio tedesco*, the German vice. The conduct of some members in Hitler's entourage at Venice disgusted the Italians. Mussolini protested against the moral character and political unreliability of the leading personnel in the Nazi Storm Troops and warned Hitler that he would have to sacrifice his favorite colleagues if he wished to save his own personal prestige and that of his regime. Among those colleagues, Roehm, Heines and Karl Ernst were mentioned (Igra:77f).

The Roehm Purge, then, was not a "moral cleansing" of the Nazi ranks, but a re-alignment of power behind the German government which was primarily forced upon Hitler by powerful political elements whose support he needed to maintain control. Igra goes on to point out that not only did the majority of the SA homosexuals survive the purge, but that the massacre was largely implemented by homosexuals. He cites Strasser's statement that "the Chief Killers of Munich [were] Wagner, Esser, Maurice, Weber and Buch." These men "were all known to be sex perverts or sexual maniacs of one type or another," concludes Igra (ibid.:80). Plant records that the larger campaign of assassinations across Germany was orchestrated by Reinhard Heydrich, also a well-known homosexual (Plant:56). Igra addresses Hitler's justification for the purge:

> In his defense before the Reichstag a week later Hitler talked of "traitors." That was his alibi...In his speech to the Reichstag he admitted that one of the motives for ordering the massacre was to get rid of the moral perverts in his party and that they were traitors because they practiced homosexualism. But under the dictatorship it was not possible for anyone to put Hitler at question. Nobody asked him to explain how it was that, if his purpose was to get rid of homosexuals, he really didn't rid himself of them but used them as the instruments of his own murder lust and still retained most of them as members of his personal entourage, as well as in key positions of the party organization and the government. Otto Strasser, in his book, *The German St. Bartholemew's Night*

(which has not been published in English), mentions sixteen of these highly placed homosexualist officials who survived the massacres of June 30 and retained their posts (Igra:82).

In the Camps

Although homosexuals were never targeted for extermination, some were interned in Nazi work camps. The actual number of pink-triangle prisoners, estimated at 5,000-15,000 by Joan Ringelheim of the US Holocaust museum (Rose:40), was a tiny fraction of the total camp population. Of these, an undetermined percentage were heterosexuals falsely labeled as homosexuals. Homosexuals who died in the camps (mostly of disease and starvation) were "a small fraction of less than 1 percent" of homosexuals in Germany (S. Katz:146), compared to more than 85 percent of European Jewry exterminated in the gas chambers. More significantly, many of the guards and administrators responsible for the infamous concentration camp atrocities were homosexuals themselves, which negates the proposition that homosexuals in general were being persecuted and interned.

While any prisoner could be chosen as a *Kapo* (a slave overseer), none of the other interned groups *except* homosexuals had counterparts among the Nazi guards and administrators. Examples of the homosexuality of the concentration camp guards can be found in many of the personal accounts of Holocaust survivors. Elie Wiesel, sent to the Buna factory camp in the Auschwitz complex, for example, acknowledges this in his book *Night*:

The head of our tent was a German. An assassin's face, fleshy lips, hands like wolf's paws. He was so fat he could hardly move. Like the leader of the camp he loved children...(Actually this was not a disinterested affection: there was a considerable traffic in young children among homosexuals here, I learned later) (Wiesel:59).

In *Treblinka*, the narrative account of the Treblinka uprising, Steiner records the story of another Nazi administrator, taken from interviews with survivors:

Max Bielas had a harem of little Jewish boys. He liked them young, no older than seventeen. He had a kind of parody of the shepherds of Arcadia, their role was to take care of the camp flock of geese. They were dressed like little princes...Bielas had a little barracks built for them that looked like a doll's house...Bielas sought in Treblinka only the satisfaction of his homosexual instincts (Steiner:117f).

The enduring "Butch/Femme" conflict among German homosexuals clearly had a substantial bearing on the treatment of pink-triangle prisoners. Plant writes of one survivor who reported that "the guards lashed out with special fury against those who showed 'effeminate traits'" (Plant:172). And Rector records an interview with a former Pink Triangle named Wolf (a pseudonym) in which the issue of effeminacy was raised. "The ones who were soft, shall I say, were the ones who suffered terribly," said Wolf. Rudolf Hoess, the infamous commandant of Auschwitz, who may himself have been a "Butch" homosexual, defined "genuine homosexuals... [by their] soft and girlish affectations and fastidiousness, their sickly sweet manner of speech, and their altogether too affectionate deportment toward their fellows" (Hoess in Rector:137f). These "genuine homosexuals" were considered incorrigible and held in special barracks, while many non-effeminate homosexuals were released (ibid.:137). Hoess, incidentally, had at one time been a close friend of Edmund Heines (Snyder:301), the procurer of boys for Roehm's pederastic orgies.

Toward the end of World War II, many homosexuals were released from the concentration camps and drafted into the German army (Shaul:688). Steven Katz cites records that "indicate that 13 percent of all homosexual camp inmates were reprieved and released" (S. Katz:146). This was happening at the same time as the Nazis' frantic push to increase their "production" in the death camps, in an effort to exterminate every last Jew in Europe before the Allies could liberate the camps.

The American Connection

While the Nazi Party was crushed as a political force in 1945, remnants of Nazism survive around the world. As in Germany, many of these fascist groups are dominated by male homosexuals.

The most famous incident in the history of the American Nazi Party resulted from its 1977 demand to stage a march through the largely Jewish neighborhood of Skokie, Illinois, a Chicago suburb and the home of many Holocaust survivors. This plan was devised by Frank Collin, who often appeared with his followers "in full Nazi regalia: brown shirts, black boots, and armbands..." Civil authorities effectively blocked the march at first, but the American Civil Liberties Union (ACLU) rose to Collin's aid and forced the City of Chicago to allow it. The subsequent event drew international media attention. Homosexualists Johansson and Percy in *Outing: Shattering the Conspiracy of Silence* have finally revealed, more than 15 years later, that Collin was a homosexual pederast. In 1979 Collin was arrested "for taking indecent liberties with boys between ages 10 and 14" and was sentenced to seven years in prison (Johansson and Percy, 1994:130).

Meanwhile, back in Germany, the alarming increase of neo-Nazi skinheads is also linked to homosexuality. Elmay Kraushaar, a journalist for *Der Spiegel*, Germany's equivalent to *TIME*, is quoted in *The Advocate*:

> There is a gay skinhead movement in Berlin. They go to cruising areas with leaflets that say, "We don't want foreigners." A major leader of the neo-Nazis in Germany, Michael Kuhnen was an openly gay man who died of AIDS two years ago. He wrote a paper on the links between homosexuality and fascism, saying fascism is based on the love of comrades, that having sex with your comrades strengthens this bond (Anderson:54).

Learning from History

Sadly, the homosexual dimension of Nazi history is overlooked by many historians. As Duberman, Vicinus and Chauncey have stated with the title to their "gay studies" text, the role of homosexuals and pederasts has been *Hidden from History*. They, of course, imagine the influence of homosexuality to be positive. From the Judeo-Christian cultural context, however, the rise of homosexuality necessarily represents the diminution of Biblical morality as a restraint on human passions. Consequently, where Judeo-Christian ideals decrease, violence and depravity increase.

It was the pederasts of the Community of the Special who sponsored the revival of Hellenic pagan ideals in German society. These men were viciously anti-Jew and anti-Christian because of the injunctions against homosexuality inherent in the Judeo-Christian sexual ethic. Homosexualist Warren Johansson notes that Hans Blueher, one of the leading theoreticians of the Community of the Special, "maintained that Judaism had suppressed the homosexual aspect of its culture, with concomitant hypertrophy [enlargement] of the family" (Johansson:816). Benedict Friedlander, in an essay for *Der Eigene* titled "Seven Propositions," chose as his first proposition an attack on Christianity. "The white race is becoming ever sicker under the curse of Christianity, which is foreign to it and mostly harmful," writes Friedlander. "That is the genuinely bad 'Jewish influence,' an opinion that has proven true, especially through the conditions in North America" (Friedlander in Oosterhuis and Kennedy:219). For his part, Adolf Brand called Christianity "barbarism" and "expressed his desire to fight 'beyond good and evil,' not for the sake of the masses, since the happiness of 'the weak' would result in a 'slave mentality,' but for the human being who proclaimed himself a god and was not to be subdued by human laws and ethics" (Oosterhuis and Kennedy:183). We should not forget Nietzsche, who called Christianity "the lie of millennia" (Macintyre: 188).

Much has been made of the reported silence, and in some cases complicity, of the supposed Christian churches during the Third Reich. But few have noted the long period of "Biblical deconstruction" that preceded the rise of Nazism, and fewer still have chronicled the diabolical perversion of German religious culture by the Nazis themselves. While the neo-pagans were busy attacking from without, liberal theologians undermined Biblical authority from within the Christian church. The school of so-called "higher criticism," which began in Germany in the late 1800s, portrayed the miracles of God as myths; by implication making true believers (Jew and Christian alike) into fools. And since the Bible was no longer accepted as God's divine and inerrant guide, it could be ignored or reinterpreted. By the time the Nazis came to power, "Bible-believing" Christians, (the Confessing Church) were a small minority. As Grunberger asserts, Nazism itself was a "pseudo-religion" (ibid.:79) that competed, in a sense, with Christianity and Judaism.

The schools were heavily targeted in order to de-Christianize the young. Mandatory prayer in schools was stopped in 1935, and from 1941 onward, religious instruction was completely eliminated for all students over 14 years old (ibid.:494f). The Nazi Teachers Association actively discouraged its members from taking religious instruction, while at the same time many teachers of religious studies (who were all required to be licensed by the state) "inculcated neo-paganism into their pupils during periods of religious instruction." Later, teachers were outright prohibited from attending voluntary religion classes organized by the Catholic church (ibid.:495).

From the early years, leading Nazis openly attacked Christianity. Joseph Goebbels declared that "Christianity has infused our erotic attitudes with dishonesty" (Taylor:20). It is in this campaign against Judeo-Christian morality that we find the reason for the German people's acceptance of Nazism's most extreme atrocities. Their religious foundations had been systematically eroded over a period of decades by powerful social forces. By the time the Nazis came to power, German culture was spiritually bankrupt. Too often, historians have largely ignored the spiritual element of Nazi history; but if we look closely at Hitler's campaign of extermination of the Jews, it becomes clear that his ostensive racial motive obscures a deeper and more primal hatred of the Jews as the "People of God."

The probable reason for Hitler's attack on Christianity was his perception that it alone had the moral authority to stop the Nazi movement. But Christians stumbled before the flood of evil. As Poliakov notes, "[W]hen moral barriers collapsed under the impact of Nazi preaching...the same anti-Semitic movement that led to the slaughter of the Jews gave scope and license to an obscene revolt against God and the moral law. An open and implacable war was declared on the Christian tradition...[which unleashed] a frenzied and unavowed hatred of Christ and the Ten Commandments" (Poliakov:300).

There is no question that homosexuality figures prominently in the history of the Holocaust. As we have noted, the ideas for disposing of the Jews originated with Lanz von Leibenfels. The first years of terrorism against the Jews were carried out by the homosexuals of the SA. The first concentration camp, as well as the system for training its brutal guards, was the work of Ernst Roehm. The first pogrom, *Kristallnacht*, was orchestrated in 1938 by the homosexual Reinhard Heydrich. And it was the transvestite Goering who started the "evolution of the Final Solution...[with an] order to Heydrich (Jan. 24, 1939) concerning the solution of the Jewish question by 'emigration' and 'evacuation'" (Robinson:25). Still, despite their disproportionate role, homosexuals did not cause the Holocaust. They, along with so many others who had lost their moral bearings, were merely instruments in its enactment. The Holocaust must be blamed on the one whom the Bible compares to "a roaring lion, seeking whom he may devour" (NKJ:I Peter 5:8).

Yet, while we cannot say that homosexuals caused the Holocaust, we must not ignore their central role in Nazism. To the myth of the "pink triangle"—the notion that all homosexuals in Nazi Germany were persecuted—we must respond with the reality of the "pink swastika."

[This article, excerpts from *The Pink Swastika: Homosexuality in the Nazi Party* by Scott Lively and Kevin Abrams (Founders Publishing Company, 1995), first appeared in *Culture Wars* (April 1996), edited by Dr. E. Michael Jones. The excerpt was prepared for *Culture Wars* by Scott Lively. *Culture Wars*, 206 Marquette Avenue, South Bend, IN 46617, phone (219) 289-9786.]

Scott Lively is co-author of *The Pink Swastika: Homosexuals and the Nazi Party* (Keizer, Oregon: Founders Publishing Company, 1995). The Pink Swastika is available by calling 1-800-828-2290. Price is $11.95 including shipping.

Bibliography:

Agonito, Rosemary. *History of Ideas on Women: A Source Book.* New York, G.P. Putnam & Sons, 1977.

Alyson Almanac. Boston, Alyson Publications Inc., 1990.

Anderson, Shelly. "Youth." *The Advocate.* January 26, 1993.

Bleuel, Hans Peter. *Sex and Society in Nazi Germany.* New York, J.B. Lippincott Company, 1973.

Burleigh, Michael, and Wipperman, Wolfgang. *The Racial State: Germany 1933-1945.* New York, Cambridge University Press, 1993.

Calic, Edouard. *Reinhard Heydrich: The Chilling Story of the Man Who Masterminded the Nazi Death Camps.* Military Heritage Press, William Morrow and Company, 1982.

Cavendish, Richard. *Man, Myth & Magic: An Illustrated Encyclopedia of the Supernatural.* New York, Marshall Cavendish Corporation, 1970.

Costello, John. *Mask of Treachery: Spies, Lies, Buggery and Betrayal.* New York, William Morrow and Company, 1988.

Crompton, Louis. "Gay Genocide: from Leviticus to Hitler." *The Gay Academic.* Palm Springs, California, ETC Publications, 1978.

Davidson, Michael. *The World, the Flesh, and Myself.* London, Arthur Baker Ltd., 1962.

Dynes, Wayne. *The Encyclopedia of Homosexuality.* New York, Garland Publishing, 1990.

Fest, Joachim C. *Hitler.* New York, Vintage Books, 1975.

Friedlander, Benedict. "Memoirs for the Friends and Contributors of the Scientific Humanitarian Committee in the Name of the Succession of the Scientific Humanitarian Committee." *Journal of Homosexuality*, January-February 1991.

Fuchs, Thomas. *The Hitler Fact Book.* New York, Fountain Books, 1990.

Gallo, Max. *The Night of the Long Knives.* New York, Warner Books, 1973.

Garde, Noel I. *Jonathan to Gide: The Homosexual in History.* New York, Vantage Press, 1969.

Goodrick-Clarke, Nicholas. *The Occult Roots of Nazism: Secret Aryan Cults and their Influence on Nazi Ideology.* New York, New York University Press, 1992.

Graber, G.S. *The History of the SS: A Chilling Look at the Most Terrifying Arm of the Nazi War Machine.* New York, Charter Books, 1978.

Greenburg, David F. *The Construction of Homosexuality.* Chicago, University of Chicago Press, 1988.

Grunberger, Richard. *The 12-Year Reich: A Social History of Nazi Germany 1933-1945.* New York, Ballantine Books, 1971.

Haeberle, Irwin J. "Swastika, Pink Triangle, and Yellow Star: The Destruction of Sexology and the Persecution of Homosexuals in Nazi Germany." *Hidden From History: Reclaiming the Gay and Lesbian Past.* Duberman, Martin, Vicinus, Martha, and Chauncey, George Jr. (Eds.). United States, Meridian, 1989.

Hartshorne, E.Y. *German Youth and the Nazi Dream of Victory.* New York, Farrar and Reinhart, Inc, 1941.

Heiden, Konrad. *Der Fuehrer: Hitler's Rise to Power.* Boston, Houghton Mifflin Company, 1944.

Heritage and S.W. Jewish Press, September 16, 1983

Hohne, Heinz. *The Order of the Death's Head: The Story of Hitler's SS.* New York, Ballantine Books, 1971.

Howard, Michael. *The Occult Conspiracy.* Rochester, Vermont, Destiny Books, 1989.

Igra, Samuel. *Germany's National Vice.* London, Quality Press Ltd., 1945.

Johansson, Warren, "Pink Triangles." In Dynes, Wayne (Ed.). *Encyclopedia of Homosexuality.* New York: Garland Publishing, 1990.

Johansson, Warren, and Percy, William A.. "Homosexuals in Nazi Germany." In Henry Friedlander (Ed.). *Simon Wiesenthal Center Annual: Volume 7.* New York, Allied Books, Ltd., 1990.

Johansson, Warren, and Percy, William A. *Outing: Shattering the Conspiracy of Silence.* New York, Harrington Park Press, 1994.

Jones, J. Sydney. *Hitler in Vienna 1907-1913.* New York, Stein and Day, 1983.

Jones, Nigel H. *Hitler's Heralds: The Story of the Freikorps 1918-1923.* London, John Murray, 1987.

Katz, Jonathan. *Gay American History.* New York, Thomas Y. Crowell Company, 1976.

Katz, Steven T. "Quantity and Interpretation—Issues in the Comparative Historical Analysis of the Holocaust." In *Holocaust and Genocide Studies: Volume 4, Number 2, 1989.* New York, Pergamon Press, 1989.

Kennedy, Hubert. "Man/Boy Love in the Writings of Karl Heinrich

Ulrichs." In Pascal, Mark (Ed.). *Varieties of Man/Boy Love*. New York, Wallace Hamilton Press, 1992.

Knickerbocker, H.R. *Is Tomorrow Hitler's?* New York, Reynal and Hitchcock, 1941.

Koehl, Robert Lewis. *The Black Corps: The Structure and Power Struggles of the Nazi SS*. Madison Wisconsin, University of Wisconsin Press, 1983.

Kogon, Eugen. *The Theory and Practice of Hell*. New York, Berkley Publishing Company, 1950.

Langer, Walter C. *The Mind of Adolf Hitler*. New York, Signet Books, 1972.

Lauritsen, John, and Thorstad, David. *The Early Homosexual Rights Movement:1864-1935*. New York, Times Change Press, 1974.

Levi, Primo. *Survival in Auschwitz*. New York, Macmillan Publishing Coompany, 1961.

Linsert, Richard. *Kabale und Liebe: Uber Politik und Geschlechtsleben*. Berlin, Man, 1931.

Lombardi, Michael A.. "Research on Homosexuality in Nineteenth Century Germany" (Parts I and II). Los Angeles, Urania Manuscripts, 1977.

MacDonald, Callum. *The Killing of SS Obergruppenfuhrer Reinhard Heydrich*. New York, The Free Press, 1989.

Macintyre, Ben. *Forgotten Fatherland: The Search for Elisabeth Nietzsche*. New York, Farrar Straus Giroux, 1992.

Miles, David H. "Stefan, George." Grolier Electronic Publishing, Inc., 1992.

Miller, Neil. *Out of the Past: Gay and Lesbian History from 1869 to the Present*. New York, Vintage Books, 1995.

Mills, Richard. "The German Youth Movement." In Leyland, Winston (Ed.). *Gay Roots: Twenty Yearsof Gay Sunshine: An Anthology of Gay History, Sex, Politics, and Culture*. San Francisco, Gay Sunshine Press, 1989.

Mosse, George L. *Nationalism and Sexuality: Respectability and Abnormal Sexuality in Modern Europe*. New York, Howard Fertig, 1985.

Nethercot, Arthur H. *The First Five Lives of Annie Besant*. Chicago, University of Chicago Press, 1960.

Newton, Michael. *Raising Hell: An Encyclopedia of Devil Worship and Satanic Crime*. New York, Avon, 1993.

Newton, Michael, and Newton, Judy Ann. *The Ku Klux Klan: An Encyclopedia*. New York, Garland Publishing, 1991.

Oosterhuis, Harry, and Kennedy, Hubert (Eds.). *Homosexuality and Male Bonding in Pre-Nazi Germany: the youth movement, the gay movement and male bonding before Hitler's rise: original transcripts from Der Eigene, the first gay journal in the world*. New York, Harrington Park Press, 1991.

Pawelczynska, Anna. *Values and Violence in Auschwitz*. Berkley, California, University of California Press, 1979.

Peters, H.F. *Zarathustra's Sister: The Case of Elisabeth and Frederich Nietzsche*. Crown Publishers, New York, 1977.

Plant, Richard. *The Pink Triangle: The Nazi War Against Homosexuals*. New York, Henry Holt and Company, 1986.

Poliakov, Leon. *Harvest of Hate: The Nazi Program for the Destruction of the Jews of Europe*. New York, Walden Press, 1979.

Read, Anthony, and Fisher, David. *Kristallnacht: The Nazi Night of Terror*. New York, Times Books,1989.

Rector, Frank. *The Nazi Extermination of Homosexuals*. New York, Stein and Day, 1981.

Reisman, Dr. Judith A. "A Content Analysis of Two Decades of The Advocate, the Gay and Lesbian National News Magazine." Work in Progress.

Reisman, Dr. Judith A., and Eichel, Edward W. *Kinsey, Sex and Fraud: The Indoctrination of a People*. Lafayette, Louisiana, Huntington House, 1990.

Reiter, Joseph A. "Death in Venice." Grolier Electronic Publishing, Inc., 1992.

Robinson, Jacob. "The History of the Holocaust." *Holocaust*. Jerusalem, Keter Publishing House, 1974.

Rose, Rick. "Museum of Pain." *The Advocate*, October 19, 1993.

Rossman, Parker. *Sexual Experience Between Men and Boys*. New York, Association Press, 1976.

Rowse, A.L. *Homosexuals in History: Ambivalence in Society, Literature and the Arts*. New York,Macmillan Publishing Company, 1977.

Schwarzwaller, Wulf. *The Unknown Hitler: His Private Life and Fortune*. National Press, Inc., and Star Agency, 1989.

Seward, Desmond. *Napolean and Hitler: A Comparative Biography*. New York, Simon & Schuster.

Shaul, Elisheva. "Homosexuality in the Third Reich." In Gutman, Israel (Ed.). *Encyclopedia of the Holocaust*. Tel Aviv, Sifria Poalim Publishing House, 198?.

Shirer, William. *The Rise and Fall of the Third Reich*. New York, Fawcett Crest, 1960.

Sklar, D. *The Nazis and the Occult*. New York, Dorset Press, 1989.

Skousen, W. Cleon. *The Naked Communist*. Salt Lake City, Utah, Ensign Publishing Co., 1958.

Snyder, Dr. Louis L. *Encyclopedia of the Third Reich*. New York, Paragon House, 1989.

Steakley, James D. *The Homosexual Emancipation Movement in Germany*. New York, Arno Press, 1975.

Steiner, Jean-Francois. *Treblinka*. New York, Simon and Schuster, 1979.

Strasser, Otto. *Hitler and I*. Boston, Houghton Mifflin Company, 1940.

Strasser, Otto, and Stern, Michael. *Flight From Terror*. New York, Robert M. McBride & Company, 1943.

Taylor, Fred. *The Goebbels Diaries: 1939-1941*. New York, G.P. Putmans' Sons, 1983.

Ulrichs, Karl Heinrich. *Forschugen uner das Ratsel der Mannmanlichen Liebe*. Leipzig, Max Spohr Verlag, 1989.

Waite, Robert G.L. *Vanguard of Nazism: The Free Corps Movement in Postwar Germany 1918-1923*. New York, W.W. Norton and Company, 1969.

Waite, Robert G.L. *The Psychopathic God Adolf Hitler*. New York, Signet Books, 1977.

Wiesel, Elie. *Night*. New York, Avon Books, 1969.

Wistrich, Robert. *Who's Who in Nazi Germany*. New York: Bonanza Books, 1984.

Same-Sex "Marriage"

by Anton N. Marco

In mid-December, 1990, three homosexual couples simultaneously applied for marriage licenses in the State of Hawaii. Their action was not unprecedented (gay couples elsewhere have made the same request), but the outcome was.

While all other previous same-sex couples have had to settle for blunt State refusals of such requests, or in gay-friendly cities like San Francisco, for so-called "domestic partnership" registration, the Hawaii Six have been able to leap several legal hurdles. They may, after an autumn 1996 trial, become the first same-sex couples in the United States to be joined in legal civil marriage.

According to the courts and a legislature-created Commission on Sexual Orientation (which refused to hear any "religious" or "health"-oriented arguments against gays or homosexual behavior[1]), despite legislative action defining marriage as the union of one man and one woman (and in the face of 74% poll-tallied public opposition to same-sex "marriage"), the State's refusal of the Hawaii Six violates Hawaii's Equal Rights Amendment (ERA) and the Six's right to equal protection, unjustly denying these (and all) same-sex couples marriage benefits in health care, insurance, joint child custody and support, tax-filing status and other critical life areas.

Some Americans might not wish to begrudge Hawaii the privilege of sanctioning same-sex marriages. But others not so "accepting" are distressed that the effects of Hawaii's decision could extend far beyond that State's borders:

> "Gay rights" activists are hoping that the U.S. Constitution's "Full Faith and Credit" clause, under whose authority States ordinarily must recognize legal licenses of other States, will mandate endorsement and "transferability" of Hawaiian same-sex marriage to every State in the Union.

> Gay activists' wished-for scenario: Gay couples by the thousands will flock from around the nation to Hawaii, be married there, then return to their home states. There, they will demand marriage recognition and broad ranges of benefits. If or when denied recognition and/or ben-

efits, gay couples will launch litigation salvos, based, as in Hawaii, on State ERAs or denial of Constitutional "equal protection." In the aftermath of these salvos, homosexuality will at last achieve equal standing with heterosexuality throughout America, culturally as well as legally.

As Mike Gabbard, who has led opposition to same-sex "marriage" in Hawaii, has reported:

> Homosexual activists are serious about legalizing same-sex "marriage." So far, seven lobby groups have been formed to convince mainstream America that homosexuals should be allowed to marry. These groups are: The Forum On the Right to Marriage (FORM), Hawaii Equal Rights Marriage Project (HERMP), Inter-National Spouses Network (INS), Lambda Legal Defense and Education Fund (LLDEF), Partners Task Force for Gay & Lesbian Couples, Same-Sex Marriage Advocates Coalition (SSMAC), and Freedom to Marry Coalition (FMC).

> The FMC is urgently attempting a massive national effort of (1) "state-by-state political organizing (i.e., coming together at a local level *now*) to start approaching non-gay and gay groups for support on marriage, building a coalition while also in a concentrated fashion developing defensive legislative strategies and (2) public education (engaging the non-gay as well as gay worlds) in understanding real-life gay and lesbian families and how we are harmed by being denied the Freedom to Marry."

> Efforts are being made to identify and enlist "key contacts" in every state to "spearhead the work in each state/community." Also organizations and individuals are being asked to sign The Marriage Resolution, which reads: "Because marriage is a basic human right and an individual personal choice, RESOLVED, the State should not interfere with same-gender couples who choose to marry and share fully and equally in the rights,

responsibilities, and commitment of civil marriage." Most groups who have signed the resolution are homosexual activist organizations, but there are others as well, including ACLU, Commission on Social Action of Reform Judaism, Japanese-American Citizens League, National Association for Women in education, and the National Organization for Women (NOW).[2]

Both gay and non-homosexual public policy observers expect a decision in favor of the Hawaii Six to produce nothing short of seismic cultural, spiritual and economic shifts in the terrain of our national life.

Gay Activists Perceive Numerous Advantages in Securing Marriage Recognition

That legitimization of gay relationships by marriage is a prime goal of gay activists is clear from numerous sources. Gay activists perceive well the advantages of such recognition. One writer in a Denver gay tabloid wrote:

The most obvious advantage [of same-sex "marriages"] is the hope that society, including but not limited to, our families, schools, and churches, will not only accept our relationships, but our homosexuality as normal...In addition to societal and religious beliefs, we will have all of the tax, insurance, and legal benefits available to "straight" married people. The marital and spousal deductions and diminished inheritance and estate taxes alone would save us millions and maybe even billions.[3]

To Have and to Hold, official same-sex marriage organizing guide of the activist National Gay and Lesbian Task Force (NGLTF), points out that...

If legally married, gay, lesbian and bisexual couples would have a greater ability to care for and protect their families, including the option to:
- file joint tax returns
- have access to joint insurance policies for home, auto and health
- inherit automatically in the absence of a will, including jointly owned real and personal property through the right of survivorship
- secure workplace and other benefits such as annuities, pension plans, Social Security, Medicare
- obtain veterans' discounts on medical care, education, and home loans
- enter jointly into leases and other contracts, such as apartment and car rental agreements, and maintain renewal rights
- raise children together including: joint adoption, joint foster care, custody, and visitation including non-biological parents
- secure wrongful death benefits for a surviving partner and children
- take bereavement leave when a partner or child dies
- handle post-mortum decisions involving deceased partners, including where to be buried and how
- receive crime victims' recovery benefits
- secure domestic violence protection orders in states where this is currently prohibited
- obtain divorce protections such as community property and child support
- establish status as next-of-kin for hospital visits and medical decisions where one partner is too ill to be competent[4]

Never before now has there been so much financial advantage to marriage itself, at least in terms of societal benefits and government-bestowed tax breaks, insurance, etc. Marriage now offers substantial benefits to people who might otherwise wish to remain single. One can understand why homosexual activists regard the issue of "lifestyle affirmation," achievable through domestic partnership or marriage recognition, as crucial to achieving "equal rights" in American society.

At the same time, activists recognize that the legitimization of same-sex "marriage" is not an idea with high approval ratings among the American public. In Hawaii, opposition to gay "marriages" has risen steadily since the Hawaii Six launched litigation to secure it.

Gay Activists' Main Arguments in Favor of Same-Sex Marriage

Basing their conclusions largely on the unquestioned acceptance of three key unspoken presuppositions, gay activists employ the following public arguments in their attempt to promote the idea of legal recognition for same-sex "marriages":

1) Gays, lesbians and bisexuals are being "discriminated against" when their unions are denied marriage recognition.

This is not the first instance of government interference in a couple's choice to marry. Less than thirty years ago interracial couples were prohibited from legally marrying. Today, very similar discriminatory arguments are being used to prohibit same-gender couples from marrying.[5]

Of course, this argument presumes a virtual legal equivalency between skin color or race and "sexual orientation."

2) Marriage is a "basic human right" and choice of marriage partners should in no way be regulated by government; therefore same-sex couples should be allowed to legally marry.

> Marriage is an important personal choice and a basic human right. The decision to get married should belong to the couple in love, not the state.[6]

Here, the operative presumption seems to be that every "sexual orientation" is fundamentally like every other, and relationships involving any and all "sexual orientations" should be freely chosen by the individuals in relationships and then recognized without question by the state.

3) Civil and religious marriage will remain separate institutions if same-sex marriages are legalized.

> Legally, religious and civil marriage are two separate institutions. Though many faiths do perform same-gender marriages now, they have no legal recognition as civil marriages. The state should not dictate which marriages any religion performs or recognizes, just as religions should not dictate who gets a civil marriage license from the state.[7]

These statements seem to presume that recognition of same-gender marriages will have little social impact, in either religious, civil or economic spheres.

4) Same-gender couples cannot legally marry in any state, despite how much they may feel a "need" to (emotionally), or how much their "families" need civil marriage's protections, benefits and responsibilities.[8]

In *Virtually Normal*, Andrew Sullivan's book-length apologia for same-sex marriage, the author asserts that...

> The introduction of gay marriage would not be some sort of leap in the dark, a massive societal risk. Homosexual marriages have always existed, in a variety of forms; they have just been euphemized. Increasingly they exist in every sense but the legal one. As it has become more acceptable for homosexuals to acknowledge their loves and commitments publicly, more and more have committed themselves to one another for life in full view of their families and friends. A law institutionalizing gay marriage would merely reinforce a healthy trend.[9]

Elsewhere, Sullivan explains further:

> In the contemporary West, marriage has become a way in which the state recognizes an emotional commitment by two people to each other for life. And within that definition, there is no public way, if one believes in equal rights under the law, in which it should legally be denied homosexuals.[10]

So long as conservatives recognize, as they do, that homosexuals exist and that they have equivalent emotional needs and temptations as heterosexuals, then there is no conservative reason to oppose homosexual marriage and many conservative reasons to support it.[11]

As mentioned, there are several unspoken presuppositions which are the foundation of these arguments.

Three Presuppositions for Gay "Marriage"

Three presumptions are critically important for gay activists taking their case for same-sex "marriage" to the public—the most crucial of which is the presumption that gays constitute some kind of immutable "minority." Possession of "minority" status is the key that will enable gay militancy to achieve all of its aims most easily and quickly, including gay "marriage." Consider how achieving even the appearance of "minority" status has already helped advance the various goals of the 1972/1993 Gay Rights/ March on Washington Platforms...

1972 Federal Demand #1:
"Minority" Status For Gays
Several cities with "gay rights" legislation in force (San Francisco and Denver to name two) have already instituted affirmative action goals for gays in city employment.

1972 Federal Demand #6:
Support for Gay/Lesbian-Taught Sex Education Of "Gayness" As Healthy, Normal
From 1993-1995, nearly $38 million worth of Federal grant money has been given to promote gay-related "health studies" in America's public schools.[12]

1972 Federal Demand #8:
Aid for Gay Organizations To Combat Effects Of "Oppressive" Society
By 1982, an exhaustive study revealed that the Federal government provided 58% of funding all American homosexual advocacy organizations.[13] It is commonly known that per-case Federal spending on AIDS research (which here in the U.S. largely benefits gay males) far exceeds spending on research for other diseases producing comparable or much larger mortality rates.

1972 State Demand #4:
"Non-Discrimination" Against Gays In
Insurance, Bonding, Etc.

"Gay rights" lobbyists were largely responsible for AIDS being declared a "disability" under the Americans with Disabilities Act (1991). Thus, AIDS has become the world's first 100% fatal disease to be protected by "minority rights," thus making "non-discrimination" against AIDS sufferers mandatory for employers, insurers, etc.

1972 State Demand #5:
No Denial Of Child Custody, Adoption,
Visitation, Foster Parenting Rights To Gays

In November, 1995, "the New York Supreme Court—noting 'fundamental changes' in the American family—ruled (4-3) that neither heterosexual nor homosexual couples have to be 'married' to adopt a child together. And, in July of last year, the Washington D.C. Court of Appeals ruled that homosexual unmarried couples in 'committed relationships' are permitted to adopt children under District law."[14]

1972 State Demand #8,
1993 Platform Demand #C-29:
Legalize Same-Sex Marriages

As public policy analyst Whitney Galbraith has observed, "[t]he key to the [Hawaii Supreme Court's] decision [regarding same-sex "marriage"] was the court's declaring same-sex couples to be part of a 'suspect class.'"[15] If gays are indeed part of a suspect class, they should not be denied such privileges as marriage either, the argument goes.

There are two other presuppositions key to gay "marriage" recognition. In addition to believing gays are a "minority," the public must presume that homosexuality is "normal and healthy" (and probably innate)—that homosexuals are "just like anyone else (in emotional needs and behavioral proclivities), except for their choice of sexual partners." If this is so, there should be little reason to deny gay unions marriage recognition.

The third presumption follows from the second: If gays are "just like everyone else," then gay activists desire the same kinds of marriages as "everyone else." Thus, placing the marriage imprimatur on gay unions will have merely negligible effects on society at large.

Gay activists arguing for same-sex "marriage" recognition now treat these presuppositions as "givens," trying as much as possible to avoid making analysis of the three a part of the debate.

Examining Presupposition One

If achieving "minority"/suspect status looms as the "fulcrum" gay activists need most to leverage the rest of their "gay rights" platforms into place, the presupposition that gays do constitute an "oppressed minority" is the first to examine. Securing suspect status in one form or another would allow gay activists, through taxpayer-funded lawsuits, to silence or punish their critics and coerce businesses and society at large to grant benefits to their "spouses" or domestic partners.

Shortly after passage of the 1964 Civil Rights Act, the U.S. Supreme Court began to issue (and reaffirm) a series of Civil Rights decisions which soon added *limitations* (to counterbalance the incentives) to the process of seeking suspect class status. In essence, the High Court put a "fence" around suspect status, in the interest of ensuring that the status remain open only to disadvantaged, politically powerless classes that truly needed government protection. The High Court did so by establishing three criteria[16] by which prospective suspect classes might be evaluated, and by which some failing to meet the qualifications might be fenced out if necessary:

Criterion #1: Prospective suspect classes should have experienced a history of severe societal oppression, evidenced by an entire "class-averaged" lack of ability to obtain economic mean income, adequate education, or cultural opportunity.

Criterion #2: Prospective suspect classes should, "averaged" as entire classes, clearly demonstrate political powerlessness.

Criterion #3: Prospective suspect classes should exhibit obvious, immutable, or distinguishing characteristics, like race, color, gender or national origin, that define them as discrete groups.

Examining Criterion #1: Low Income, Inadequate Education, Lack of Opportunity

For decades homosexual activists have fostered the impression that gays are economically, educationally and culturally disadvantaged. Yet recent marketing studies, done by gay-run marketing agencies and boasting scientific accuracy above 99%, roundly refute those claims.[17]

- Homosexuals have an average annual individual income of $36,800-$41,000, depending on which study one cites (an estimated 55% of gay individuals earn more than $50,000 per year), versus $12,287 for the general population and $3,041 for disadvantaged African Americans. Thus, gay individuals' average income is at least 300% higher than average Americans' and more than 1,200% higher than that of disadvantaged African Americans.

- More than three times as many gays as average Americans are college graduates (59.6% v. 18%)—a percentage dwarfing that of truly disadvantaged African Americans and Hispanics.

- 65.8 % of homosexuals are overseas travelers—more than four times the percentage (14%) of average Americans. More than thirteen times as many homosexuals as average Americans (26.5% vs. 1.9%) are frequent fliers.

- 7% of gays live in households with annual income of over $100,000. Gay households are four times as likely as average Americans to be earning in excess of $100,000 annually.

- 56.2% of cohabiting lesbian/gay couples' household incomes top $50,000 a year. Almost 30% of lesbian households earn over $50,000 annually.

- While, in 1989, 32.8% of African Americans lived below the poverty line ($8,343 annually for two-person households under age 65[18]), 62% of gay households earned more than the average American household, and more than 95% of gay households lived above the poverty line.[19]

Also, according to Michael's (et al) landmark survey *Sex In America*, self-identified gays and lesbians tend to be far better educated than the general population. Twice as many college men identify themselves as gay as do non-college men, and with lesbians, there is an even greater contrast. Women with college educations are eight times more likely than high school-educated women to identify themselves as lesbians.[20]

Also contradicting the "severe oppression" complaints of gay activists, avowedly gay writer Ed Mickens, employment and business commentator for *The Advocate*, has admitted that gay people do not suffer greatly in the workplace: "Today, it's rare that anyone gets fired just for being gay."[21] Gay activist/journalist Andrew Sullivan commented:

Unlike blacks three decades ago, gay men and lesbians suffer no discernible communal economic deprivation and already operate at the highest levels of society: in boardrooms, governments, the media, the military, the law and industry. They may have advanced so far because they have not disclosed their sexuality, but their sexuality as such has not been an immediate cause for their dis-

charge. In many cases, their sexuality is known, but it is disclosed at such a carefully calibrated level that it never actually works against them.[22]

Syndicated columnist Mike Royko, generally regarded as liberal in political philosophy, agrees that gays scarcely seem "oppressed":

[Gays'] difficulties look pretty meager compared to those of the poor, the uneducated and the unemployed. It may be a politically incorrect risk to disagree with those hundreds of thousands of homosexual demonstrators who gathered in Washington, but, no, this decade will not be "The Gay '90s." That's because there are so many people in this country who have far worse problems than do homosexual men and lesbians.[23]

Overwhelmed by the weight of such evidence, self-identified gay activists and journalists like Jonathan Rauch have as much as conceded that, by virtue of their failure to meet Criterion #1 alone, gay activists should abandon their "minority" claim:

The standard political model sees homosexuals as an oppressed minority who must fight for their liberation through political action. But that model's usefulness is drawing to a close. It is ceasing to serve the interests of ordinary gay people, who ought to begin disengaging from it, even drop it. Otherwise, they will misread their position and lose their way, as too many minority groups have done already....[24]

Examining Criterion #2: Political Powerlessness

Far from being politically powerless, allegedly gay activists have in recent years demonstrated enormous political clout relative to their numbers. Combining economic and educational advantage with high-pressure lobbying tactics, gay activists have ridden waves of tolerance emanating from the sexual revolution, plus the presumption that gays are some kind of "minority," to a position of almost irresistible influence in today's America. They have:

- Won passage of legislation granting homosexuals suspect-equivalent status in eight states, more than 135 cities across America, plus our nation's capitol.

- Secured political office both in the U.S. Congress and on numerous major U.S. city councils.

- Pressured the medical community to discard well-established public health measures and treat AIDS as history's first "politically protected" 100% fatal plague.

- Received benefits for "domestic partners" identical to those of married couples, and other kinds of preferential treatment in numerous major U.S. corporations.

- Implemented gay activist-created curricula representing homosexual sex as a "valid, healthy alternative" to heterosexuality.

- Gained ordination in mainline church denominations. Case in point: On April 1, 1991, a prominent Marin County, Calif., lesbian minister became a co-pastor of the Downtown United Presbyterian Church of Rochester, N.Y.

- Won National Endowment for the Arts (NEA) grants for "works of art" that graphically portray homosexual sex and savagely ridicule traditional "family" and religious values.

As recently as 1987, a report issued by the Federal Elections Commission stated that "The Human Rights Campaign Fund" [HRCF], the national gay activist political action committee (PAC), was at that time the "16th largest independent political action committee (PAC) in the nation" and "the 39th largest PAC overall." Considering that more than 4,500 PACs had registered with the FEC at the time, this represents enormous political power.

During the 1986 elections, HRCF raised more than $1.4 million. This put it in the top 1% of PACs nationwide. HRCF funded candidates in 112 political races— "an incredible political achievement," according to political experts.

By fiscal year 1991-1992, the HRCF's budget had grown to nearly $4 million and announced a 1992-1993 projected budget of over $5 million.[25] Gay activists have now established a Washington, D.C.-based "Victory Fund" to empower local, openly homosexual candidates, with a current operating budget of between $650,000 and $1 million.

Giving to the top 12 "gay rights"-promoting PACs now ranges in the top tenth of one percent of *all* PAC giving in the United States.

Examining Criterion #3: Immutable Characteristics

Attempting to satisfy this criterion, gay militants claim that "gayness" is genetically determined. Gay activist protestations aside, there is simply no credible scientific evidence to support their assertions.

"The genetic theory of homosexuality has been generally discarded today... Despite the interest in possible hormone mechanisms in the origin of homosexuality, no serious scientist today suggests that a simple cause-effect relationship applies" according to *Human Sexuality*, a 1984 textbook written by Masters, Johnson and Kolodny.

How sexual orientation evolves is a debatable question, but that it can (and does) change is a well-observed fact. A recent study by the gay-friendly Kinsey Institute found that 84% of homosexuals and 29% of heterosexuals shifted or changed their "sexual orientation" at least once in a lifetime; 32% of homosexuals and 4% of "straights" reported a second shift; and 13% of homosexuals and 1% of heterosexuals claimed at least five changes in sexual orientation during their lifetimes.[26]

Scientific literature is filled with evidence of permanent change from initial homosexual orientation to exclusive heterosexual orientation:

> Sexual behavior may or may not correlate with sexual orientation. Furthermore, an individual's sexual behavior and orientation may vary over time.

> The scientific literature indicates that homosexual feelings are more frequent than homosexual behavior and that same-sex behavior is more frequent than lasting homosexual identification.[27]

> Approximately thirty percent of male homosexuals who come to psychotherapy for any reason (not just for help with their sexual preference) can be converted to the heterosexual adaptation.[28]

> Five years after publishing our study, a follow-up of patients showed that the one-third whose adaptation had shifted to heterosexuality remained so. And we have personally followed some patients for as long as 20 years who remained exclusively heterosexual.[29]

> Treatment using dynamic individual psychotherapy, group therapy, aversion therapy, or psychotherapy with an integration of Christian principles will produce object-choice reorientation and successful heterosexual relationships in a high percentage of persons....Homosexuals can change their orientation.[30]

Dr. Judd Marmor, past president of the American Psychiatric Association and the American Academy of Psychoanalysis, has said:

> The myth that homosexuality is untreatable still has wide currency among the public at large and among homosexuals themselves....

> There is little doubt that a genuine shift in prefer-

50

ential sex object choice can and does take place in somewhere between 20 and 50 per cent of patients with homosexual behavior who seek psychotherapy with this end in mind. The single most important prerequisite to reversibility is a powerful motivation to achieve such a change.

Although some gay liberationists argue that it would be preferable to help these persons accept their homosexuality, this writer is of the opinion that, if they wish to change, they deserve the opportunity to try, with all the help that psychiatry can give them....[31]

Dr. Reuben Fine, director of the New York Center for Psychoanalytic Training, has written:

I have recently had occasion to review the result of psychotherapy with homosexuals, and been surprised by the findings. It is paradoxical that even though politically active homosexual groups deny the possibility of change, all studies from Schrenk-Notzing on have found positive effects, virtually regardless of the kind of treatment used...a considerable percentage of homosexuals became heterosexual....

If the patients were motivated, whatever procedure is adopted, a large percentage will give up their homosexuality. In this connection, public information is of the greatest importance. The misinformation spread by certain circles that "homosexuality is untreatable by psychotherapy" does incalculable harm to thousands of men and women.[32]

Nevertheless, gay activists insist publicly that homosexuality is innate and immutable—and cite "scholarship" to "prove" their contention. One highly-publicized study by an avowed homosexual, reported in a cover article in the Feb. 24, 1992 edition of *Newsweek*, claimed to discover "homosexual brains."[33] However, on closer examination the study does not hold up. Simon LeVay's study of the brains of 19 homosexual male corpses (who died of AIDS complications) noted a difference in size of a specific neuron group, INAH3, compared with that of a group comprised of 16 *presumably* heterosexual male and six female corpses.

One problem with LeVay's study is that the researcher presumed that the control group of 16 corpses had been heterosexual. Avowedly homosexual reporter Michael Botkin wrote, shortly after the study's publication:

It turns out that LeVay doesn't know anything about the sexual orientation of his control group, the 16 corpses "presumed heterosexual." A sloppy control like this is...enough by itself to invalidate the study. LeVay's defense? He knows his controls are het[erosexual] because their brains are different from the HIVer corpses. Sorry, doctor; this is circular logic. You can use the sample to prove the theory or vice versa, but not both at the same time.[34]

Similarly, a much-publicized "gay twin" study (by avowedly gay researchers Bailey and Pillard) suggested genetic origins for "gayness." The study, however, did not examine twins raised in different environments. Thus, the study cannot prove any genetic connection. Developmental biologist Anne Fausto Stirling put it simply:

In order for such a study to be meaningful, you'd have to look at twins raised apart. It's such badly interpreted genetics.[35]

Though another "genetic origins of homosexuality" study, by Dean Hamer, has also been widely (and uncritically) reported in the media, minuscule coverage has been given to the fact that the study, done under the auspices of the National Cancer Institute, is, according to syndicated columnist Cal Thomas, "under investigation for alleged fraud by the federal Office of Research Integrity and that a colleague of Mr. Hamer has charged that Mr. Hamer selectively reported data in ways that enhanced the study's thesis...."[36]

Also of note, though several studies have been undertaken, none has ever been published advancing an even nearly credible claim that lesbianism is genetically determined.

More astounding is the enormous weight of evidence available from *gay and lesbian activist* sources that the issue of gay "innateness and immutability" is in serious doubt among gay activists themselves. According to "Queer Nation" pioneer Jonathan Ned Katz:

Contrary to today's bio-belief, the heterosexual/ homosexual binary is not in nature, but is socially constructed, therefore deconstructable.

In other words, human beings make their own different arrangements of reproduction and production, of sex differences and eroticism, their own history of pleasure and happiness.[37]

In an Afterword to Katz' book, lesbian activist Lisa Duggan frankly explores the reasons why some activists make so-called "innateness" arguments: They are politically expedient...

...Katz will...be challenged by lesbian and gay "essentialists" who believe that sexual identity is fixed, perhaps inborn. Understandably, these advocates of equality believe that their kind of argument works better against the conservatives who would banish them from the earth. If lesbians, gay men, and bisexuals are born, not made, then the wish to ban or punish them is itself *against nature* and thus wrong as well as mean.

But such arguments are short-sighted as well as a-historical. All they can win is tolerance for a supposedly fixed minority called "lesbian" and "gay." What they can't do is change the notion that "heterosexuality" is "normal" for the vast majority of people, and shift social, cultural, and political practices based on that assumption. Nor can they destabilize the rigid notions of gender that underlie sexual identity categories.[38]

Lesbian activists Sue O'Sullivan and Pratibha Parmar comment on the raging debate among lesbians about who is a "real lesbian":

That a woman can spend half her adult life seeing herself as a heterosexual, marrying and bearing children, and then, in mid-life, become a lesbian puzzles most observers and quite often the woman herself. Yet from rural Idaho to Metropolitan New York, women are redefining their sexuality and becoming lesbians in mid-life.

What are the social dynamics involved in this process of change? We will discuss this question in light of a survey of over 30 American women who had recently changed their sexual identity. Their experiences challenge the common assumption that sexuality is "set" at an early stage of the life cycle. They also illuminate the social context which was supportive to the redefinition of the lesbian stereotype and their own sexuality.

From the same article: "Several women followed what we might call a 'feminist path' to lesbianism, a pattern for 'coming out' that has been known since the early days of the women's movement. For these women, becoming a lesbian was a direct and conscious outgrowth of their commitment to feminism. For them, lesbianism was a deliberate choice, the logical last step in the process of political analysis."[39]

A recently published survey also calls the "innateness" of lesbianism into question:

There's a big controversy now: Is lesbianism hereditary? People are trying to find a genetic predisposition to being gay. I think part of this is positive in that researchers are trying to tell the establishment, "Don't try to cure homosexuality. They were born this way. A certain percent of the population is going to be this way, no matter what you do."

But even if they're right, what about those for whom it's not hereditary? Many women say it's a choice. They have chosen lesbianism because of positive experiences with women...Why are we so afraid to say we chose it? It's so scary to take that chance and say, "I am choosing it. It's really what I want to do. It's not because my DNA is making me. DNA be d[—]ed, I think I'll be a lesbian."[40]

Lesbian activist Donna Minkowitz would also seem to affirm a "non-innateness" perspective, in an article entitled "Recruit, recruit, recruit!":

Remember that most of the line about homosex[uality] being one's nature, not a choice, was articulated as a response to brutal repression. "It's not our fault!" gay activists began to declaim a century ago, when queers first began to organize in Germany and England. "We didn't choose this, so don't punish us for it!" One hundred years later, it's time for us to abandon this defensive posture and walk upright on the earth. Maybe you didn't choose to be gay—that's fine. But I did.[41]

Public policy author and American University professor Jerry Z. Muller observes, of gay activist "sexual politics":

In political arguments toward the non-homosexual public, the homosexual movement has tended toward a deterministic portrait of homosexuality as grounded in irrevocable biological or social-psychological circumstance. Yet among homosexual theorists in the academy, the propensity is toward the defense of homosexuality *as a voluntarily affirmed "self-fashioning."*

The confluence of feminism and homosexual ideology has now led to a new stage, in which the politics of stable but multicultural and multisexual identities is being challenged by those who regard all permanent and fixed identity as a coercive restriction of autonomy, which is thought to include self-definition and redefinition.[42]

Lastly, a number of prominent gay activists have recently attempted to disparage LeVay, Hamer and their "findings," holding that homosexuality is indeed non-innate and mutable, for a curious reason: They fear that if "gayness" can be proved to be genetically determined, it will therefore be "surgically correctable, or alterable by genetic engineering." They fear "fascists" and/or "homophobes" may try to round up gays and "correct" their sexual orientation "under the knife" or "in the test tube"—even kill infants determined genetically to be homosexual.

In any event, it must be observed that if gay activists themselves, strongest advocates of the "innateness and immutability" of homosexuality, cannot agree on this question, and if what "science" there is supporting their thesis is faulty if not fraudulent, it would be foolhardy to make sweeping public policy decisions based on the dubious presumption that gays are "born that way" and cannot change their sexual orientation.

Examining Presupposition Two

For arguments in favor of same-sex "marriage" to be valid, the presupposition that gays are "just like everyone else, except for their desire for same-sex partners" must be proved valid. Does such a presupposition have a basis in truth? Has the "homosexualization of America" (Americans, in general, becoming more promiscuous and more favorable toward casual and anyonymous sex) proceeded so far that there are indeed no essential remaining differences between the ways "gays and straights" conduct their lives and loves?

To address these questions one can examine the scientific literature and gays' and lesbians' own self-admissions with regard to *dominant lifestyle patterns* within gay and lesbian populations. Then, one can compare these findings with evidence regarding lifestyle behaviors in the general population.

Promiscuity and Relational Instability: Dominant Features of Gay, Lesbian Lifestyles

Gay apologists attempt to make the prospect of same-sex "marriage" seem as harmless and appealing as possible. For instance, Andrew Sullivan asserts that "many" gay relationships are "virtual textbooks of monogamy." However, the available research on gay lifestyles does not back up that assertion. Psycho-sociological studies and gay/lesbian self-admissions reveal that if any two factors most accurately characterize gay and lesbian lifestyles, they are: sexual promiscuity and relational instability.

AIDS research released in 1982 by the U.S. Centers for Disease Control reported that the typical gay man interviewed claimed to have had more than 500 different sexual partners in a 20-year span. Gay people with AIDS studied averaged more than 1,100 "lifetime" partners.

Some reported as many as 20,000. (A psychologist we interviewed personally told of counseling a gay clergyman who admitted to having had more than 900 sexual partners to date.)

From perhaps the most comprehensive study of gay lifestyles ever undertaken before 1980, we learn that:

- 43% of white male homosexuals estimated they'd had sex with 500 or more different partners

- 75% had had 100 or more sexual partners; 28% (the largest subcategory) reported more than 1,000 partners

- 79% said more than half their partners were strangers

- 70% said more than half their sexual partners were men with whom they had sex only once[43]

A study of San Francisco gay men published in *Psychology Today* (Feb. 1981) also reported that 28% of gay men surveyed had engaged in sex with more than 1,000 partners.

In a 1986-published gay tabloid, Dr. Will Handy, former co-chair of Wisconsin's Governor's Council on Lesbian and Gay Issues and an avowed homosexual, detailed his objections to "contact tracing" of HIV-positive people as follows:

Contact tracing has not proved very effective among gay men, even for those diseases (syphilis and gonorrhea) which are, in a sense, "designed" for it. In the three weeks incubation period for syphilis, the average gay man will have three sexual partners to report. Wisconsin's HTLV-III contact tracing proposal calls for the tracing of partners back to 1980: that suggests quite a large pool of people to contact for each positive test given to a gay/bisexual man. But the reality is that many of those contacts would have been anonymous or so casual that memories of names, addresses, and dates would be long lost. The Division of Health can't trace my partners if I can't recall who they were.[44]

In one of medical literature's only studies reporting on homosexuals who kept sexual "diaries," the number of annual sexual partners was nearly 100.[45]

Studies reported by Bell and Weinberg (Bloomington: Indiana University Press, 1981) indicated that only 3% of gay men they surveyed had had fewer than 10 "lifetime" sexual partners. Only about 2% could be classified as either "monogamous" or even "semi-monogamous." Even "monogamy" seems to lack traditional meaning in gay male circles. Studies have indicated that "monogamy" for gay men tends to last from between 9 and 60 months.[46]

A study by McKusick, et al, of 655 San Francisco gay men[47] recommended that homosexuals limit their sexual expression to committed monogamy. McKusick reported responses to this suggestion he received from avowedly gay men:

...[T]he recommendation that gay men limit themselves to committed monogamy was discussed [among survey participants] and found to lack creativity...and to reflect the simple insensitivity of an outsider approaching the gay world. Although most of our subjects have expressed a desire for more primary partnering in response to AIDS, there has been no significant increase in these bonds during the [three year] period of our investigation.[48]

Weinberg and Williams (op. cit.) reported that two-thirds of 1,117 gay males they had surveyed answered "no" when asked whether they or their present sexual partner were currently "limiting your sexual relationships primarily to each other." Only a third of gay males surveyed claimed they had "ever" been involved in such a mutually exclusive relationship.

Gay activist marketing experts Kirk and Madsen admit in *After the Ball* (op. cit., p. 330), "...[T]he cheating ratio of 'married' gay males, given enough time, approaches 100%...Many gay lovers, bowing to the inevitable, agree to an 'open relationship,' for which there are as many sets of ground rules as there are couples."

"Reparative therapist" Joseph Nicolosi writes:

The fact is, a committed, monogamous gay relationship is very rare. Sometimes good friends make a commitment to share a home and care for and support each other, but as gay literature itself tells us, these relationships characteristically include an understanding that there will be outside sexual relationships.

In *The Male Couple*, by David McWhirter and Andrew Mattison, the authors—a gay couple themselves—could find no gay relationship in which fidelity was maintained more than five years. In fact, the authors tell us, "the single most important factor that keeps couples together past the ten-year mark is the lack of possessiveness they feel. Many couples learn very early in their relationship that ownership of each other sexually can become the greatest internal threat to their staying together."[49]

A 1984 study by the American Psychological Association's Ethics Committee, reported in *USA Today* (November 21, 1984), indicated that fear of AIDS had lowered gay men's promiscuity rate from 70 different partners in 1982 to 50 partners per year by 1984. (Even at this "safer sex" rate, a gay male would still total over 600 sexual partners between ages 18-30.)

A University of Chicago study[50] concluded that the estimated number of lifetime sexual partners since age 18 for the U.S. population as a whole is 7.15 (only 8.67 for those who never marry).

In *American Couples* (1983)—"A major enlightening report on how Americans live their private lives," according to the *Philadelphia Inquirer*—authors Philip Blumstein, Ph.D. and Pepper Schwartz, Ph.D. state:

If a gay man is monogamous, he is such a rare phenomenon, he may have difficulty making himself believed.

[and]

Gay men can make non-monogamy part of everyday life. They have no trouble incorporating casual sex into their relationships. Since their partner is male, they are not called on to honor the female preference for monogamy...

Gay authors David P. McWhirter, M.D., and Andrew M. Mattison, M.S.W., Ph.D. (*The Male Couple*) confirm homosexual promiscuity:

Only seven couples [out of the 156 interviewed] have a totally exclusive sexual relationship, and these men have all been together less than 5 years. Stated in another way, all couples with a relationship lasting more than 5 years have incorporated some provision for outside sexual activity in their relationships. That translates into 5 percent monogamous, 95 percent non-monogamous.[51]

Isolated studies of interviews conducted since 1987 suggest that gay men may have lowered the number of their sexual contacts to around 10 per year. Even a reduction of this magnitude would mean gay males, on average, have more sexual partners in one year than the average American male (and this estimate is probably raised somewhat by factoring in the partnering of promiscuous gay men) has in a lifetime.

Evidence also exists in the literature and in gay self-admissions that lesbians exhibit high levels of promiscuity relative to the general female population. Jay and Young's *Gay Report*[52] revealed that 38% of lesbians surveyed claimed to have had between 11 and more than 300 sexual partners lifetime. In *Homosexualities* (op. cit.), Bell and Weinberg reported that 41% of Caucasian lesbians admitted to having had between 10 and 500 sexual partners lifetime.

There is also much evidence of lesbian relational instability. An article entitled, "Maintaining Our Equilibrium in Couples—Or Not," by Clare Coss, quotes a writer named Alison as saying:

> I met somebody the other day and she's been in and out of relationships as I have. She said, "You know, I'm so jaded now I think if I ever got into a relationship it would be about six weeks." I said, "That long?"[53]

Also, from the book *Lesbian Passion*...

> Everyone wants to know: How come lesbian relationships don't last long? They forget that these days, no relationships last long. We're in a fast-paced, fast-moving world. Things change all the time...
>
> Today, everybody's moving all the time. Who even knows her neighbors? Relationships of all persuasions aren't lasting very long. Some lesbians have unreal expectations that because we're lesbians, our relationships are going to be better. They're going to be different. They're going to be stronger. They're going to last longer. All the while, somewhere inside of us, we don't believe that for an instant. We need only look at the relationships of our friends to see how flimsy that belief is.[54]

The authors of *Lesbian Passion* spend considerable time writing about the instability and transitory nature of many lesbian relationships. According to their survey, many lesbians (69%) who'd been couples had been couples for fewer than three years. Only 7% had been couples for nine or more years.[55]

> When thinking about [sexual] satisfaction it's important to remember that most of the lesbians in this survey had been in their current situations (single, casually involved, coupled) for fewer than three years... No matter how many questionnaires were analyzed, the statistics did not change significantly, so it seems likely that lesbians generally do not stay in their situations for long.[56]

Lifestyle Behaviors in the General Population

Attempting to shore up their claim to be "just like everyone else," homosexual activists argue that (1) wildly promiscuous heterosexuals also exist, and (2) the scope of "normality" is vast. Do these claims have substance?

Sex In America, conducted by Michael, Gagnon, Laumann and Kolata, published in 1994, and claiming to be the most comprehensive report ever conducted of American sexual life and habits[57], calls these claims and the entire "homosexualization of America" concept into serious question. According to Michael, et al:

> America has a message about sex, and that message is none too subtle. Anyone who watches a movie, reads a magazine, or turns on the television has seen it. It says that almost everyone but you is having endless, fascinating, varied sex.
>
> But, we have found, the public image of sex in America bears virtually no relationship to the truth. The public image consists of myths, and they are not harmless, for they elicit at best unrealistic and at worst dangerous misconceptions of what people do sexually. The resulting false expectations can badly affect self-esteem, marriages, relationships, even physical health.[58]
>
> Our study, called the National Health and Social Life Survey, or NHSLS, has findings that often directly contradict what has become the conventional wisdom about sex. They are counterrevolutionary findings, showing a country with very diverse sexual practices but one that, on the whole, is much less sexually active than we have come to believe.[59]

For instance, the survey revealed that 67.6% of men and 75.5% of women surveyed had had only one sex partner in the past year. The survey found that only 2.6% of men and only 1.2% of women had only same-sex partner(s) during the past year.[60]

The survey also revealed that Americans tend to establish long-term relationships in marriage with people much like themselves, i.e., people largely choose marriage partners and "significant others" from the same socioeconomic and educational strata they themselves "fall into." And people tend to have little sex while establishing those relationships. Obviously, for most Americans, other factors than sheer sexual attraction play a major role in the making of long-term, committed relationships.

Contrary to some expectations, the survey found very little incidence of adultery in traditional marriage. And, according the survey, in 1992, more than half of men and women in America between the ages of 18-26 had had just one sex partner in the past year, and another 11% had *none*. The same kinds of results are reported in British and European sex surveys. Michael, et al, find that...

...nearly all Americans have a very modest number of partners, whether we ask them to enumerate their partners over their adult lifetime or in the past year. The number of partners varies little with education, race, or religion. Instead, it is determined by marital status or by whether a couple is living together. Once married, people tend to have one and only one partner, and *those who are unmarried and living together are almost as likely to be faithful.*[61]

The survey's findings...

...give no support to the idea of a promiscuous society or of a dramatic Sexual Revolution reflected in huge numbers of people with multiple casual sex partners. The finding on which our data give quite strong and amazing evidence is not that most people do, in fact, form a partnership, or that most people do, in fact, ultimately get married. That fact was also well documented in many previous studies. Nor is it news that more recent marriages are much less stable than marriages that began 30 years ago. That fact, too, was reported by others before us. But we add a new fact, one that is not only important but is striking.

Our study shows clearly that no matter how sexually active people are before or between marriages, no matter whether they lived with their sexual partners before marriage or whether they were virgins on their wedding day, marriage is such a powerful social institution that, essentially married people are nearly all alike—they are faithful to their partners as long as the marriage is intact....Once married, the vast majority have no other sexual partners; their past is essentially erased. Marriage remains the great leveler.[62]

The old standards of sexual behavior are not so much gone as made more fuzzy, more diffuse, in the time before and between marriages. But there are definitely standards of behavior. And if society's goal is to get people safely married and procreating and faithful to their spouses, the standards have been a roaring success.[63]

The survey revealed that overall, married people are those most physically pleased and emotionally satisfied with the sex they are having. The lowest rates of satisfaction are among the unmarried or those who are not living with someone. Interestingly, *satisfaction declines when people have more than one sex partner.* The *least* satisfied are the unmarried or non-cohabiting *who have two or more sex partners at any one time.*

More interestingly, the survey revealed that conservative, Protestant married women claimed the highest rate of orgasms during sexual relations. The sexually-active unmarried and the non-religious, non-cohabiting, reported the lowest incidence of orgasms.

Not surprisingly, most people in the survey who identify themselves as faithful partners or mates also have faithful partners or mates. It also showed that only 4.1% of men and 1.6% of women had five or more sexual partners during the last 12 months. And only 15.1% of men and 2.7% of women had 5 or more partners *lifetime.*[64] Very few Americans had five or more sex partners in the past year of the survey, and these were mostly young, mostly male, and we may be safe in assuming, mostly gay.

When the survey inquired about the *kinds* of sex practices engaged in by Americans, heterosexuals showed very little interest in "kinky" or unusual sexual behaviors, like sado-masochism. Heterosexuals report very little drug or alcohol use before sex, and, except for religious liberals and libertarians, Americans overwhelmingly think same-gender sex is *always* wrong.

Significantly, the National Health and Social Life survey did not find gays numbering anywhere near the 10% of the general population figure usually cited by gay activists. In fact, researchers found very small percentages of both men and women who have had exclusively gay sex and lesbian relationships and even a much smaller percentage of people who have been involved in bisexual relationships. Only 1.4% of women and 2.8% of men identified themselves as homo- or bisexual:

No matter how we define homosexuality, we come up with small percentages of people who are currently gay or lesbian. These numbers, in fact, may sound astonishingly low, especially to residents of cities like New York or San Francisco, where there are large lesbian and gay communities. But, we found, gays and lesbians are not evenly distributed across the country. They tend to live in large cities and to avoid or leave small towns and rural areas...[65]

Certainly, *Sex In America's* sexual and relational portrait of the married and cohabiting general American population presents a striking contrast, in sexual/relational fidelity, to the "open" nature of gay relationships, even those characterized as "monogamous." Gay lifestyles appear to be much more promiscuous than "straights'." There appears to be a marked transitoriness in both gay and lesbian relational patterns, and a great deal more sheer sexual preoccupation.

Avowedly gay activist leaders themselves admit the deficiencies of gay life. Kirk and Madsen say: "In short, the gay lifestyle—if such a chaos can, after all, legitimately be called a lifestyle—just doesn't work: it doesn't serve the two functions for which all social frameworks evolve: to constrain people's natural impulses to behave badly and to meet their natural needs."[66]

Examining Presupposition Three

If gays are not "just like everyone else," then gay activists' third major unspoken presupposition—that gay activists will desire the same kinds of marriages as "everyone else," and that the legalization of same-sex "marriage" will have minimal effects on society at large—must be examined carefully before America proceeds to make public policy decisions we may deeply regret. Granting same-sex unions legal recognition may have much greater "ripple effects" than gay activists would have us believe.

Andrew Sullivan is the most prominent avowedly gay spokesman who says the effects of same-sex "marriage" recognition will not be serious. In his *Virtually Normal,*[67] Sullivan assures us that:

(1) Same-sex "marriage" would certainly not be "a massive societal leap in the dark."

(2) Same-sex "marriage" would not radically alter the nature of marriage as society has known it; instead, marriage would bring "stability" to gays, "domesticate them" and bring them closer to society's mainstream.

(3) Churches, synagogues and other religious organizations would not be forced to enact or recognize same-sex civil "marriages."

(4) Granting same-sex "marriage" recognition would not exacerbate the tumultuous struggle over "gay rights"; it would actually *defuse* the conflict.

Sullivan's assertions demand responses.

Sullivan's Assertion 1: Same-sex "marriage" would be no "leap in the dark" for society.

From all the evidence we have reviewed so far, it should be clear that same-sex "marriage" surely *would* be "a massive societal leap in the dark." Social critics recognize same-sex "marriage's" potential, just for starters...

...to have enormous impact on the broad range of rights and benefits associated with marriage. These range from income tax and estate tax law, communal property ownership, inheritance and probate law, divorce and child custody regulations, and insurance benefits.[68]

...to unleash avalanches of gay activist lawsuits, against employers, landlords, school authorities, insurance companies, churches, governmental authorities and more which refuse to recognize same-sex "marriages."

...to force the rewriting of business employment policies, insurance actuarial tables and government regulations at every level of society. "Mega"-businesses may be able to afford to subsidize and create benefit structures for same-sex "marriages" and "domestic partnerships" (some large companies are already providing employee benefits for partners of gay employees[69]), but small businesses will not likely be able to survive with these kinds of added burdens.

...to coerce public and private schools to rewrite curricula to include materials showing gay and lesbian lifestyles in a favorable light. As Mike Gabbard, who has led statewide opposition to same-sex "marriage" recognition in Hawaii, points out: "Compulsory education forces all children— a truly captive audience—to [be educated]. If same-sex 'marriages' become legal, children would be taught in health ed, sex education, and marriage/family courses that so-called homosexual 'marriage' is the equivalent of heterosexual marriage."[70]

...to, as numerous gay activists have predicted, begin "blowing the doors" off traditional marriage and family definitions and boundaries, to accommodate the vagaries of gay and lesbian lifestyles.

California Attorney General Dan Lundgren observes:

If you have the legal determination that there cannot be a preferred status for heterosexual marriage, you open yourself up to all sorts of other [legal] attacks...We go all the way to the question of bigamy, we go to the question of marrying between cousins and so forth and so on once you eliminate this preferred status.[71]

In raising such issues, have opponents, as columnist Stephen Chapman says in an article supporting same-sex "marriage," "passed into outright hallucination"[72]? One wonders how much "gay theory" about marriage and relationships Chapman has read. Activist Paula Ettelbrick, currently policy director for the National Center for Lesbian Rights, formerly legal director of the Lambda Legal Defense and Education Fund (formerly the Lambda Legal Defense Fund), is tactically "for" same-sex "marriage," but shares these *caveats*:

Being queer is more than setting up house, sleeping with a person of the same gender, and seeking state approval for doing so....Being queer means pushing the parameters of sex, sexuality, and family, and in the process, transforming the very fabric of society....

As a lesbian, I am fundamentally different from non-lesbian women....In arguing for the right to legal marriage, lesbians and gay men *would be forced to claim that we are just like heterosexual couples*, have the same goals and purposes, and vow to structure our lives similarly....We must keep our eyes on the goals of providing *true alternatives to marriage* and of radically reordering society's view of reality.[73]

Both the National Center for Lesbian Rights and the Lambda Legal Defense and Education Fund are considered, not "fringe," but "mainstream" gay activist groups. Former Lambda Legal Defense Fund president Thomas Stoddard also expresses lukewarm support for same-sex "marriages":

I must confess at the outset that I am no fan of the "institution" of marriage as currently constructed and practiced....Why give it such prominence? Why devote resources to such a distant goal? *Because marriage is, I believe, the political issue that most fully tests the dedication of people who are not gay to full equality for gay people*, and also the issue most likely to lead ultimately to a world free of discrimination against lesbians and gay men.[74]

The New American has reported:

In his 1990 book *An End to Shame: Shaping Our Next Sexual Revolution*...sociologist Ira Reiss describes..."a true sexual democracy [in which] all of us can achieve a much higher level of well-being—an ability to satisfy one's sexual interests without guilt or anxiety...."

Reiss points out that extending the social privileges associated with marriage to homosexuals and unmarried couples would be a major step toward the establishment of that "sexual democracy":

We should develop some kind of religious and civic ceremony that will sanctify and recognize a non-marital love relationship between two gays, two lesbians, or two straights. The registration of domestic partners so they may claim legal rights of inheritance and health benefits is a step in

this direction which some cities have taken. Discrimination on the basis of sexual orientation must join the list of forbidden discrimination like race, religion, and creed.

Unlike some...Reiss is refreshingly candid about the totalitarian nature of the reforms he recommends: "To build [sexual] pluralism we must firmly root out the narrow thinking about sex that exists in all of our basic institutions—family, political, economic, religious and educational. We need to change our whole basic social institutional structure...."[75]

Activist Donna Minkowitz says:

We [gay and lesbian activists] have been on the defensive too long. It's time to affirm that the Right is correct in some of its pronouncements about our movement. Pat Buchanan said there was a "cultural war" going on "for the soul of America" and that gay and lesbian rights were the principal battleground. He was right. Similarly, [homo]'phobes like Pat Robertson are right when they say that we threaten the family, male domination, and the Calvinist ethic of work and grimness that has paralyzed most Americans' search for pleasure.

Indeed, instead of proclaiming our innocuousness, we ought to advertise our potential to change straight society in radical, beneficial ways. Het[erosexual]s have much to learn from us: first and foremost, the fact that pleasure is possible (and desirable) beyond the sanction of the state. Another fact gleaned from gay experience—that gender is for all intents and purposes a fiction—also has the potential to revolutionize straight lives.[76]

Writing in *Out* magazine, regular contributor Michelangelo Signorile (quoted *supra*) has described a strategy in which homosexuals "fight for same-sex marriage and its benefits and then, once granted, redefine the institution of marriage completely...to debunk a myth and radically alter an archaic institution....The most subversive action lesbians and gays can undertake—and one that would perhaps benefit all of society—is to transform the notion of 'family' entirely."[77]

Sullivan's Assertion 2: Same-sex "marriage" would not radically alter the nature of marriage as society has known it; rather, marriage would bring "stability" to gays, "domesticate them" and bring them closer to society's mainstream.

Do gay activists truly want gays and lesbians to benefit from "the stability of marriage"—or do they want to destabilize the very foundation of marriage in order to accommodate their own oft-demonstrated relational instability?

As we have seen, not only married couples, but also cohabiting *singles* in the general population overwhelmingly practice fidelity during their committed relationships. Gays enjoy the same opportunity to be "domesticated" as general-population singles, yet they do not seem to be "domesticating"—and do not, for the most part, seem to desire "domestication." In fact, gay promiscuity and its consequences are generally highest in cities that are most "gay friendly."[78]

Even "conservative" same-sex "marriage" apologist Andrew Sullivan "fudges" when it comes to the idea of pinning gays down to the same marriage relationship standards by which the general population abides. Early in *Virtually Normal*, Sullivan says conservatives should welcome same-sex "marriage," because it would "harness one minority [?] group—homosexuals—and enlist them in a conservative [social] structure." But, by his book's end, Sullivan coyly hints heterosexuals might learn a lot from gay open-style "marriages":

> At times among gay male relationships, the openness of the contract makes it *more likely to survive than many heterosexual bonds.* Some of this is unavailable to the male-female union: there is more likely to be greater understanding of the need for extramarital outlets between two men than between a man and a woman...

> ...I believe strongly that marriage should be made available to everyone, in a politics of strict public neutrality. But within this model, there is plenty of scope for cultural difference. There is something baleful about the attempt of some gay conservatives to educate homosexuals and lesbians *to an uncritical acceptance of a stifling model of heterosexual normality.* The truth is, homosexuals are not entirely normal; and to flatten their varied and complicated lives into a single, moralistic model is to miss what is essential and exhilarating about their otherness.

> This need not mean, as some have historically claimed, that homosexuals have no stake in the sustenance of a society, but that their role is somewhat different...they may be able to *press the limits of the culture* or the business infrastructure, or the boundaries of intellectual life, in a way that heterosexuals by dint of a different type of calling, cannot.[79]

To date, no such "essential and exhilarating" allowances have been made for heterosexual marriages.

On the one hand, Sullivan and other gay activists imply that gays are promiscuous because they cannot marry. On the other hand, they say, "Change the basis of marriage to suit the way *we* are. It's heterosexual society that needs changing, not us!" They say, "We can't develop stable relationships because we can't marry." But to other audiences they say, "We don't want to form stable relationships, so change the definition of marriage so we don't have to live in sexually faithful relationships."

Sullivan says gays should not be pressed into the "stifling mold of heterosexual normality" (though the "straight" world has also experimented with "open marriages"—with less-than-happy results). But if gays and their relationships aren't "entirely normal," why should either gays or their relationships be recognized as legal "minorities" or equals of heterosexual marriages?

In effect, Sullivan has just pulled the rug out from under his own argument: Do gay activists want to stretch marriage barriers to include all kinds of relationships and combinations of same that would not now be accepted under that "tent"? Evidently, the "ripple effects" of same-sex "marriage" will by no means be as gentle as Sullivan is purringly trying to make them seem!

If gay activists are not trying to effect a radical demolition and re-establishment of the basic foundations of marriage, just to accommodate themselves, why do they seem so unwilling to accept the same standards of sexual fidelity as heterosexuals? Do gay activists want new marriage definitions, not just so marriage can include them, but also so marriage can include the vagaries of their lifestyles?

Ironically, Sullivan finds himself willing to apply the very kind of practical, lifestyle-pattern analysis considerations we have applied to gay unions to disqualify incest and near-kin sexual attraction as bases for marriage. Would he be willing to accept our analysis of homosexual lifestyles in evaluating "gayness" as a basis for marriage? Somehow, we doubt it.

Sullivan himself also admits that no two gay men or lesbians can be parents in the way heterosexual men and women can, so in what way would same-sex "marriage" and parenthoods be comparable to heterosexuals'?

Sullivan's Assertion 3: Churches, synagogues and other religious organizations would not be forced to recognize same-sex civil "marriages."

Sullivan nimbly dodges the question of whether religious organizations will have to recognize or perform same-sex "marriages." Since all gay activists are asking for, Sullivan says, is the privilege of enjoying *civil* marriage, *religious* organizations would not be forced to recognize or perform same-sex "marriages." One senses Sullivan knows better. As public policy analyst Robert K. Knight explains:

Although the [Hawaii Commission on Sexual Orientation] majority report recommends that religious institutions not be forced to perform same-sex ceremonies, it offers no defense for the conscientious Christian, Jew or Muslim (or Hindu or atheist, for that matter) who will not legally recognize same-sex "marriage." Law carries the potential use of force against those who will not abide by it....

All institutions except specifically religious ones would be subjected to state enforcement [according to the Commission]. That would include [religious] bookstores, radio and TV stations, and other nondenominational businesses owned by religious people.[80]

In fact, shortly after the State of Hawaii passed S.B. No. 1181, its comprehensive "gay rights" legislation, Hawaii Attorney General Warren Price answered by letter an inquiry regarding the bill's effects on religious organizations' hiring practices as follows:

Non-sectarian employees of the church, church-sponsored activities or programs are not exempt. This would include janitors, gardeners, teachers, etc.[81]

At present, Hawaii requires clergy to obtain a State license in order to perform marriages. The legal "machinery" is already in place to compel Hawaiian clergy to recognize and perform same-sex "marriages" or forfeit licensure.[82]

Gay activists have been known in the past to renege on promises not to disturb religious organizations. When Wisconsin's former governor, Lee Sherman Dreyfus, signed that State's "gay rights" bill into law, he was assured by gay activists that the bill would have no effect on religious institutions.

Shortly after Dreyfus left office, two allegedly gay men appeared at the 40-year-old Rawhide Boys' Ranch, a Christian home for troubled youths, demanding to be hired as counselors. When refused, the gay men took legal action. Evidence later surfaced indicating that not only was this action deliberate, it was planned by the Wisconsin Governor's Council on Lesbian and Gay Issues. A copy of minutes (obtained by this writer) of the October 19, 1985, meeting of the Council, under the heading "RAWHIDE" contains the following words:

Jim Thideman [one of eight Council members present] has asked some people to apply for a job [at Rawhide] and pursue filing a discrimination report with ERD [Equal Rights Division] upon refusal of employment, assuming it will be that

clear cut. Kathleen Nichols [another Council member] reported that Char McLaughlan is acquainted with a lesbian with a son at Rawhide who has been refused family counseling sessions if accompanied by her lover. Follow-up is necessary to see if this woman would be willing to file a complaint.

According to sources at the Rawhide Ranch, heading off these conspiratorial actions has cost the home in excess of $30,000. Former governor Dreyfus later wrote the "gay rights" bill's promoters, expressing his sense of betrayal at "gay rights" activists' flagrant breach of promise. Relief for Rawhide came only through passage of additional legislation that "exempted" religious institutions like it. But, for significant reasons, "religious exemptions" in "gay rights" or same-sex "marriage" legislation may only bring temporary relief from enforcement of such measures.

It is difficult to believe that Andrew Sullivan does not perceive the potential for coercion religious organizations will face in these kinds of dilemmas. Same-sex civil "marriage" recognition might well predicate these dilemmas and others. Yet while Sullivan decries as "anti-liberal" the potential coercion of "gay rights" legislation, he insists same-sex "marriage" recognition will not have the same effects.

Whether Sullivan believes so or not, same-sex "marriage" recognition would indeed "legislate private tolerance" by religious organizations, just as the acceptance of openly gay persons into America's military forces would "legislate tolerance" in that environment. Both of these eventualities would have the effect of saying to all touched by them, "Either accept gay 'marriages' or else!"

Sullivan's Assertion 4: Granting same-sex "marriage" recognition would not exacerbate the tumultuous struggle over "gay rights"; it would actually DEFUSE the conflict.

Since same-sex "marriage" recognition would render "gay rights" legislation unnecessary, moves allowing gays to marry would also defuse the rancorous national "gay rights" debate, Sullivan insists. Sullivan here writes disingenuously, if anywhere in his book. Surely he knows that many States recognize "marital status" as a "protected" (though not suspect) classification. Protected classes also possess the ability to claim discrimination—which is precisely the ability gay activists have been seeking to acquire through gaining suspect class recognition!

So long as gay activists can "claim discrimination" on some grounds, they can still use government and taxpayers' dollars to sue others and advance gay activist interests. "Marital status" will serve as well as suspect status in many states for that purpose. Furthermore, if the Hawaii Supreme Court ruling that *gender* is a suspect class holds up, "married" gay activists will be able to claim discrimination on "gender" grounds wherever marital status is not a protected class.

In any event, same-sex "marriage" recognition will simply "grandfather" gay activists into a position where they can use government to sue resistors and opponents and advance their political and social interests, just as well as they might by wielding "gay rights" legislation. Thus the "gay rights" struggle will continue, though in a slightly different guise, every bit as fervently and rancorously as before.

If the three gay activist presuppositions we have examined cannot stand scrutiny, the rest of gay activists' *apologia* will not likely persuade, either. We conclude that gays do *not* constitute a true suspect minority; gays are *not* "just like everyone else" in terms of relational lifestyle stability; and gay activists do *not* desire the same kinds of "marriages" as "everyone else"; therefore, the changes in marriage brought about by same-sex "marriage" recognition would have cataclysmic effects for society at large. Same-sex "marriage" recognition:

- would be a "massive societal leap" into a "darkness" of radical social experimentation, endless litigation and drastic business, economic and public policy reorganization

- would radically alter the institution of marriage as we have known it

- would be highly unlikely to change gay/lesbian lifestyle patterns

- would force churches, synagogues and other religious institutions to either recognize and perform same-sex "marriage" rites or be attacked by gay activists

- would perpetuate, and probably intensify, the "gay rights" controversy, on national and local levels

In addition, gay activists themselves are sharply divided on some of the most crucial issues surrounding same-sex "marriage": Whether homosexuality is innate and immutable; whether gays are truly an "oppressed class"; whether marriage would be an advantage or a threat to gay and lesbian relationships; and much more. If gay activists themselves cannot make up their minds on these issues, they have scarcely laid a solid foundation for implementation of the major public policy decisions they are asking society-at-large to make—strictly for their benefit.

Re-Examining the Four Major Arguments

With all this in mind, we will now briefly re-examine gay activists' four primary arguments in favor of same-sex "marriage recognition."

1) Gays, lesbians and bisexuals are being "discriminated against" when their unions are denied marriage recognition.

In essence, to make a claim of discrimination, one must be a member of a protected or suspect class. In saying they are being "discriminated against," gay activists are *already* claiming to be a protected or suspect class, in most cases *without having first earned the status that allows the claim.*

Since gay activists cannot make a valid claim to be recognized as a suspect class, they cannot properly make "claims of discrimination." Also, not being able to make "claims of discrimination" does not prove that one is being "discriminated against." The Civil Rights Act of 1964 and other state and local Civil Rights statutes simply do not provide extraordinary protection for every conceivable group that might at some time or other be looked down upon by some person or other group. Laws designed to specially protect the truly disadvantaged and politically powerless must be based on criteria of some sort. "Sexual orientation" simply does not meet the established criteria. It is not a racial, color or even religious category. It is not even, as gay activists define it, a *behavioral* category.

If gay activists are not part of a suspect class, they have no "right to claim discrimination," nor, in Civil Rights terms, can they be "discriminated against." Therefore, they do not have to be treated as if they *were* a suspect class—or anything other than people who claim to experience a certain sexual proclivity to an intense degree.

Are gays being denied benefits available to the married? An understanding of "minority" Civil Rights law should be sufficient to close the "discrimination" issue, but gay activists press further by insisting they are being denied benefits heterosexual married couples now enjoy. (They fail to mention that most of the benefits they feel they are lacking are also equally unavailable to unmarried *heterosexual* couples.) Is gay activists' claim in this regard true? For one thing, the argument itself smacks of circular reasoning: It presumes *a priori* that gays, lesbians and bisexuals *deserve* these benefits and are being willfully and unjustly denied them.

We also learn from numerous avowedly gay/lesbian sources that gay activists are aware of their ability to avail themselves of a host of substitutes for traditional marriage "benefits" now available through tort law. Gay activist Eric Marcus discusses several under the heading, "Legal Options for Formalizing Your Relationship."[83] Activist Paula L. Ettelbrick also reports, in a *Lesbians at Midlife* article entitled, "Legal Protections for Lesbians," that lesbians and gays have many legal options that can almost fully compensate for the lack of a marriage privilege. One of Colorado's chief avowedly gay same-sex "marriage" advocates, a Boulder activist named Rick Cendo, feels that he already has, in effect, "a working same-sex marriage."[84]

In the final analysis, to claim that opponents of "gay rights" or same-sex marriage recognition are "discriminating against gays and lesbians" is begging the question: assuming gays already possess universally accepted suspect status, which, as we have seen, is not the case. Criticism of, or legal action contrary to, the whims of affluent special interest groups which do not possess or qualify for suspect status does not constitute "discrimination." Saying that wealthy Caucasian corporation presidents as a class do not qualify for suspect status does not "discriminate" against the white and well-heeled. It simply states a fact. No amount of non-actionable verbal "millionaire-bashing" will compel government to declare Caucasian plutocrats a suspect class. They simply do not qualify for that status, nor do gay activists or other wealthy, powerful special interest groups. Gay activists have ample resources to secure virtually all the benefits they might desire—without tapping the public till or using government as a billy club to punish their opponents.

Refusing to grant special status (suspect or marital) to gay activists does not deny gay people a single fundamental Constitutional right. Suspect and marital status bestow privileges *additional* to the U.S. Constitution's fundamental protections. Again, Caucasian males under age 40 with no disabilities or firm ethnic identities are not beneficiaries of suspect status; nevertheless, it cannot be said that they do not possess all fundamental Constitutional rights because they do not enjoy special status.

In fact, it is gay activists who seem most eager to practice *reverse* discrimination against other Americans, by using suspect or marital status leverage to force society to subsidize and advance gay lifestyles and to institutionalize their own political goals, using government to advance their interests. Opposing gay activist special interests is not "discriminating against gays;" it is preserving rational and just Civil Rights policies; it is simply saying, "no special status and benefits" to a powerful special interest group which already shares the fundamental rights of American citizenship and enjoys far more advantages than most American citizens.

2) Marriage is a "basic human right" and choice of marriage partners should in no way be regulated by government; therefore same-sex couples should be allowed to legally marry.

One will search the Constitution of the United States in vain for a "fundamental right to marry," or even for a mention of marriage. It is true that numerous U.S. Supreme Court decisions have referred to the extraordinary significance of marriage; the High Court has called marriage "one of the basic civil rights of man" (see *Skinner vs.*

Oklahoma, 1942; *Zablocki vs. Redhail*, etc.). But perhaps David Shapiro, managing editor of *The Honolulu Star-Bulletin*, has answered this argument as pointedly as is necessary:

> There's no civil right to marry *whomever you wish*. Gay and lesbian couples aren't the only ones who can't get marriage licenses. You can't get a license to marry your brother or sister. You can't get a license to marry more than one person at a time. You can't get a license to marry a 9-year-old child or your horse.
>
> Every man and woman in Hawaii has the exact same right to get married. It just has to be to an individual of the opposite sex who is of age, is not a close relative and is human.
>
> If men and women are treated the same, there's no sex discrimination unless you hold that gay men and lesbian women are the third and fourth genders. There's a lot of legal ground to plow between here and there.[85]

Far less likely will one be to discover in the Constitution any "right" to marry *whomever one wishes* based on particular self-alleged varieties of sexuality alone.

Republican Presidential candidate Alan Keyes has said, "...[I]f we allow people to redefine marriage as an institution in such a way as to make it consistent with life sensuousness instead of responsibility, then I think we will have destroyed not only this important institution, but all the things in society that depend on it."[86]

To oppose the aims of affluent gay activist special interests may violate their *wishes* and deprive them of undeserved status and benefits, including marital; it does not, however, violate their fundamental *rights*.

3) Civil and religious marriage will remain separate institutions if same-sex marriages are legalized.

If gay activists gain suspect status and sufficient political leverage, America can count on it: Gay activists will show up at religious organizations' doors with lawyers in tow, followed by process servers with subpoenas to "equal protection" lawsuits against organizations that refuse to recognize and enact same-sex "marriages."

4) Same-gender couples cannot legally marry in any state, despite how much they may feel a "need" to (emotionally), or how much their "families" need civil marriage's protections, benefits and responsibilities.

Like gay activists' second argument, this one also presumes that it is perfectly right and just for gay activists to demand marriage recognition for same-sex unions. We think we have shown that this demand is neither right nor just, and is no more appropriate than for consensual sado-masochists, or hair, foot or underwear fetishists to make, based solely on their self-alleged sexual fantasy proclivities.

Gay Activists' Unspoken "Fifth Argument"

Stripped of all their pseudo-merit, gay activists' arguments in support of same-sex "marriage" boil down to one unspoken "fifth argument," which happens to be a classic non-sequitur known as *argumentum ad misericordiam*, or the "argument to pity." Applied to "gay rights" issues, it goes something like this:

Gay people have suffered emotional torment because society does not smile on their "sexual orientation." Gay activists complain loudly about this "oppression." Therefore, society "owes" gays suspect status, marital status and all accompanying benefits, to redress injuries done to gays and to make them feel better.

Or, as one observer has put gay activists' position more colloquially, "We feel bad, we shout loud, give us 'perks'!"

Of course, injured feelings *per se* offer no compelling reason to bestow favors on anyone. If they did, every child's tantrum would be rewarded. Doubtless many imprisoned criminals feel bad because they are behind bars. This fact alone does not entitle them to automatic release. Nor do gay activists' hurt feelings alone entitle them to get away with perpetrating massive Civil Rights fraud.

———————————————

Anton N. Marco is founder of Colorado for Family Values and America for Family Values. He was the author of Colorado's Amendment 2 campaign against "protected class" status for gays, and, with his wife, Joyce, runs DoveTail Ministries, a ministry to gays.

Endnotes:

[1] According to avowed gay activist attorney Evan Wolfson, arguments rooted in "morality" or "religion" should not be recognized in public debate on this issue. Wolfson has said, "For government to interfere with the freedom of an individual—whether religious or personal—there must be valid secular reasons."

[2] "Homosexual Activists Start 'Marriage' Lobby Groups," *SPHA Bulletin*, December 1995, p. 6.

[3] "Gay and Lesbian Marriages: To Be Or Not To Be," *Quest*, February 1992, p. 20.

[4] "To Have and to Hold," (Washington, D.C.: The National Gay and Lesbian Task Force, 1995), p. 6.

[5] Ibid. p. 15.

[6] Ibid. p. 15.

[7] Ibid. p. 15.

[8] Cf. "To Have and to Hold," p. 15.

[9] Andrew Sullivan, *Virtually Normal* (New York: Alfred A. Knopf, 1995), p. 183.

[10] Ibid. p. 112.

[11] Ibid. p. 185.

[12] Cf. "A healthy dose of homosexuality?" *The Washington Times*, National Weekly Edition, May 26, 1996, p. 33.

[13] Cf. Enrique Rueda, *The Homosexual Network: Private Lives and Public Policy* (Washington: Devin Adair Co., 1982).

[14] "The Family Defined," *Chalcedon Report*, June 1996, p. 9.

[15] Cf. "Matrimony in Hawaii: Marriage On the Rocks?" *Rights in America* newsletter, Vol. 2, No. 5, p. 1.

[16] Cf. *San Antonio Independent School District vs. Rodriguez*, 1973; *Massachusetts Board of Retirement vs. Murgia*, 1976; *Plyler vs. Doe*, 1982; *City of Cleburne vs. Cleburne Living Center*, 1985; reaffirmed in *Jantz vs. Muci*, 1991, denied cert., U.S. S.Ct.; cf. also *Frontiero vs. Richardson*, 1973.

[17] See the following articles, among many: "Overcoming a Deep Rooted Reluctance, More Firms Advertise to Gay Community," *The Wall Street Journal*, July 18, 1991; "The Gay Nineties," *The Marketer*, September 1990 (reporting findings by the Simmons Market Research Bureau and the U.S. Census Bureau). Other market research, produced by Overlooked Opinions, a Chicago firm (boasting 99%+ accuracy), are reported in: "Gay Market a Potential Gold Mine," *The San Francisco Chronicle*, August 27, 1991; "For Gays, Ship Charters Are a Boon, Say Two Travel Companies," *Travel Weekly*, August 5, 1991; and "Where the Money Is: Travel Industry Eying Gay/Lesbian Tourism," *The Bay Area Reporter* (a gay/lesbian newspaper), September 19, 1991.

[18] Source: *The Statistical Abstract of the United States, 1990.*

[19] Op. cit., Overlooked Opinions survey.

[20] Robert T. Michael, John H. Gagnon, Edward O. Laumann and Gina Kolata, *Sex In America* (Boston: Little, Brown & Co., 1994), cf. p. 182.

[21] "Can I come out at work and be secure?" *The Advocate*, March 22, 1994, p. 20.

[22] "Beyond Oppression," *The New Republic*, May 10, 1993, pp. 34-35.

[23] "Gays' problems not all that bad," Colorado Springs *Gazette Telegraph*, April 30, 1993.

[24] "Beyond Oppression," pp. 18ff.

[25] "Activists from around the country descend on the Hill," *The Washington Blade*, May 8, 1992.

[26] Bell and Weinberg, *Homosexualities: A Study of Diversities Among Men and Women* (New York: Simon and Schuster, 1978); Hammersmith, S.K., *Sexual Preference: Its Development in Men and Women* (Bloomington: Indiana University Press, 1981).

[27] "Health Care Needs of Gay Men and Lesbians in the United States," *JAMA*, May 1, 1996, Vol. 275, No. 17, p. 1354.

[28] Ruth Tiffany Barnhouse, *Homosexuality: A Symbolic Confusion* (New York: The Seabury Press, 1977), p. 97.

[29] Tom Morey, Committee to Study Homosexuality of the United Methodist Church, General Conference of Ministries, Chicago Meeting on the Sciences, August 1990, p. 19.

[30] Charles W. Keysor, ed., *What You Should Know About Homosexuality* (Grand Rapids: Zondervan Publishing House, 1979), p. 167.

[31] "Homosexuality and Sexual Orientation Disturbances," in Alfred M. Freedman, Harold I. Kaplan and Benjamin J. Saddock, eds., *Comprehensive Textbook of Psychiatry II*, second edition (Baltimore: The Williams & Wilkins Co., 1975), p. 1519.

[32] Fine, *Psychoanalytic Theory, Male and Female Homosexuality: Psychological Approaches* (pamphlet), pp. 84-86.

[33] See LeVay, *Science*, 253 (1991): 1034.

[34] "Salk and Pepper," *The Bay Area Reporter*, September 5, 1991, pp. 21, 24.

[35] See *Newsweek*, Feb. 24, 1992, p. 48.

[36] Cf. "Not-so-straight news: "Reporting" on genetic research tells only half the story," *World* magazine, November 11, 1995.

[37] Op. cit. Katz, *The Invention of Heterosexuality*, p. 190.

[38] Ibid. p. 195, emphasis Duggan's.

[39] Op. cit., *Lesbians at Midlife*, "Redefining Sexuality: Women Becoming Lesbians in Mid-Life," Charbonneau and Lander, p. 35.

[40] Op. cit. *Lesbian Passion*, p. 35.

[41] Cf. *The Advocate*, December 29, 1992.

[42] "Coming Out Ahead: The Homosexual Movement in the Academy," *First Things*, August-September 1993, p. 20, emphasis added.

[43] Cf. op. cit., Bell and Weinberg, *Homosexualities, a Study of Diversity Among Men and Women* (New York: Simon and Schuster, 1978), p. 308-309.

[44] Source: *In Step*, May 28, 1986.

[45] Corey, L. and Holmes, K.K., "Sexual transmission of hepatitis A in homosexual men," *New England Journal of Medicine*, 1980, 302, pp. 435-438.

[46] Gebhard, P.H. and Johnson, A.B., *The Kinsey Data* (Sanders, 1979); Bell, Weinberg and Hammersmith, *Sexual Preference*, op. cit.

[47] "AIDS amd sexial behavior reported by gay men in San Francisco," *American Journal of Public Health*, December 1985, 75, pp. 493-496.

[48] Letters to the Editor, *American Journal of Public Health*, December 1985, 75, pp. 1449, 1450.

[49] Joseph Nicolosi, "Let's Be Straight: A Cure Is Possible," *Insight*, December 6, 1993, p. 24.

[50] *Adult Sexual Behavior in 1989: Number of Partners, Frequency and Risk*, presented February 1990 to the American Association for the Advancement of Science, published 1990 by NORC, University of Chicago.

[51] Eric Marcus, *The Male Couple's Guide to Living Together* (New York: Harper & Row, 1988), pp. 26-27.

[52] Summit Books, 1979, a survey by avowedly gay researchers.

[53] Op. cit., Sang, Warshow and Smith, *Lesbians at Midlife: The Creative Transition*, p. 134.

[54] Op. cit., Loulan/Nelson, *Lesbian Passion*, p. 35.

[55] Ibid. ref. p. 194.

[56] Ibid. pp. 202,203.

[57] Cf. Robert T. Michael, John H. Gagnon, Edward O Laumann, Gina Kolata, *Sex In America* (Boston: Little, Brown & Co., 1994).

[58] Ibid. p. 1.

[59] Ibid. p. 25.

[60] Ibid. p. 35, Table 1.

[61] Ibid. p. 101, emphasis added.

[62] Ibid. p. 105.

[63] Ibid. p. 110.

[64] Ibid. ref. p. 109.

[65] Ibid. p. 177.

[66] Marshall Kirk and Hunter Madsen, *After the Ball* (New York: Doubleday, 1989), p. 363.

[67] Op. cit.

[68] Whitney Galbraith, "Merits of amendment prohibiting gay marriage debated," *Colorado Springs Gazette Telegraph*, January 1, 1996, p. B-5.

[69] Walt Disney, for example.

[70] As quoted in "Same-Sex Marriage," *The New American*, April 1, 1996, p. 5.

[71] "Congress considers bill to ban same-sex marriages," *Colorado Christian News*, June 1996, p. 7.

[72] "Why shouldn't gay couples be able to marry?" *Colorado Springs Gazette Telegraph*, January 28, 1996, p. B-7.

[73] "Since When Is Marriage a Path to Liberation," essay in William B. Rubenstein, ed., *Lesbians, Gay Men and the Law* (New York: The New Press, 1993), pp. 401-405, emphasis added.

[74] Ibid. essay entitled "Why Gay People Should Seek the Right to Marry," pp. 398, 400, emphasis added.

[75] Op. cit., *The New American*, pp. 6, 7.

[76] Op. cit., Donna Minkowitz, "Recruit, Recruit, Recruit!"

[77] Quoted in "What's wrong with this picture," *Citizen* magazine, Vol. 10, No. 4, April 22, 1996, p. 3.

[78] Cf. *The San Francisco Examiner*, April 23, 1979; "CDC Hepatitis A among homosexual men—United States, Canada and Australia," *MMWR*, 1992: 41: 155-164, 12.

[79] Op. cit., Sullivan, pp. 203, 204, emphasis added.

[80] "Homosexual 'Marriage,'" *AFA Journal*, April 1996, p. 15.

[81] A copy of this correspondence has come into the possession of this writer.

[82] Cf. *Biblical Baptist Press*, March-April 1996, p. 5.

[83] Op. cit., *The Male Couple's Guide to Living Together*, p. 161 ff.

[84] "Same-sex couples register commitment," Colorado Springs *Gazette Telegraph*, July 2, 1996, p. B-2.

[85] Editorial, December 16, 1995, enmphasis added.

[86] Statement to press, January 27, 1996, quoted in *SPHA Bulletin*, January/February 1996, p. 6.

The Gay Youth Suicide Myth

by Peter LaBarbera

The rate of suicide has nearly tripled among young people since 1965.[1] Efforts to discover the root causes of this epidemic of self-inflicted violence must be dispassionate and free of politics. However, homosexual activists have manipulated this national tragedy to promote their political agenda.

Voicing concern over suicide risk for "gay youth," homosexual activists are pushing pro-homosexual programs in the schools, which will invariably ensnare vulnerable teens who might otherwise have avoided the destructive homosexual lifestyle. Their diagnosis: gay youths need affirmation of their homosexuality in a "homophobic" world, or they may become suicidal. The proffered solution: affirmation programs that make gay youths comfortable with being homosexual and the rest of the student population comfortable with the concept of homosexuality. Once everyone accepts homosexuality as "normal" and "natural," gay youth will achieve high self-esteem and avoid suicidal behavior.

But this view is based on the aims and values of the gay activist movement, not on any solid scientific assessment. For starters, it ignores the possibility that homosexuality is a condition—apart from societal acceptance or nonacceptance—that often leads to unhealthy behavior, which leads to unhappiness.

The genesis of the homosexual teen suicide myth lies in a deeply flawed and pro-homosexual report by San Francisco homosexual activist Paul Gibson. The paper, "Gay Male and Lesbian Youth Suicide," was included, as a supporting document, in a 1989 report by a special federal task force on youth suicide reporting to Dr. Louis Sullivan, former Secretary of Health and Human Services (HHS). However, Secretary Sullivan repudiated and distanced his department from the Gibson paper:

> ...the views expressed in the paper entitled 'Gay Male and Lesbian Youth Suicide' do not in any way represent my personal beliefs or the policy of this Department.[2]

Sullivan went on to say:

> Indeed, I am strongly committed to advancing traditional family values. Federal policies must be crafted with great care so as to strengthen rather than undermine the institution of the family. In my opinion, the views expressed in the paper run contrary to that aim.[3]

Dr. David Shaffer, one of the country's leading authorities on suicide among youth, notes that Gibson's paper "was never subjected to the rigorous peer review that is required for publication in a scientific journal and contained no new research findings."[4]

The following are some of Gibson's most tendentious and oft-repeated claims:

- gay and lesbian youths may account for one third of all youth suicides;

- homosexual youths are two to three times more likely to attempt suicide than their heterosexual peers;

- suicide is the leading cause of death among gay and lesbian youth; and

- gay youth suicide is caused by the internalization of "homophobia" and violence directed at gays.[5]

Although Gibson's report was denounced by Secretary Sullivan, homosexual activists have skillfully used it to claim that "government statistics" support their suicide assertions. Pro-gay articles routinely (and mistakenly) cite Gibson's unproven statistics as part of the HHS task force's official conclusions on youth suicide.[6] Gibson himself has declined an interview with the author to discuss his controversial assertions.[7]

In Massachusetts, a recently established Commission on Gay and Lesbian Youth set up by Republican Gov. William Weld relied almost exclusively on Gibson's unpublished HHS paper to warn ominously of a gay teen suicide epidemic. Gibson's exaggerated claims became the central rationale for creating a sweeping pro-gay counseling program in the state's schools.[8] In an interview in *The Advocate*, a national gay magazine, Governor Weld, curiously, uses a Gibson-derived statistic to justify the program while at the same time seemingly acknowledging that this program may have credibility problems: "They say the harassment is one of the reasons gays and lesbians account for 30% of teenage suicides. That doesn't even need to be true for me to say that fighting anti-gay discrimination in the schools is absolutely necessary."[9]

Lobbying by public school students was the key to passage of a student "gay rights" bill in Massachusetts, and, again, Gibson's "30 percent" statistic was a factor. According to *The New York Times*, a student stood outside the State House for several weeks leading up to the December 6, 1993 Senate passage of the bill holding a sign that said "Gays Make Up 30 Percent of Completed Teen Suicides."[10] David LaFontaine, a gay activist who is now the director of Weld's youth commission, went so far as to say, "Gay youth suicide is like a hidden holocaust in America."[11]

Notwithstanding such wild exaggerations, there is no consensus among experts that anything resembling an "epidemic" of gay teen suicides even exists. Moreover, many observers are aghast that, in this age of AIDS, the danger of suicide would be used to confirm confused youths in an unhealthy, destructive lifestyle that is fraught with anxiety and disease and that often leads to early death.[12]

Due in large part to the effective use of the suicide scare, Massachusetts teenagers in public schools are now facing an array of pro-gay counseling programs similar to Project 10—the Los Angeles school program set up by a lesbian teacher with the goal of "validating the feelings" of "lesbian and gay youth." Project 10's blatant pro-gay bias is exemplified by its name, which is based on the now-repudiated myth that homosexuals make up 10 percent of the population.

GIBSON'S SKEWED RESEARCH

The myth of a gay teen suicide epidemic is built upon a flimsy statistical foundation. Gibson, a homosexual social worker in San Francisco, uses statistics from mainly homosexual sources and then extrapolates them to the general youth population using the discredited Kinsey estimate of a 10 percent gay population.

A perusal of Gibson's report turns up numerous contradictions and statistical impossibilities. For example, he refers to one author who speculated in 1985 (in the gay newspaper, *The Washington Blade*) that as many as 3,000 gay youths kill themselves a year—a number that exceeds the *total* number of annual teen suicides by more than a thousand.[13]

To reach his core conclusions on the high rate of homosexual suicides, Gibson points to assorted gay survey studies that claim homosexual youth are far more likely than their heterosexual counterparts to have considered or to have attempted suicide. These studies rely on surveys of troubled and often runaway youth. Generally, they have found a much higher rate (two to four times higher) of suicidal tendencies in their "gay" respondents compared with their "straight" respondents. Gibson then multiplies this higher rate by the disputed Kinsey figure of a 10 percent homosexual population to produce his figure that 30 percent of all youth suicides involve homosexual youth.

David Shaffer, a Columbia University psychiatrist and specialist on adolescent suicide, has said, "I struggled for a long time over [Gibson's] mathematics, but, in the end, it seemed more hocus-pocus than math."[14] Nevertheless, Gibson's claims have been repeated over and over as homosexual activists have made them part of their lore.

In his paper, Gibson writes that "there are far more gay youth than you are aware of." He notes that "Kinsey found a significant amount of homosexual behavior among adolescents surveyed with 28 percent of the males and 17 percent of females reporting at least one homosexual experience." Finally, he posits that "a substantial minority of youth—perhaps one in ten as one book suggests—have a primary gay male, lesbian, or bisexual orientation."[15] But since Gibson wrote his paper, there has been widespread repudiation of the Kinsey-based "10 percent" myth. One recent survey of nearly 35,000 Minnesota adolescents found only half of one percent described themselves as predominantly homosexual.[16] And studies from many countries are finding that homosexuals comprise less than 2% of any population and, often, less than 1%.[17]

In addition to his reliance on the false Kinsey estimate of the homosexual population, Gibson's study is fraught with difficulties that should disqualify its findings, among them:

Problem #1: Small Percentage of Suicides Found Gay

Perhaps the most damaging blow to the gay teen suicide myth comes from the studies of completed suicides, in which nothing close to Gibson's 30 percent figure has been found. Keeping in mind the difficulties of assessing whether or not a deceased person was homosexual, Shaffer cites three major studies analyzing factors behind a consecutive number of youth suicides:

- A "psychological autopsy" study in 1959 by researcher Eli Robins—one of the first of its kind—of 133 consecutive suicides in St. Louis. No cases of known homosexuality were found;[18]

- A 1986 study of San Diego youth led by Charles Rich and researchers with the University of California, San Diego, who interviewed the survivors of 283 consecutive suicides—133 of whom were under 30. Only nine (7 percent) were found to be homosexual, and none of these suicides was under age 21. Shaffer grants that it is possible ("even likely") that the San Diego study undercounts the homosexual factor behind the deaths, but notes it is, nevertheless, far from Gibson's claim of 30 percent of suicide victims being gay;[19]

- A study conducted by Shaffer and his colleagues at Columbia University of 107 consecutive New York City suicides. Shaffer notes that his research team inquired about a much broader group of behaviors than the San Diego study to ascertain whether the victim was homosexual. For example, surviving relatives and acquaintances were asked if the victim had any gay friends or ever voiced concerns about sexuality.

Shaffer writes:

By broadening the definition, we therefore ran the risk of over-determining the number of gay suicides. In spite of this, out of 107 male teen suicides, only three were known to have talked to others about a homosexual experience (2.7%) and 2 of these 3 died together in a suicide pact. A further four showed some behavior that could have been indicative of homosexuality. None of the female suicides were thought to have been lesbian. If all of the teenagers who showed any evidence of homosexual behavior were indeed gay, then a total of 6% of the suicides in our study would have been gay. Once again, no evidence that a large proportion of suicides are gay, but [6% is] more or less [what] we would expect in the general population.[20]

Beyond the studies cited by Shaffer, a 1991 survey by the respected Gallup Organization found little support for the theory that homosexuality is a prime cause of teen suicide. Gallup polled a random sample of 1,152 teenagers, 60 percent of whom said they knew a teen who had attempted suicide; although 10 causes were cited, none specifically mentioned that the person's sexuality problems were the impetus for his suicidal behavior.

A more telling finding from the Gallup report was the view of the 15 percent of respondents who said they had actually come close to committing suicide. (Six percent reported attempting to kill themselves.) These teenagers were asked the open-ended question of what factors led them to their act of desperation. The most commonly cited causes were such things as family problems, depression, "boy/girl relationships," and low self-esteem, but gender or sexuality crises were not reported as a cause.[21]

"That was asked as an open-ended question and nobody answered, 'because I'm gay,'" recalled Howard "Red" Smith, senior market manager at Gallup who oversaw the poll.[22]

Problem #2: Gibson Cites Gay Studies with Unrepresentative Samples

In what has become a defining characteristic of pro-gay scholarship (e.g., Simon LeVay's flawed study of brain structure), Gibson errs in supporting his thesis with data collected from institutions whose clientele do not represent the overall homosexual population. Writes Shaffer:

Where did the idea that gay suicide is common come from? There have been a series of unusual groups of gays that provide an excellent example of how bad research provides misleading answers that can come home to roost. All were among what epidemiologists call "convenience samples," that is, the studies used subjects that were easy to find, but who were almost certainly not representative of gays at large.[23]

As noted above, the foundation of Gibson's claim of a soaring rate of gay teen suicides is data culled from surveys at youth assistance or "drop in" centers. Many of the centers studied are gay-oriented establishments for homeless youth or those facing severe crises, such as the Institute for the Protection of Gay and Lesbian Youth in New York City. Such sample groups skew the results because they reflect a pool of troubled youth who are naturally more suicidal than a random sample of teens.

Another study cited by Gibson is the 1978 report by Kinsey Institute researchers A.P. Bell and M.S. Weinberg, which found that 38 percent of lesbians and 35 percent of gay men had attempted or seriously considered suicide. But Shaffer notes that about 40 percent of the male subjects for this study were recruited from bars or bathhouses, and another quarter were recruited from gays with personal contacts in such places. Thus a high proportion of men interviewed had an alcohol problem. Shaffer writes:

...gays who hang out in bars will likely include a

disproportionate number of alcoholics and almost every study on suicide shows that alcohol is strongly associated with suicide.[24]

Problem #3: Gibson's Supporting Studies Lack Control Groups

A critical error in the works used by Gibson to show a preponderance of gays among suicide attempters is their lack of a heterosexual control group to put their findings in context. Shaffer writes:

> Drop-in centers are places of comfort and shelter for unsupported and neglected youngsters, whether gay or straight. To make sense of a high rate of suicide attempts in gays who use shelters, you would need to see if the rate was higher than in a control or comparison group of non-gay shelter users, which these studies have not done.[25]

Researcher Susan Blumenthal of the National Institutes of Mental Health concurs, noting with regard to the studies cited by Gibson:

> ...many of these studies have a small sample size, lack comparison groups, and have difficulties ascertaining the prevalence of homosexuality in the population being studied.[26]

Interestingly, a recent unpublished study of high-risk youth found a much lower incidence of youths citing homosexuality as a factor in their suicide attempts. Leona L. Eggert, a researcher at the University of Washington, Seattle, questioned 64 students who were screened as "high risk" suicidal youth. The youngsters were asked questions about various aspects of their lives to find out what "stressors" may have contributed to their suicidal behavior. Only one student said that sexual orientation problems contributed to his attempted suicide.

In an interview, Eggert said she was wary of making the 1 in 64 data public because it offers no definitive picture of the role that homosexuality plays. She noted that the purpose of the study was to evaluate suicide prevention programs and not to assess homosexuality specifically. She said that the lone question relating to sexual orientation did not "properly set the stage" for a thorough analysis of sexual orientation as a factor in suicide.

Eggert said the question did come toward the end of the survey—when respondents would be more comfortable with the interviewer and presumably more truthful. But she said that a thorough effort would have involved several questions about the stigmatized factor of homosexuality.

Keeping Eggert's reservations in mind, findings such

as the 1-in-64 statistic deserve public airing, particularly since gay activists irresponsibly promote the fiction that 30 percent of all youth suicides are gay.[27]

With regard to the "30 percent" assertion, Peter Muehrer, chief of the youth mental health program in the Prevention Research Branch of the National Institutes of Mental Health, said that nobody can make definitive claims about the percentages of "gay" youth suicides. No national or statewide studies published in peer-reviewed journals have analyzed completed suicides of homosexual youths during the past 30 years, he noted. The closest thing, Muehrer said, was the Charles Rich study cited above, and that was limited to San Diego. Muehrer noted that Paul Gibson's HHS paper is merely an "essay" that presents no new data on completed suicides.[28]

Problem #4: Gibson Is Too Simplistic, Neglecting Other Psychological Factors Behind Most Suicides

Gibson, like many other homosexual advocates, assumes that the cause of suicide in alleged gay youth is internalized "homophobia." But, as Shaffer notes, the assumption that the "humiliation, abuse and isolation" experienced by gay adolescents leads to suicide "would be at variance with what we usually see among suicides....Sheer adversity of life does not in itself seem to lead to suicide."[29] He writes that the evidence from completed suicides and suicide-attempting youth suggests that they fall into three main categories: "hot-headed," aggressive males; teenagers who are "chronically and irrationally anxious;" and the woefully depressed who plan their suicides carefully.

According to Shaffer, who has spent a career studying the thought and mental feelings of troubled teens, "gay" suicide victims are not distinguished among the larger pool of suicide victims. Regarding his study of "gay" New York teenagers who killed themselves, he writes:

> ..I have leafed through their sad case records and there seemed little to differentiate them from the straight suicides. The stories were the same: a court appearance scheduled for the day of the death; prolonged depression; drug and alcohol problems; etc.[30]

Most studies of homosexual suicide attempts find other influencing factors present in their backgrounds that are common to all cases of suicide. For example, one 1989 study of suicidal behavior in young adult gay men found that the "suicidal" men were more than three times as likely as the "non-suicidal" men to have alcoholic fathers, and more than twice as likely to have no religious affiliation and a family history of suicide. Other harmful factors such as divorce were found to be disproportionate among the suicidal men.[31]

Blumenthal writes that although the humiliation related to homosexuality may be a precipitant of a suicide attempt, that does not make it the *cause:* "...[T]he most important risk factor is the presence of mental illness ...those gay and heterosexual youths at highest risk may have certain predisposing factors, such as a family history of suicide and a biological vulnerability that interacts with risk factors developed later in life, including a psychiatric illness, substance abuse, and poor social supports."[32]

Note that while some observers might classify homosexual desires as a "mental illness" leading to increased suicidal behavior, that classification is emphatically rejected by Gibson and other gay academics who insist that homosexuality is a normal condition.

Problem #5: Gibson Assumes a Permanent Homosexual "Orientation" Fixed at Birth

On page (3)-114 of his study, Gibson writes, "A gay or lesbian adolescence is not just a phase the youth is going through." Although he asserts this as fact, it is nothing more than a judgment—and one that is contradicted by recent *gay* research. Gary Remafedi, a homosexual researcher at the University of Minnesota, recently published a study in the journal *Pediatrics* which found that students' confusion with regard to their "sexual orientation" decreased with age. Significantly, the survey of nearly 35,000 Minnesota youth (grades 7 through 12) found that older students were less likely to identify themselves as homosexual or bisexual than younger students:

> The percentage of students reporting a predominantly ("mostly" or "100%") heterosexual orientation increased slightly with age from 98.4% at age 12 to 99.2% at 18 years of age, with a corresponding decline in the percentage who adopted the bisexual label.[33]

A significant body of evidence exists that a sizeable percentage of men and women experiment with homosexual acts in their youth but go on to lead normal, heterosexual lives. Such evidence is resisted by the gay lobby, which increasingly argues that one's homosexual "identity" is fixed at birth or in one's very early years and *cannot be changed*. In Massachusetts, Gov. Weld's Commission on Gay and Lesbian Youth was presented with testimony from men and women who had experimented with homosexuality in their youth but abandoned such behavior and found happiness. But the commission rejected such testimonies in preparing its report calling for pro-gay school programs, apparently because it did not fit the objective of confirming "gay and lesbian youth" in their homosexuality.[34]

Alan Medinger, a former homosexual and director of

Regeneration, an ex-gay ministry based in Baltimore, said that, given the evidence of changed lives and research suggesting that students' views about their sexuality are fluid, "It is absolutely criminal to take a confused kid and lead him into a life that could kill him."[35] Yet a pro-homosexual orientation is precisely the goal of counseling programs like Project 10.

Problem #6: Gibson's Study Embraces Radical Homosexual Agenda

Beyond the shoddy methodology, Gibson's paper and his motives must be assessed within the context of his recommendations—several of which are sweeping in scope. Since he attributes the homosexual's anxiety and depression to a "homophobic" culture that forces gays into self-hatred, Gibson proposes to help the aggrieved homosexual by proposing that society offer "positive" reinforcement to his gayness.

Even churches that oppose homosexuality on biblical grounds need to "reassess" their views, he says, or they risk contributing to the violence and hatred against gays. Gibson writes:

> Many traditional (e.g., Catholicism) and fundamentalist (e.g., Baptist) faiths still portray homosexuality as morally wrong or evil...These beliefs can also create unresolvable internal conflicts for gay youth who adhere to their faith but believe they will not change their sexual orientation. They may feel wicked and condemned to hell and attempt suicide in despair of ever obtaining redemption...

> Religions need to reassess homosexuality in a positive context within their belief systems... Religions should also take responsibility for providing their families and membership with positive information about homosexuality that discourages the oppression of lesbians and gay men. Faiths that condemn homosexuality should recognize how they contribute to the rejection of gay youth by their families and suicide among lesbian and gay male youth.[36]

On the supposed normalcy of homosexuality, Gibson again reveals his militancy:

> Homosexuality...is a natural and healthy expression of human sexuality. If homosexuality is not an illness or disorder, it cannot be regarded as such to the extent that it occurs in the young...

> Transsexual youth who are open about their identity face extreme abuse and rejection from

their families...The only known course of treatment is to help transsexuals adjust to their believed gender identity and obtain sex-assignment surgery. Most transsexual youth, however, are unable to obtain or afford the help they need in resolving their identity conflicts.

There is nothing inherently self-destructive in homosexual feelings and relationships that could be a source of suicidal behavior...

...[m]arriages between homosexuals should be recognized...A conscious effort must be made to dispel the destructive myths about homosexuality at all levels of society...Massive education efforts need to take place that would provide people with accurate information about homosexuality. These efforts need to be directed to those who have responsibility for the care of the young including families, clergy, teachers, and helping professionals...

All youth need to be presented with positive information about homosexuality that presents it as a viable adaptation. We must accept a homosexual orientation in young people in the same manner we accept a heterosexual orientation...

It is important for schools to hire openly gay male and lesbian teachers to serve as role models and resource people for gay youth.[37]

These and other radical statements expose Gibson as an ardent activist—not a dispassionate researcher. Yet his paper and statistics have been quoted by gay leaders and liberal educators as if they were the work of a renowned statistician. Meanwhile, the work of academics who find a much lower incidence of homosexuality among suicidal teens is ignored.

Perhaps the myth of a gay teen suicide "holocaust" is irresistible to gay activists because it squares so perfectly with their strategy of embracing victim status to gain sympathy with the general population. That strategy was eloquently stated by homosexual authors Marshall Kirk and Hunter Madsen:

..In any campaign to win over the public, gays must be portrayed as victims in need of protection so that straights will be inclined by reflex to adopt the role of protector. ...The purpose of victim imagery is to make straights feel very uncomfortable; that is, to jam with shame the self-righteous pride that would ordinarily accompany and reward their antigay belligerence, and to lay the groundwork for the process of con-

version by helping straights identify with gays and sympathize with their underdog status.[38]

Trojan Horse for More Gay-Positive Programs

The fact that gay activists would use a discredited and sloppy study like Gibson's to advance their agenda shows there is more to their apocalyptic warnings of a gay teen suicide "epidemic" than mere concern for troubled youth. Since these activists cling so stubbornly to Gibson's study as evidence of the need for pro-gay intervention programs in schools, it is only fair to assume they will follow the rest of his guidelines for expanding the pro-homosexual message to schoolchildren. In fact, this is clearly the case.

In Massachusetts, pro-family activists warn that gay activists are already using the heart-tugging teen suicide issue as a Trojan horse to bring their destructive agenda into the public school system. Such fears are borne out in the report issued by the state's Commission on Gay and Lesbian Youth, which contains a long-term recommendation for teachers to "integrate gay and lesbian themes and issues into their subject areas."[39]

Massachusetts pro-family activist Nancy Sutton notes that under the state's new "education reform" law, schools are being pressured into starting pro-gay counseling programs (similar to Project 10) through the threat of withholding state funds to school districts that fail to comply.[40] Among the groups that have volunteered to help schools comply with the "Project Teen Health" guidelines (that include pro-gay suicide prevention) are pro-homosexual outfits like the Boston Alliance of Gay & Lesbian Youth.[41]

Conclusion

There appears to be evidence that youth confused about their sexuality are at greater risk for suicide. But it is foolhardy to use the polemical work of Paul Gibson as proof that there is an "epidemic" (or worse, a "holocaust") of gay youth suicides that requires drastic action. Homosexual activists who do so risk expanding the cracks in their already fractured credibility.

Further research and careful debate on this issue are warranted. Ann Garland of the Department of Psychology at Yale University wrote recently, "There is considerable debate over whether homosexuality is a risk factor for suicide."[42] There is also great disagreement among psychiatrists over whether suicide intervention programs in schools actually work; some believe they cause more harm by *implanting* the idea of suicide in the minds of impetuous youth. Shaffer, Garland, and other specialists on suicide write that "to date there is no evidence of even marginal efficacy" of school-based suicide intervention programs.[43]

Although the increase in general youth suicides in recent years certainly warrants concern, Shaffer notes that "suicide is a relatively uncommon cause of death; fewer than 20 boys out of every 100,000 who are alive, will commit suicide in a year."[44] Great care must be taken not to endanger youths who otherwise would not be touched by suicide in the name of "rescuing" a tiny portion of the teen population who, in reality, are not best or most accurately identified by their struggles over sexuality.

Moreover, Gibson himself cites Remafedi in noting that the "earlier a youth is aware of a gay or lesbian orientation, the greater the problems they face and more likely the risk of suicidal feelings and behavior."[45] Paradoxically, programs like Project 10 *encourage* impressionable teens to take that potentially lethal step of "identifying" themselves as homosexuals at a young age.

The dangers of pro-homosexual counseling programs of the type envisioned by homosexual activists to "rescue" suicidal "gay and lesbian teens" is perhaps best described by former homosexual Alan Medinger:

> In schools all over the country, children...are being labelled "sexual minority" students and are being led to counselors drawn from the gay community. How often are the deeply rooted needs and biases of these "counselors" going to lead them to counsel the "unsure" that they are gay? "Unsure" in their minds often means that the youngster is simply afraid of coming to terms with his or her homosexuality...
>
> From every medical and health aspect—up to and including the probability of becoming infected with AIDS—it is tragic, even criminal to lead a child into homosexuality because he or she showed some degree of sexual confusion in adolescence.[46]

[This article first appeared in the Family Research Council's *Insight*, February 1994. Used by permission.]

Peter LaBarbera, a former reporter for *The Washington Times*, is executive director of Accuracy in Academia, a Washington, D.C.-based group that monitors bias in higher education. He is also publisher of *The Lambda Report on Homosexuality*, a quarterly newspaper focusing on the activities of the homosexual rights movement. For information on AIA or *The Lambda Report on Homosexuality*, call Mr. LaBarbera at 202-364-3085.

Endnotes:

[1] Table 5-1, Deaths of People Aged 15 to 24, by Age and Cause of Death, 1965-1988, Office of Education Research and Improvement, U.S. Department of Education, cited in *Losing Generations: Adolescents in High-Risk Settings*, Commission on Behavioral and Social Sciences and Education, National Research Council (National Academy Press: Washington, D.C.), 1993, p. 83.

[2] Dr. Louis W. Sullivan, M.D., Secretary of Health and Human Services, letter to Representative William E. Dannemeyer, October 1989.

[3] Ibid.

[4] David Shaffer, "Political Science," *The New Yorker*, May 3, 1993, p. 116.

[5] Paul Gibson, "Gay Male and Lesbian Youth Suicide," originally contained in "Report of the Secretary's Task Force on Youth Suicide," January 1989.

[6] A good example is an essay by Del Stover which appeared in *Education Digest* (May 1992), condensed from *The Executive Educator* (March 1992). Mr. Stover writes: "The U.S. Department of Health and Human Services reported in 1989 that 30 percent of all teens who commit suicide are gay and that gay teens are two to three times more likely than other teens to attempt suicide."

[7] Phone interview with author, March 8, 1993.

[8] Report issued by (Massachusetts') Governor's Commission on Gay and Lesbian Youth, "Making Schools Safe for Gay and Lesbian Youth," February 25, 1993, p. 5. The Massachusetts document stated regarding Gibson's paper: "In 1989, the U.S. Department of Health and Human Services issued a stunning report on youth suicide, with a chapter on gay and lesbian youth suicide. Pressure from anti-gay forces within the Bush/Quayle administration led to suppression, not only of the controversial chapter, but also of the entire report."

[9] Chris Bull, "Hetero Heroes: William Weld," *The Advocate*, cover story, November 16, 1993, p. 58.

[10] Sara Rimer, "Gay Rights Law for Schools Advances in Massachusetts," *The New York Times*, December 8, 1993, p. A-10.

[11] David LaFontaine, director of the Coalition for Lesbian and Gay Civil Rights, quoted in *New York Native*, February 24, 1992. Gov. Weld's Task Force on Gay and Lesbian Youth is the first government agency of its kind in the nation.

[12] Paul Cameron, "Study on Gay Death Rates/Age," Family Research Institute, 1992. Ironically, Cameron notes that a proclivity towards suicide among gay adults contributes toward their early death rates.

[13] Gibson, *op. cit.*, p. (3)-115, citing Parris, F., "Some Die Young," *Washington Blade*, May 17, 1985. In 1988, a total of 2,059 adolescents ages 15-19 and 243 children under age 15 committed suicide, according to the National Center for Health Statistics. These figures were reported by Ann F. Garland and Edward Zigler ("Adolescent Suicide Prevention," *American Psychologist*, February, 1993). The National Center for Health Statistics reports that in 1991, the latest year for which suicide statistics are available, the breakdown is as follows according to age categories: 5-9 (1); 10-14 (265); 15-19 (1,899); 20-24 (2,852) for a total of 5,017 (phone interview with author, January 31, 1994). Even if we accept this expanded definition of "youth" to include 24-year-olds, the figure in Gibson's report of 3,000 annual gay youth suicides would mean that well over half of all youth suicides are by homosexuals—a patent absurdity.

[14] David Shaffer, interview with author, April 22, 1993.

[15] Gibson, *op. cit.*, p. (3)-115.

[16] Gary Remafedi, MD, MPH, Michael Resnick, PhD, Robert Blum, MD, PhD, Linda Harris, *Pediatrics*, April 1992, pp. 714-721.

[17] A good summary of the studies can be found in J. Gordon Muir, "Homosexuals and the 10% Fallacy," *The Wall Street Journal*, March 31, 1993, p. A-14.

[18] David Shaffer, "Teen Suicide and Gays in the Military," unpublished paper from which the article in *The New Yorker* above (see footnote no. 1) was derived, March 22, 1993, p. 6. Shaffer is Irving Philips Professor of Child Psychiatry at Columbia University.

[19] Shaffer, *Ibid*, pp. 6-7, citing Charles Rich, Richard Fowler,

and Mary Benkush (1986), *Suicide & Life-Threatening Behavior*, Vol. 16, issue 4, pp. 448-457.

[20] Shaffer, *Ibid*, pp. 7-8.

[21] Narrative Summary of Teenage Suicide Study, The Gallup Organization, January 1991, p. 7.

[22] Howard "Red" Smith, phone interview with author, April 14, 1993.

[23] Shaffer, "Teen Suicide and Gays in the Military," p. 10.

[24] Shaffer, *Ibid*, p. 11

[25] Shaffer, *Ibid*, p. 11.

[26] Susan J. Blumenthal, MD, MPA, letter to *Journal of the American Medical Association*, June 5, 1991, pp. 2806-2807.

[27] Leona L. Eggert, interview with author, January 27, 1994.

[28] Peter Muehrer, interview with author, January 28, 1994.

[29] Shaffer, unpublished paper, March 22, 1993, p. 12.

[30] Shaffer, p. 14

[31] Stephen G. Schneider, PhD, Norman L. Farberow, PhD, and Gabriel N. Kruks, "Suicidal Behavior in Adolescent and Young Adult Gay Men," *Suicidal and Life-Threatening Behavior*, Winter 1989, pp. 381-394.

[32] Blumenthal, *op. cit.*, pp. 2806-2807.

[33] Remafedi, et al, *op. cit.*

[34] Nancy Sutton, director of Family First, a pro-family group based in Needham, Massachusetts that opposes Gov. Weld's pro-gay initiatives. Ex-gay testimonies were sent through Family First. Phone interview with author, August 4, 1993.

[35] Alan Medinger, interview with author, July 27, 1993.

[36] Gibson, *op. cit.,* p. (3)-128, (3)-135.

[37] Gibson, *ibid.*, pp. (3)-115, 24, 126, 133, 134, 135.

[38] Marshall Kirk and Hunter Madsen, *After the Ball: How America Will Conquer Its Fear & Hatred of Gays in the 1990s* (Doubleday: New York: 1990), p. 183.

[39] "Making Schools Safe for Gay and Lesbian Youth," the Governor's Commission on Gay and Lesbian Youth, Recommendation Five, p. 30.

[40] Nancy Sutton, phone interview with author, August 5, 1993.

[41] List of Project Teen Health groups provided by Sutton.

[42] Ann F. Garland, "Adolescent Suicide Prevention," *American Psychologist*, February 1993, p. 173.

[43] Shaffer, Garland, Veronica Vieland, PhD, Mary Rojas, PhD, Maureen Underwood, MSW, Cary Busner, MPH, letter to *Journal of the American Medical Association*, June 5, 1991, p. 2805.

[44] Shaffer, unpublished paper, *op. cit.*, p. 5.

[45] Gibson, *op. cit.*, p. 3-125.

[46] Alan Medinger, *Regeneration News*, February 1993, p. 1-2.

Responding to Pro-Gay Theology

by Joe Dallas

Major denominations ordaining homosexuals, priests and clergy presiding over same-sex weddings, sanctuaries invaded by boisterous gay activists, debates over homosexuality ripping congregations apart—who would have guessed we would ever reach such a point in church history?

A vigorous debate between Christians and homosexuals shouldn't be surprising in and of itself. If author and commentator Dr. Dennis Praeger is right when he says the Judeo-Christian ethic is responsible for the Western World's disapproval of homosexuality,[1] then conflicts between the Church and the gay rights movement are not only understandable, they are inevitable. (While acceptance of homosexuality in ancient cultures is well documented,[2] the past 2000 years of Western thought have, by and large, rejected it,[3] and the influence of both Old and New Testaments can be credited for that.)[4]

What is surprising, though, is the current trend in which these ethics are not only being challenged, but rewritten as well, most notably in the form of the pro-gay theology.

The pro-gay theology is much like the broader gay rights philosophy, in that it seeks legitimization (not just tolerance) of homosexuality. Gay spokesmen have made no secret of this as being their goal in secular culture; activist Jeff Levi put it plainly to the National Press Club during the 1987 Gay Rights March on Washington:

> We are no longer seeking just a right to privacy and a protection from wrong. We also have a right—as heterosexual Americans already have—to see government and society affirm our lives. Until our relationships are recognized in the law—in tax laws and government programs to affirm our relationships, then we will not have achieved equality in American society.[5]

But pro-gay theology takes it a step further by redefining homosexuality as being God-ordained and morally permissible:

> "I have learned to accept and even celebrate my sexual orientation as another of God's good gifts."
> —gay author Mel White[6]

When God is reputed to sanction what He has already clearly forbidden, then a religious travesty is being played out, and boldly. Confronting it is necessary because it (the pro-gay theology) asks us to confirm professing Christians in their sin, when we are Biblically commanded to do just the opposite. As Christ's ambassadors on earth, we unfaithfully represent Him if a professing believer's ongoing sin has no effect on our relationship with that believer...which is, in essence, what Paul told the Thessalonians:

> In the name of the Lord Jesus Christ, we command you, brothers, to keep away from every brother who is idle and does not live according to the teaching you received from us. If anyone does not obey our instruction in this letter, take special note of him. Do not associate with him, in order that he may feel ashamed. Yet do not regard him as an enemy, but warn him as a brother. (2 Thes 3:6, 14-15)

Likewise, when Paul heard of a Corinthian church member's incestuous relationship with his stepmother, he ordered the man be excommunicated (1 Cor 5:1-5), then explained the principle of confrontation and, if necessary, expulsion from the community of believers:

> Don't you know that a little yeast works through the whole batch of dough? Get rid of the old yeast that you may be a new batch without yeast. (1 Cor 5:6-7)

A healthy body purges itself of impurities; the Body of Christ cannot afford to do less. Error, like leaven, has a toxic effect.

The pro-gay theology is a strong delusion—a seductive accommodation tailor-made to suit the Christian who struggles against homosexual temptations and is considering a compromise. Some who call themselves gay Christians may be truly deceived into accepting it; others might be in simple rebellion. What compels them to believe a lie we cannot say. What we *can* say is that they are wrong...dead wrong.

But even as we say so, the caution of a proper spirit is in order. When we answer the pro-gay theology, we do so as sinners approaching other sinners, nothing more. Rev. Andrew Aquino of the Columbus Baptist Association expressed it perfectly during a recent interview:

> My message to the homosexual is: We love you. Come and struggle with us against sin. Don't give in to it.[7]

The Pro-Gay Theology in Brief

Exactly *what* do the "gay Christians" believe, and *how* did they come to believe it? The first question is more easily answered than the second. Explaining *what* a group believes is not hard. Explaining *how* they have come to believe it is another matter.

We cannot read minds or motives. That, I am sure, is one reason Jesus warned against judging (Mt 7:1). We *can* be certain the teachings themselves are false; *why* people have accepted them is something we cannot prove one way or another. Yet the Bible offers clues, and testimonies from members of the gay Christian movement are also enlightening, in helping to understand *what* the gay Christian movement believes, and what *personal* and *spiritual* factors may have influenced their beliefs.

The pro-gay theology is the cornerstone of the "gay Christian" movement (which is comprised of whole denominations, like the Universal Fellowship of Metropolitan Community Churches, as well as gay caucuses within mainline denominations) just as the Athanasian and Nicene Creeds are the foundation of most Protestant's beliefs.[8] The movement is diverse; some of its spokespersons—Episcopal Priest Robert Williams and Bishop John Shelby Spong, for instance —promote flamboyant and blatantly heretical ideas. But most groups within the gay Christian movement ostensibly subscribe to traditional theology. (The Statement of Faith of the Metropolitan Community Churches, for example, is based on the Apostles and Nicene Creeds.)[9]

Although the pro-gay theology claims a conservative theological base, it includes additions and revisions to basic, traditional ethics. First, homosexuality is seen as being God ordained. As such, it's viewed as being on par with heterosexuality. Gay author Mel White points out, quite accurately, that "if you don't see that premise (that God created homosexuality) then gay marriage looks ridiculous, if not insane."[10]

But to be seen as created by God, the traditional understanding of homosexuality needs to be discredited. This is done four basic ways within the "gay Christian" movement. First, prejudice against homosexuals is blamed for the understanding most Christians have of the Biblical references to it. The founder of the Metropolitan Community Churches, Rev. Troy Perry, asserts this is his writings:

> To condemn homosexuals, many denominations have intentionally misread and misinterpreted their Bibles to please their own personal preferences.[11]

So, according to Perry and others, not only are most Christians wrong about homosexuality, but many or most are *intentionally* wrong—deliberately reading their prejudice against gays into the Bible.

White goes even further, stating that major leaders in the Christian community—Jerry Falwell, James Kennedy and Pat Robertson—take public stands against the gay rights movement for the sake of raising funds and increasing their visibility.[12]

Casting doubt on the motives of conservative leaders, and numerous denominations, makes it easier to discount their Bible-based objections to homosexuality. No wonder this tactic is so common in the "gay Christian" movement. Others within the movement contend the scriptures we understand to condemn homosexuality have actually been mistranslated. According to this view, the Bible should be taken literally *in its original language;* the problem with most Christians, they say, is that they don't know Biblical Greek and Hebrew well enough to realize our modern translations on homosexuality are all wrong.

Another claim pro-gay theorists make is that the Bible verses (Lev 18:22 and 20:13; Rom 1:26-27; 1 Cor 6:9-10; 1 Tim 1:9-10) which seem to prohibit homosexuality have actually been yanked out of context from their original meaning, or that they only applied to the culture existing at the time they were written. (Professor Robin Scroggs of Union Theological Seminary, for example, claims, "Biblical judgments about homosexuality are not relevant to today's debate."[13])

These arguments do not sit well with most serious Christians. The scriptures mentioned earlier are so clear and specific they defy interpretation of any sort. "Thou shalt not lie with a man as with a woman" requires no more interpretation than "Thou shalt not kill." It is intellectually dishonest to say conservatives "interpret" such verses out of prejudice against homosexuals. Those same "prejudiced" conservatives (Falwell, Kennedy, Robertson et al) also take scriptures against heterosexual sins quite literally. If they only prohibit homosexuality out of their own prejudice, why on earth do they, as heterosexuals, also condemn heterosexual sins? The argument makes no sense.

Neither does the "mistranslation" argument. We can allow some discrepancy in minor areas of translation, but, on something as important as sexual ethics, are we really to believe the Bible translators we rely on got it wrong five different times, in two different testaments? And *only* on the scriptures regarding homosexuality? (Pro-gay apologists seem to have no problem with the other scriptures condemning sins like adultery and child abuse.)

Equally poor is the "out-of-context" argument. The fact is, in Leviticus, Romans, 1 Corinthians and 1 Timothy, homosexuality is mentioned *in the context of sexual and immoral behavior!* The context is quite clear—a variety of behaviors are prohibited; homosexuality—along with adultery, fornication and idolatry—is one of them.

The "cultural" argument fares no better. In some cases, a scripture may seem culturally bound (injunctions against long hair on men, or women speaking to their husbands during church.) But again—five times? Five different scriptures, from both testaments, addressed to highly different cultures (from the Hebrew to the Roman) are obviously not culturally bound. The cultures they address are just too different.

All of which leaves conservatives highly skeptical of the "gay Christian" movement's claim to respect Biblical authority. It takes mental gymnastics to accept these inadequate arguments; those not having a stake in accepting them are unlikely to do so. But those having a personal interest the pro-gay theology are another matter. Twist the Scriptures hard enough and you can make them appear to say anything you please. Author Paul Morris raises this very issue when he warns:

> But if I were a Christian homosexual, I think this one question would disturb me most: Am I trying to interpret Scripture in the light of my proclivity; or should I interpret my proclivity in the light of Scripture?[14]

An unfortunate pattern of doing the former can be seen in the "gay Christian" movement's testimonials. Rev. Troy Perry writes about having already decided homosexuality was acceptable, *then* searching the Bible to equip himself to answer conservatives.[15] Mel White alludes, in his book, to some earlier studies of the destruction of Sodom[16] but his turning point seems to have come not from a careful, prayerful study of scripture, but from a psychologist who encouraged him to accept his homosexuality and find a lover![17] And gospel musician Marsha Stevens (composer of the beloved song "For Those Tears I Died" and now openly lesbian) gives a lengthy account of her acceptance of homosexuality without once explaining how she reached the point of believing homosexuality was scripturally acceptable. (The closest she comes is in telling how she prayed one night for confirmation that lesbianism was okay; the next morning someone gave her a pin saying "Born Again Lesbian.")[18] Considering the background and theological training of the above-mentioned believers in pro-gay theology, their acceptance of it is astounding.

Or maybe it is not. Paul predicts an abandonment of truth for the sake of personal fulfillment:

> For the time will come when men will not put up with sound doctrine. Instead, to suit their own desires, they will gather around them a great number of teachers to say what their itching ears want to hear. They will turn their ears away from the truth and turn aside to myths. (2 Tim 4:3-4)

Self over truth, man over God—can a Christian be so deceived? Evidently—Paul referred to the Galatian church as having been "bewitched" (Gal 3:1), and Jesus warned that a prominent sign of the days before His coming would be an increase in deception (Mt 24:14). To confront the pro-gay theology, then, is to confront a deceptive element of our time—the tendency to subjugate objective truth to subjective experience.

That is one reason confrontation is not enough to change a heart. Being knowledgeable enough to dismantle all the "gay Christian" movement's claims will not be enough to persuade a homosexual to repent. The heart, having been hardened through deception or rebellion or both, has to be softened. And that is the work of God alone. Ours is to simply speak the truth, trusting Him to quicken it to our hearers.

To that end, this three-part series will address the pro-gay theology by dividing its arguments—or tenants—into three categories: social justice arguments, general religious arguments, and scriptural arguments. A brief description of these arguments will be provided, followed by a response/rebuttal to each.

SOCIAL JUSTICE ARGUMENTS

Social justice arguments are effective because they sound so good. They demand an end to homophobia and insensitivity; who wants to say they are against such goals? But just as the question "When did you stop beating your wife, Mr. Jones?" assumes (without proof) that Mr. Jones *has* been beating his wife, so the pro-gay social justice arguments assume (without proof) that gays are victims, and that the conservative church is largely responsible for their victimhood.

These arguments are most effective in secular discussions (talk shows, interviews, university debates) where listeners are unlikely to judge them by Biblical standards. Instead of discerning which side is theologically correct, non-Christian audiences tend to side with whoever seems "nicest." Usually, that means the gay spokesman asking for anti-discrimination laws or support clubs for gay teenagers. The person against these things—usually a conservative Christian—does not seem "nice," no matter how nice he or she may truly be.

That is not to say pro-gay social justice arguments are unwinnable; answered properly and politely, un-Biblical ideas can be challenged in the secular arena. Paul proved that with the citizens at Mars Hill (Acts 17:22). But the challenger needs to be aware that often, because of his position, he will be seen as the bad guy. And that is all the more reason to speak with an equal measure of clarity and politeness.

Social Justice Argument #1: "Homosexuality Is Inborn."

ARGUMENT #1-A:
Simon LeVay And the Hypothalamus

In 1991 Dr. LeVay, a neuro-scientist at the Salk Institute of La Jolla, California, examined the brains of 41 cadavers: 19 allegedly homosexual men, 16 allegedly heterosexual men, and 6 allegedly heterosexual women. His study focused on a group of neurons in the hypothalamus structure called the interstitial nuclei of the anterior hypothalamus, or the INAH3.

He reported this region of the brain to be larger in heterosexual men than in homosexuals; likewise, he found it to be larger in heterosexual men than in the women he studied. For that reason, he postulated homosexuality to be inborn, the result of size variations in the INAH3, and his findings were published in *Science* in August of 1991.[19] This is the study most often quoted when people insist homosexuality has been "proven" to be inborn.

Response: This argument is *exaggerated* and *misleading* for six reasons:

First, LeVay did not prove homosexuality to be inborn; his results were not uniformly consistent. On the surface it appears *all* of LeVay's homosexual subjects had smaller INAH3's than his heterosexual ones; in fact, three of the homosexual subjects actually had *larger* INAH3's than the heterosexuals. Additionally, three of the heterosexual subjects had *smaller* INAH3's than the average homosexual subject. Thus, six of LeVay's 35 male subjects (17% of his total study group) contradicted his own theory.[20]

Second, LeVay did not necessarily measure the INAH3 properly. The area LeVay was measuring is quite small—smaller than snowflakes, according to scientists interviewed when his study was released. His peers in the neuroscientific community cannot agree on whether the INAH3 should be measured by its size/volume or by its number of neurons.[21]

Third, it's unclear whether brain structure affects behavior or behavior affects brain structure. Dr. Kenneth Klivington, also of SALK Institute, points out that neurons can change in response to experience. "You could postulate," he says, "that brain change occurs throughout life, as a consequence of experience."[22] In other words, even if there is a significant difference between the brain structures of heterosexual and homosexual men, it is unclear whether the brain structure caused their homosexuality, or if their homosexuality affected their brain structure.

In fact, one year after LeVay's study was released, Dr. Lewis Baxter of UCLA obtained evidence that behavioral therapy can produce changes in brain circuitry, reinforcing the idea that behavior can and does affect brain structure.[23] Therefore, even if differences *do* exist between the INAH3's of homosexual and heterosexual men, it is possible that the diminished size of the homosexual's is caused by his behavior, rather than his behavior being caused by the INAH3's size.

Fourth, LeVay was not certain which of his subjects were homosexual and which were heterosexual. Dr. LeVay admits this represents a "distinct shortcoming" in his study. Having only case histories on his subjects to go by (which were by no means guaranteed to provide accurate information about the patient's sexual orientation), he could only assume that, if a patient's records did *not* indicate he was gay, he must have been heterosexual.

Yet 6 of the 16 reportedly heterosexual men studied had died of AIDS, increasing the chances their sexual histories may have been incompletely recorded.[24] If it is uncertain which of LeVay's subjects were heterosexual and which were homosexual, how useful can his conclusions about "differences" between them really be?

Fifth, LeVay did not approach the subject objectively. Dr. LeVay, who is openly homosexual, told *Newsweek* that, after the death of his lover, he was determined to find a genetic cause for homosexuality or he would abandon science altogether. Furthermore, he admitted, he hoped to educate society about homosexuality, affecting legal and religious attitudes towards it.[25] None of which diminishes his credentials as a neuroscientist. But his research can hardly be said to have been unbiased.

Sixth, the scientific community did not by any means unanimously accept Dr. LeVay's study. Comments from other scientists in response to LeVay's work are noteworthy. Dr. Richard Nakamura of the National Institute of Mental Health says it will take a "larger effort to be convinced there is a link between this structure and homosexuality."[26] Dr. Anne-Fausto Sterling of Brown University is less gentle in her response:

My freshman biology students know enough to sink this study.[27]

Dr. Rochelle Kliner, at Psychiatrist at Medical College of Virginia, doubts we will "ever find a single cause of homosexuality."[28] And *Scientific American* sums up the reason many professionals approach the INAH3 theory with caution:

LeVay's study has yet to be fully replicated by another researcher.[29]

ARGUMENT #1-B: Twins

In 1991, psychologist Michael Bailey of Northwestern University (a gay rights advocate) and psychiatrist Richard Pillard of Boston University School of Medicine (who is openly homosexual) compared sets of identical male twins to fraternal twins (whose genetic ties are less close). In each set, at least one twin was homosexual.

They found that, among the identical twins, 52% were both homosexual, as opposed to the fraternal twins, among whom only 22% shared a homosexual orientation.[30]

Pillard and Bailey suggested the higher incidence of shared homosexuality among identical twins meant homosexuality was genetic in origin.

Response: The argument is *misleading* and *exaggerated* for four reasons:

First, Pillard and Bailey's findings actually indicate that something besides genes must account for homosexuality. If 48% of identical twins, who are closely linked genetically, do NOT share the same sexual orientation, then genetics alone CANNOT account for homosexuality. Bailey admitted as much by stating, "There must be something in the environment to yield the discordant twins."[31]

Second, all of the twins Pillard and Bailey studied were raised in the same household. If the sets of twins in which both brothers were homosexual were raised in *separate* homes, it might be easier to believe genes played a role in their sexual development. But since they were all raised in the same households, it's impossible to know what effect environment played, and what effect, if any, genes played.

Dr. Fausto-Sterling summarized the problem: "In order for such a study to be at all meaningful, you'd have to look at twins raised apart."[32]

Third, Drs. Pillard and Bailey, like Dr. LeVay, did not approach their subject objectively. Their personal feelings about homosexuality, like Dr. LeVay's, certainly do not disqualify them from doing good research on the subject. But they must be, at the very least, considered. Pillard said, in fact: "A genetic component in sexual orientation says, 'This is not a fault,'" and both he and Bailey stated they hoped their work would "disprove homophobic claims."[33]

Fourth, a later study on twins yielded results differ-

ent from Pillard and Bailey's. In March of 1992, the British Journal of Psychiatry published a report on homosexuals who are twins (both fraternal and identical) and found that only 20% of the homosexual twins had a gay co-twin, leading the researchers to conclude that "genetic factors are insufficient explanation of the development of sexual orientation."[34] Not only, then, has Pillard and Bailey's work not been replicated; when a similar study was conducted, it had completely different results.

ARGUMENT #1-C: Genes

In 1993, Dr. Dean Hamer of the National Cancer Institute studied 40 pairs of non-identical gay brothers and claimed that 33 of the pairs had inherited the same X-linked genetic markers, thus indicating a genetic cause for homosexuality.[35]

Response #1: The argument is *misleading* and *exaggerated* for two reasons:

First, like LeVays' study, Hamer's results have yet to be replicated. Again, it should be noted a lack of replication does NOT mean a study is invalid; it only means the study's conclusions have not been confirmed by further research.

Second, a later, similar study actually contradicted Hamer's conclusions. George Ebers of the University of Western Ontario examined 52 pairs of gay brothers, and found "no evidence for a linkage of homosexuality to markers on the X-chromosome or elsewhere."[36]

Ebers also, with an associate, studied 400 families with one or more homosexual male, and found "no evidence for the X-linked, mother-to-son transmission posited by Hamer."[37] Again, like Pillard and Bailey's earlier work, a later study similar to Hamer's yielded clearly different results.

Response #2: This argument, like those based on LeVay, Pillard, and Bailey's work, is *illogical* in that it assumes *inborn* means *normal* or *morally acceptable* . That assumption is faulty, for three reasons:

First, "inborn" and "normal" are not necessarily the same. Even if homosexuality is someday proven to be inborn, *inborn* does not necessarily mean *normal*. Any number of defects or handicaps, for example, may be inborn, but we'd hardly call them normal for that reason alone. Why should we be compelled to call homosexuality normal, just because it may be inborn?

Second, inborn tendencies towards certain behaviors (like homosexuality) do not make those behaviors moral. Studies in the past fifteen years indicate a variety of behaviors may have their roots in genetics or biology. In 1983 the former Director of the National Council on Alcoholism reported on a number of chemical events that can produce alcoholism;[38] in 1991, the City of Hope Medical Center found a certain gene present in 77% of their alcoholic patients.[39] Obesity and violent behavior are now thought to be genetically influenced,[40] and even infidelity, according to research reported in *Time*, may be in our genes![41]

Surely we're not going to say that obesity, violence, alcoholism and adultery are legitimate because they were inherited. So it is with homosexuality. Whether inborn or acquired, it is still, like all sexual contact apart from marriage, immoral. And immoral behavior cannot be legitimized by a quick baptism in the gene pool.

Third, we are a fallen race, born in sin. Scripture teaches we inherited a corrupt sin nature affecting us physically and spiritually (Ps 51:5; Rom 5:12). We were born spiritually dead (Jn 3:5-6) and physically imperfect (1 Cor 15:1-54). We cannot assume, then, that because something is inborn, it is also God ordained. There are mental, psychological, physical and sexual aspects of our beings that God never intended us to have. "Inborn," in short, does not mean "divinely sanctioned."

Response #3: Professional opinion is by no means unanimously convinced of the "Homosexuality is Inborn" Argument.

Some researchers, according to the *Chronicle of Higher Education*, actually say the "born gay" theories are "unfounded and politically dangerous."[42] Dr. William Byne of Columbia University calls the "inborn" evidence "inconclusive" and compares it to "trying to add up a hundred zeroes so you can get 1."[43] Dr. Fausto-Sterling says the studies, and ensuing debate, are not even about biology but about politics,[44] and Professor John D'Emilio of the University of North Carolina, while willing to consider the possibility of inborn homosexuality, says there's "too much else we haven't explored."[45]

Social Justice Argument #2:
"Homosexuality Cannot Be Changed."

"Sexual orientation simply cannot be changed," a gay psychiatrist says confidently,[46] warning "there may be severe emotional and social consequences in the attempt to change from homosexuality to heterosexuality."[47] This argument draws heavily from the social sciences, as it must; the Bible supports no such claim. Indeed, St. Paul makes the opposite remark, clearly stating homosexuals *can* change, when he asserts:

Do you not know that the wicked will not inherit the kingdom of God? Do not be deceived: Neither the sexually immoral nor idolaters nor adulterers nor male prostitutes nor homosexual offenders... will inherit the kingdom of God. And that is what some of you *were*. But you were washed, you were sanctified, you were justified in the name of the Lord Jesus Christ and by the Spirit of our

God. (1 Cor 6: 9-11; emphasis added)

Still, the "I-tried-to-change-but-I-couldn't" argument is quite popular among homosexuals who have accepted their orientation and insist others do the same.

Response #1: The "unchangeable" argument is *misleading*. While many mental health authorities believe homosexuality is unchangeable, many others believe it *can* be changed.

In 1970, the Kinsey Institute reported that 84% of the homosexuals they studied had shifted their sexual orientation at least once; 32% of them reported a second shift, and 13% reported *five changes*, during their lifetime, in their sexual orientation![48]

The Director of the New York Center for Psychoanalytic Training, no doubt aware such changes occur, remarked on the "misinformation spread by certain circles that homosexuality is untreatable," saying it did "incalculable harm to thousands."[49]

Dr. Irvine Bieber concluded (after treating over a hundred homosexuals) that "a heterosexual shift is a possibility for all homosexuals who are strongly motivated to change."[50]

Sex researchers Masters and Johnson (hardly a pair of standard-bearers for the traditional view!) said the "homosexuality cannot be changed" concept was "certainly open to question."[51] Drs. Wood and Dietrich, writing about the effectiveness of treatment for homosexuality, confirmed "all studies which have attempted conversions from homosexuality to heterosexuality have had significant success."[52] And the New Report of the Kinsey Institute explains people do not "necessarily maintain the same sexual orientation throughout their lives," then explained that "programs helping homosexuals change report varying degrees of success."[53]

But no one says it better than Stanton Jones, Chair of Psychology at Wheaton College:

Anyone who says there is no hope (for change) is either ignorant or a liar. Every secular study of change has shown some success rate, and persons who testify to substantial healings by God are legion.[54]

Response #2: This argument is *illogical* in that it assumes if a condition is *unchangeable* it is therefore *desirable*.

For the sake of argument, suppose it *could* be proven that homosexuality, as a condition, is unchangeable—that no amount of prayer, counseling or efforts of any sort could make a homosexual become attracted to the opposite sex. What then? Should that change our view of homosexual behavior as being sinful? Hardly. There's no contingency in any scriptural reference to any kind of sin, in the Old or New Testament, saying: "Thou shalt not do thus and so!" ("Unless, of course, you tried hard to change, went for prayer and counseling, and found you just could not stop wanting to do thus and so. If that's the case, then thus and so is no longer a sin. It's an inborn, immutable gift and you can indulge it!")

The Apostle Paul's thorn in the flesh, whatever it may have been, was unchangeable; despite his prayers for deliverance, God allowed it to remain. But it certainly was not desirable (2 Cor 12:7-9). Other conditions—alcoholism, for example, or various addictions—are widely believed to be unchangeable, and have to be coped with daily. That hardly makes them desirable, natural or God-ordained.

Social Justice Argument #3:
"10% of the Population Is Gay. Could So Many People Be Wrong?"

This argument has been so roundly disproved, in secular, clinical and theological sources worldwide, that it may be unnecessary to mention it. But on the chance that the reader may need to confront it in future discussions, we will briefly review what is commonly called the "10% Myth" and how to respond to it.

In 1948, sex researcher Alfred Kinsey published *Sexual Behavior in the Human Male*, which listed his findings after taking the sexual histories of 5,300 American men. The findings, especially on homosexuality, shocked American sensibilities: 37% of the subjects admitted at least one homosexual experience since their adolescence,[55] and 10% claimed to have been homosexual for at least three years.[56]

Word was out—ten percent of the male population was homosexual! Knowing there is power in numbers, pro-gay theorists and spokesmen repeated the statistic relentlessly until it became a given: one out of every ten males was gay; therefore, homosexuality was much more common than anyone had previously thought. The concept was extremely useful to activists when, decades later, they would ask how anyone could believe ten percent of the population was abnormal, immoral or just plain wrong.

Response #1: The argument is *exaggerated*; Kinsey did NOT claim 10% of the male population was homosexual.

Kinsey's wording was plain—10% of the males surveyed claimed to have been homosexual for at least three years. They had not necessarily been homosexual all their lives, nor would they necessarily be homosexual in the future. Future studies by the Kinsey Institute, in fact, would confirm that sexual orientation is not necessarily fixed, and may change throughout a person's lifespan. The 1990 *Kinsey Institute New Report on Sex* states:

Some people have consistent homosexual orientation for a long period of time, then fall in love with a person of the opposite sex; other individuals who have had only opposite-sex partners later fall in love with someone of the same sex.[57]

Response #2: The "10%" is misleading for two reasons:

First, Kinsey's data was not taken from a population accurately representing American men. Dr. Judith Reisman, in her book *Kinsey, Sex and Fraud: The Indoctrination of a People* has soundly discredited Kinsey's conclusions and methods. One of her important findings was that 25% of the men he surveyed were prisoners, many of whom were sex offenders.[58] Naturally, a higher incidence of homosexuality would be found among prisoners, especially sex offenders, many of whom may have been in prison for homosexual behavior. (In the 1940s that was quite possible; today, thankfully, people are not incarcerated for homosexuality.)

Second, subsequent studies have disproved the 10% claim. *USA Today* reported on April 15, 1993, a new survey of 3,321 American men indicating 2.3% of them had engaged in homosexual behavior within the previous ten years; only 1.1% reported being exclusively homosexual.

This was only the latest in a series of studies proving Kinsey wrong. In 1989, a U.S. survey estimated no more than 6% of adults had any same-sex contacts and only 1% were exclusively homosexual; a similar survey in France found 4% of men and 3% of women had ever engaged in homosexual contacts, while only 1.4% of the men and 0.4% of the women had done so within the past five years. The article concluded, not surprisingly, that the 10% statistic proposed by Kinsey was "dying under the weight of new studies."

A candid remark by a lesbian activist explains how the 10% figure stayed in the public's awareness for so long:

The thing about the 'one in ten'—I think people probably always did know that it was inflated. But it was a nice number that you could point to, that you could say 'one in ten,' and it's a really good way to get people to visualize that we're here.[59]

If what she's saying is true, gay spokesmen were willing to repeat something they knew to be false, for the sake of furthering their cause. With that in mind, one wonders what other "facts" on homosexuality ("gays are born gay," "gays cannot change") will someday be disproved as well—exposed as propaganda that people "always knew was inflated," but promoted anyway because the end justified the means.

We can accept some parts of these pro-gay arguments. We can allow, for example, the *possibility* of genetics someday being found to play a role in the development of homosexuality. We can agree that, in many cases, the homosexual condition—sexual attractions to the same sex rather than the opposite one—begins very early in life. And while it's common knowledge that ten percent of the population is not, nor ever has been, gay, we'll admit there are probably far more homosexuals in the population than we're aware of. Their claim of not having asked for their orientation is, in most cases, true; we ought to feel genuine compassion for people struggling with, or mistreated for, something they never chose. Stanton Jones of Wheaton College puts it well:

> If you cannot empathize with a homosexual person because of fear of, or revulsion to, them, then you are failing our Lord.[60]

But where we must part company with promoters of the pro-gay theology is in the conclusions they've drawn. We cannot rewrite scripture, as they have, to accommodate a sin simply because it has been shown to be inborn, unchangeable or common. On this point, we might well borrow a quote from, of all people, the liberal playwright Lillian Hellman:

> I cannot and will not cut my conscience to suit this year's fashions.

GENERAL RELIGIOUS ARGUMENTS

A recent poll showed 66% (two thirds) of Americans no longer believe there is such a thing as "absolute truth." More disturbing, though, was the fact that 53% of those not believing in absolute truth identified themselves as born again Christians; 75% of whom were mainline Protestants.[61]

If "absolute truth" no longer exists, even in the minds of half the "born-again" population, it logically follows that doctrine, and the Bible itself, is given less credence. Pollster George Gallup Jr. noticed this in *The People's Religion: American Faith in the 90's.* "While religion is highly popular in America," he states, "it is to a large extent superficial. There is a knowledge gap between American's stated faith and the lack of the most basic knowledge about that faith."[62]

In short, self-identified Christians in the 90s are Biblically ignorant. Doctrine has become less important than good feelings; indeed, a *USA Today* survey found that, of the 56% of Americans who attend church, 45% did so because "it's good for you," 26% went for peace of mind. Specific doctrines, the pollster noted, seemed unimportant.[63]

If the notions of "truth" and "doctrine" are becoming unimportant to Christians, can the idea of "sin" hope to survive? Probably not; 25% of Christians polled in 1993 believed sin to be "an outdated concept."[64]

"The awareness of sin used to be our shadow," Cornelius Plantinga writes in *Christianity Today.* "Christians hated sin, feared it, flew from it. But now the shadow has faded. Nowadays, the accusation you have sinned is often said with a grin."[65]

But the gospel truth is never so accommodating. John the Baptist was ferocious with the Pharisees (Mt 3:7-8), Jesus trounced Peter when he tried to interfere with the His mission, (Mt 16:22-23) and Paul was willing to publicly rebuke hypocrisy, even when committed by a respected disciple (Gal 2:11-14). To be sure, there is a place for gentleness. But never at the expense of truth.

Yet today the gap between truth and modern practice has been large enough to allow any number of false (albeit "nice") ideas to enter the church, creating a mentality that says, "Let's all get along without conflict, shall we?" Author J. Stephen Lang attempts to explain this phenomenon:

> Love is understandable—warm and fuzzy. Doctrine, on the other hand, sounds cold, difficult and demanding.[66]

A desire for "warm and fuzzy" without a commitment to truth makes the general religious arguments of the pro-gay theology all the more palatable. Unlike the social justice arguments, these arguments are more "religious"; that is, they appeal to general religious themes of harmony and goodwill, while bypassing issues of the fallen nature, sin and obedience. To the Biblically ignorant they can pass for truth; in the light of scripture, though, they have no leg on which to stand.

Since they are more religious in tone than social arguments, these arguments can be answered almost exclusively in Biblical terms. Remembering that members of the gay Christian movement say they believe in Biblical authority, these arguments are best answered with a call to return to the objective truth of the Bible, in lieu of the subjective winds of human experience and understanding.

Religious Argument #1:
"Jesus Said Nothing About Homosexuality."

This argument is a favorite at gay parades. Invariably, when the "gay Christian" movement is represented, someone in their group will hold up a sign saying, "WHAT JESUS SAID ABOUT HOMOSEXUALITY: _____." The idea, of course, is that if Jesus did not specifically forbid a behavior, then the behavior must not have been important to Him. Stretching the point further, this argument assumes if Jesus was not manifestly concerned about something, we should not be, either.

Troy Perry (as most gay Christian leaders do) makes

much of this argument based on silence:

> As for the question, 'What did Jesus say about homosexuality?", the answer is simple. Jesus said nothing. Not one thing. Nothing! Jesus was more interested in love.[67]

So, according to the argument of silence, if Jesus did not talk about it, neither should we.

Response: The argument is misleading and illogical for four reasons:

<u>First, the argument assumes the gospels are more authoritative than the rest of the books in the Bible.</u> The idea of a subject being unimportant just because it was not mentioned by Jesus is foreign to the gospel writers themselves. At no point did Matthew, Mark, Luke or John say their books should be elevated above the Torah or, for that matter, any writings yet to come. In other words, the gospels—and the teachings they contain—are not more important than the rest of the Bible. *All* scripture is given by inspiration of God. The same spirit inspiring the authors of the Gospels also inspired the men who wrote the rest of the Bible.

<u>Second, the argument assumes the gospels are more comprehensive than they really are.</u> Not only are the gospels no more authoritative than the rest of scripture, they are not comprehensive either. That is, they do not provide all we need to know by way of doctrine and practical instruction.

Some of the Bible's most important teaching, in fact, does not appear in the gospels. The doctrine of man's old and new nature (outlined by Paul in Romans 6); the future of Israel and the mystery of the Gentiles (hinted at by Christ but explained more fully in Romans 9-11); the explanation and management of the spiritual gifts (detailed in 1 Corinthians 12 and 14); the Priesthood of Christ (illustrated in Hebrews)—all of these appear after the accounts of Christ's life, death and resurrection. (And we have not even mentioned the entire Old Testament.) Would anyone say none of these doctrines are important because they were not mentioned by Jesus?

Or, put another way, are we really to believe that Jesus did not care about wife beating or incest, just because He said nothing about them? Are not the prohibitions against incest in Leviticus and 1 Corinthians, as well as Paul's admonition to husbands to love their wives, enough to instruct us in these matters without being mentioned in the gospels? There are any number of evil behaviors that Christ did not mention by name; surely we don't condone them for that reason alone! Likewise, Jesus' silence on homosexuality in no way negates the very specific prohibitions against it which appear elsewhere, in both Old and New Testaments.

<u>Third, this argument is inaccurate, in that it presumes</u> <u>to know all of what Jesus said.</u> The gospels do not profess to be a complete account of Jesus' life or teachings. Whole sections of His early years are omitted; much of what He did and said remains unknown.

Luke wrote his gospel so Theophilus would "know the certainty of those things wherein he had been instructed" (Lk 1:4). John's motives are broader: "These are written that ye might believe that Jesus is the Christ, and that believing, ye might have life through His name" (Jn 20:31). But none of these authors suggested they were recording all of Christ's words. John, in fact, said that would have been an impossibility:

> Jesus did many other things as well. If every one of them were written down, I suppose that even the whole world would not have room for the books that would be written. (Jn 21:25)

If that is the case, how can we be certain He said nothing about homosexuality? No one can say. But we know there are other equally important subjects left undiscussed in the gospels, but mentioned in detail in other books of the Bible. Homosexuality, while absent from Matthew, Mark, Luke or John, is conspicuously present in both testaments and, just as conspicuously, it is forbidden.

<u>Fourth, this argument assumes, because Jesus said nothing specific about homosexuality, that He said nothing about heterosexuality as a standard.</u> Jesus referred in the most specific of terms to God's created intent for human sexuality:

> But at the beginning of creation God "made them male and female. For this reason a man will leave his father and mother and be united to his wife, and the two will become one flesh." So they are no longer two, but one. Therefore what God has joined together, let man not separate." (Mk 10:6-9)

In this passage, Jesus had been presented with a hypothetical question: Is divorce lawful? Instead of giving a simple yes or no, He referred to Genesis and, more specifically, to *created intent* as the standard by which to judge sexual matters. By repeating the Genesis account, He emphasizes four elements of the created intent for marriage and sexual relating: *independence* was one—a man was to leave his own home to establish his own family with his wife; a *"one flesh"* sexual union was another; and, of course, *monogamy*. But the first element of created intent Jesus stressed was the complimentary factor: it was to be a union of *male* and *female, man* and *wife*.

Homosexuality may not have been mentioned by Jesus—many other sexual variations were not, either. But He could not have spelled out the standard for sexual expression more clearly: male to female, joined as God intended them to be. He cannot be assumed to have approved of anything less.

Religious Argument #2:
"I'm a Born-Again Believer *and* I'm Gay. How Can That Be, If Homosexuality Is Wrong?"

This argument is most often promoted by a declaration: *I'm gay and Christian, which is living proof you can be both!* Mel White, upon his installation as pastor of America's largest gay congregation, made a similar affirmation:

> Now, thank God, after thirty years of struggle, I can say at last who I really am. I am gay. I am proud. And God loves me without reservation.[68]

The message, then, is that if a person is truly born again and homosexual, the two must be compatible.

Response: The argument is illogical in that it assumes if one is a Christian, and if one is loved by God, then what one does must be all right in God's sight.

We can assume Dr. White's assertions are true: he is gay, he says he is proud (and no one is in a position to say otherwise) and God loves him. But does God's love for him, or Dr. White's pride in being gay, justify homosexuality itself?

Hardly. And while it is beyond the scope of this article to enter into the debate over eternal security ("once saved, always saved"), let us remember that Christians do not automatically become non-Christian just because they are sinning. The fact they are sinning— even if they do not realize it—does not automatically nullify their salvation.

But neither does their salvation legitimize their sin. A Christian may, indeed, be openly homosexual; that is no proof homosexuality and Christianity are compatible. In fact, a Christian may be openly sinning; that is no proof sin and Christianity are compatible, either.

Ananias and Sapphira, a husband and wife mentioned in Acts Chapter 5, were evidently believers. Yet their sin of hypocrisy (pretending to give more money to the church than they actually did) cost them their lives. They were Christians, and they were in serious error. Their error did not mean they were not Christian; their Christianity did not legitimize their error.

The Apostle Peter was, on one occasion at least, afraid to be seen associating with Gentiles, for fear of reprisals from Jews who felt Jews and Gentiles should never mix. So when Jewish people were not around, he was willing to eat with Gentile friends; when Jews were present, he avoided Gentiles (Gal 2:11-13). His hypocrisy in the face of prejudice was wrong, yet no one doubts he was a Christian. Yet that in no way justified his hypocrisy.

In other words, being a Christian is no indication, in and of itself, that your life is pleasing to God. And any honest believer knows that. It is a waste of time to argue intangibles, such as whether or not a 'gay Christian' is *truly* born again, or "saved." We may argue that if he continues in sin, he risks hardening his heart toward God, or reaping corruption, since God is not mocked. But we cannot see inside his soul to determine how hardened or deceived he may be.

No matter how proud, confident or loved by God a person is, he can be walking in darkness without knowing it. That is exactly why we have an objective standard by which to judge our actions. "Take heed unto thyself," Paul told Timothy, "and unto the doctrine. Continue in them, for in doing this thou shalt both save thyself, and them that hear thee" (1 Tim 4:16).

Saying "I'm Christian and gay" proves nothing. The question shouldn't be *Can a person be homosexual and still belong to God?* But rather, *Is homosexuality right or wrong according to the Bible?*

Religious Argument #3:
"I Attend a Gay Church Where the Gifts of the Spirit and the Presence of God Are Manifest. How Can That Be, If Homosexuality Is Wrong?"

When the late Rev. Sylvia Pennington, a defender of the pro-gay theology, attended her first gay church, she still believed homosexuality was wrong. But something happened to change her mind:

> I became aware of the Holy Spirit's presence hovering around, about and within me. They [gay Christians] were sensing the same Spirit that I sensed and loving God back as I was. They were actually worshiping God. And God was there— undeniably there![69]

The argument, then, is that if God's presence and gifts are manifest in a gay church, it is evidence that God accepts and blesses homosexuality.

Response: The argument is misleading in that it assumes God's gifts or presence are an indication of His approval.

By Rev. Pennington's description of a gay church, we can assume one of three things: either God's presence was not there at all, and what she felt was just emotion; or what she (and the others present) felt was a demonic counterfeit; or, in fact, God's presence *was* there.

I find it useless to argue over whether or not the presence of God can actually be found in gay churches. Instead, it is best to ask, "So what?" Even if God *is* present in gay churches and if His gifts *are* manifest there, does that prove He condones homosexuality?

Not at all. God's presence, wonderful as it is, and His

gifts, valuable as they are, are given freely. They are neither a reward for, nor evidence of, righteousness. (I am not arguing that God IS present in gay churches; I'm only saying that, like the "I'm gay and Christian" argument, it is best to stick to the bottom line issue: *Is homosexuality right or wrong?*)

To illustrate this, look at the Corinthian church. No one could doubt they were genuine believers; Paul opens his letter to them addressing them as "sanctified in Christ Jesus" (1 Cor 1:2). Further, the gifts of the Spirit—teaching, preaching, prophetic words and so forth—were manifest there; Paul spent all of Chapters 12 and 14 teaching them how to manage these gifts. So God's presence, and His gifts, were clearly a part of the Corinthian church's life.

And the Corinthian church was a mess. They were, by Paul's own account, carnal and full of divisions (1 Cor 3:3-4), incest was openly committed among them (5:1-5), they were hauling each other to court over lawsuits (6:1-3), and getting drunk at the communion table (11:21). Yet God's presence was at Corinth. Because He approved of their behavior? Of course not. But His gifts and calling, as Paul said in Romans 11:29, are without repentance. He would not remove them, even when the church they operated in was in serious error.

Modern examples abound. By now we have all heard of evangelists or preachers whose ministries thrived even when, unfortunately, they were involved in sexual immorality. For years, in some cases, God's presence and blessing was on their work, even as they continued their secret sin. Yet none of us would assume God approved of their behavior.

What, then, *can* we assume? Two things: first, if God has given someone a gift of the Spirit, that gift may continue to operate even if the person is willfully sinning. Second, the gift, or God's presence, is a sign of grace, not approval. It cannot be said that, because the gifts are operating in a church, the church's activities are legitimate. Legitimacy is determined by scripture, not spiritual dynamics.

Religious Argument #4:
"My Lover and I Are in a Monogamous Relationship, and We Truly Love Each Other. That Can't Be Wrong!"

As the gay rights and gay Christian movements have evolved, more emphasis has been put on the quality of homosexual relationships. Initially, gay apologists argued for sexual freedom; today, they argue for legitimacy. As this is being written, in fact, the nation is holding its breath to see how the Hawaii Supreme Court will rule on the legality of gay marriages.

"God is ecstatic that I'm so happy in a relationship with a woman," a lesbian member of the Metropolitan Community Church gushed on a recent news program.[70] A stable relationship, then, is seen as evidence of God's

blessing. And if true love is involved, so the argument goes, it must be right.

Response: The argument is misleading in that it assumes love sanctifies a relationship.

It is hard these days to say love is not the final standard for right and wrong. Love is *nice*, after all; in our culture, it has been nearly deified as something so intense and beautiful, it justifies almost anything done in its name. And with all the hatred and violence in the world, why knock a loving relationship between any two people? Because love, in and of itself, does not make a relationship right. In fact, contrary to the touchy-feeling wisdom of the times, love is not always such a good thing.

An essay on homosexuality and ethics puts it well:

One of the most popular errors in the realm of Christian ethics has been the effort to make love an omnipotent spiritual quality which has the power to sanctify anything that is done its name.[71]

Love can, according to Jesus, interfere with God's plan for an individual. He warns His followers that love for anyone, no matter how legitimate the relationship, becomes sin when it surpasses our love for Him (Mt 10:37). King Solomon, in a similar vein, loved his foreign wives. Problem was, they turned his heart away from God (1 Ki 11:3-4). In his case, love became a snare.

Love is not enough to justify a relationship. An unmarried Christian couple may be very much in love; if they become sexually involved before marriage, it will still be sin, no matter how much love went into it. And it will still be wrong. A married man can fall deeply in love with a woman other than his wife; that will never sanctify adultery.

Likewise, two men, or women, may be in love. Their love may run very deep, they may pledge fidelity to each other and live as happily as any married heterosexual couple. Again, that will not, of itself, justify a homosexual relationship. Scripture places boundaries on human relationships, offering no compromise, even if love is present and desires to cross those boundaries. If a form of sexual relating is wrong, it remains wrong no matter what degree of love goes along with it.

We would rather be nice. That is a strange tendency creeping into the church: "niceness" is taking precedence over truth. Immorality—even among Christian leaders—is going unconfronted, and many churches seem more concerned with making people comfortable than arousing in them a sense of their need for God. In such an environment, it is no wonder erroneous teachings like the pro-gay theology are flourishing. Evangelist and Pastor Greg Laurie summed up the problem nicely:

What is being depicted to individuals is a 'user-friendly' God who will smile benignly down upon their lifestyles of choice, as they continue to live as they like.[72]

But, however the social justice arguments of the pro-gay theology compel us towards "niceness," the God we represent places a higher premium on truth than accommodation. May we, by His grace, never shun the two-fold mandate to speak the truth, in love.

SCRIPTURAL ARGUMENTS

This part of the pro-gay theology offers what appears to be a series of conservative, fundamentalist responses to conservative, fundamentalist objections. That is, it meets every Bible verse referring to homosexuality head on, and attempts to explain why each verse is misunderstood today. It is the boldest part of pro-gay theology, and, for many Christians, the most difficult for which to give response.

That is because these arguments take what is obvious and claim to have discovered it has a different, heretofore hidden meaning. To illustrate, let us take a fairly straight-forward scripture:

Come unto me, all ye that labour and are heavy laden, and I will give you rest. (Mt 11:28, KJV)

The meaning is clear: Jesus invites the weary to come to Him for rest. No need to check the original Greek or review the cultural context; the scripture is clear.

Now suppose someone tells you they have done an extensive word study on this verse, and discovered Jesus was *really* inviting pregnant women to stay at His maternity ward in Nazareth. It seems ridiculous; the context so clearly points to something else. But if you have not taken the time to study the original Greek in this verse, you cannot technically refute the "maternity ward" idea, though common sense tells you it is nonsense.

That is the power of the pro-gay theology. It takes scriptures we are all familiar with, gives them an entirely new interpretation, backs its claims with well-credentialed scholars, and gives birth to a new sexual ethic. Common sense may reject it, but until it is examined a bit more closely, it is difficult to refute.

To approach this portion of the pro-gay theology, we will review each scripture referring to homosexuality, establish the traditional view of the scripture, name the pro-gay arguments against that view, and offer a response to each.

CREATION/CREATED INTENT
Genesis 1:27-28; 2:18, 23-24

So God created man in his own image, in the im-

age of God he created him; male and female he created them. God blessed them and said to them, "Be fruitful and increase in number; fill the earth and subdue it. Rule over the fish of the sea and the birds of the air and over every living creature that moves on the ground."

The LORD God said, "It is not good for the man to be alone. I will make a helper suitable for him." The man said, "This is now bone of my bones and flesh of my flesh; she shall be called 'woman,' for she was taken out of man." For this reason a man will leave his father and mother and be united to his wife, and they will become one flesh.

Traditional View:

God's intention for human sexual relationships is limited to heterosexual union between a man and a woman in marriage.

Pro-Gay Argument:

The Genesis account does not *forbid* homosexuality; it simply does not refer to it, for obvious reasons. A gay couple could hardly begin the population process. But these verses cannot be seen as a model for all couples: many heterosexual couples are childless, or unable to have sexual relations. Are they in sin because they do not conform to the Genesis account?

Response #1:

While it is true this passage does not forbid homosexual relations, it does provide the primary model for sexuality by which other forms of sexual expression must be judged. Thomas Schmidt puts it well:

It [Genesis] provides a basis for Biblical commands and for subsequent reflection on the part of those who wish to construct a sexual ethic to meet changing situations—it is appropriate for us to explore the relevance of Biblical commands about marriage and to evaluate modern homosexuality in light of Genesis.[73]

Stanton Jones, regarding creation as a model for sexuality, adds:

The heart of Christian morality is this: God made sexual union for a purpose—the uniting of husband and wife into one flesh in marriage. God uses sexual intercourse, full sexual intimacy, to weld two people together.[74]

Response #2:

The male-female union, introduced in Genesis, is the only model of sexual behavior consistently praised in both

Old and New Testaments. While other forms of behavior (polygamy and the use of concubines, for example) are introduced and even allowed in the Old Testament, a monogamous relation between husband and wife is the standard upheld as the ideal within scripture. While the old phrase, "God created Adam and Eve, not Adam and Steve" seems flippant, it is a fair assessment of created intent: whereas heterosexuality is commended throughout the Bible, not once is a homosexual relationship mentioned in anything but negative terms.

THE DESTRUCTION OF SODOM
Genesis 19:4-9

Before they [the angels visiting Lot to judge the wickedness of Sodom and determine whether or not to spare it] had gone to bed, all the men from every part of the city of Sodom—both young and old—surrounded the house. They called to Lot, "Where are the men who came to you tonight? Bring them out to us *so that we can have sex with them* [lit., 'so we may know them']." Lot went outside to meet them...and said, "No, my friends. Don't do this wicked thing. Look, I have two daughters who have never slept with a man. Let me bring them out to you, and you can do what you like with them. But don't do anything to these men...." ...And they said, "We'll treat you worse than them."

Traditional Position:

The men of Sodom were attempting homosexual contact with Lot's visitors. Sodom was subsequently destroyed for its great wickedness, homosexuality playing a major role in its destruction.

Pro-Gay Argument #1:

Sodom was destroyed because of the inhospitality of its citizens, not because of homosexuality.

Professor John Boswell, in *Christianity, Social Tolerance and Homosexuality* (University of Chicago Press 1980), supports this view, basing it on two assumptions: first, that Lot was violating Sodom's custom by entertaining guests without the permission of the city's elders,[75] thus prompting the demand to bring the men out "so we may know them"; second, that the word "to know" did not necessarily have a sexual connotation.

The Hebrew word *yada* appears 943 times in the Old Testament; it carries a sexual meaning perhaps 10 of those 943 times. The argument, then, is that the men of Sodom had no sexual intentions towards Lot's visitors.

Response:

The argument makes no sense in light of Lot's responses. His first response, "Don't do this wicked thing,"

could hardly apply to a simple request to "get to know" his guests. His second response is especially telling: he answered their demands by offering his two virgin daughters—another senseless gesture if the men wanted only a social knowledge of his guests. And why, if these men had innocent intentions, was the city destroyed for inhospitality? Whose rudeness was being judged—Lots', or Sodom's citizens?

The theory raises more questions than it answers. While Boswell and Bailey are correct in pointing out the seriousness of inhospitality in Biblical times, inhospitality alone cannot account for the severity of Lot's response to the men, or for the judgment that soon followed.

Pro-Gay Argument #2:

Sodom was destroyed for attempted rape, not homosexuality.

This argument is more common; it is proposed by lesbian author Virginia Mollenkott and others, and is far more plausible than the "inhospitality" theory.

"Violence—forcing sexual activity upon another—is the real point of this story," Mollenkott explains.[76] Accordingly, homosexuality had nothing to do with Sodom's destruction; had the attempted rape been heterosexual in nature, judgment would have fallen just the same. Violence, not homosexuality, was being punished when Sodom fell.

Response:

The argument is partially true; the men of Sodom certainly were proposing rape. But for such an event to include "all the men from every part of the city of Sodom—both young and old," homosexuality must have been commonly practiced. Mollenkott makes a persuasive case for the event being much like a prison rape, or the kind of assaults conquering armies would commit against vanquished enemies,[77] but her argument is weakened by Professor Thomas Schmidt's cited evidence in early literature connecting Sodom with more general homosexual practices:

The second-century BC Testament of the Twelve Patriarchs labels the Sodomites 'sexually promiscuous' (Testimony of Benjamin 9:1) and refers to 'Sodom, which departed from the order of nature' (Testament of Nephtali 3:4). From the same time period, Jubilees specifies that the Sodomites were 'polluting themselves and fornicating in their flesh' (16:5, compare 20:5-6). Both Philo and Josephus plainly name same-sex relations as the characteristic view of Sodom.[78]

Pro-Gay Argument #3:

The real sins of Sodom, according to Ezekiel 16:49, were that it was "arrogant, overfed and unconcerned; they did not help the poor and needy." These have nothing to do with homosexuality.

Response:

Again, the argument is partially true. When Sodom was destroyed, homosexuality was only a part—or symptom—of its wickedness. Romans Chapter One gives a similar illustration, describing the generally corrupt condition of humanity, while citing homosexuality as a symptom of that corruption. But Ezekiel also says of the Sodomites: "They were haughty and did detestable things before me" (16:50). The sexual nature of these "detestable" things is suggested in 2 Peter 2:6-7:

If he [God] condemned the cities of Sodom and Gomorrah by burning them to ashes, and made them an example of what is going to happen to the ungodly; and if he rescued Lot, a righteous man, who was distressed by the filthy lives of lawless men…

And again in Jude 7:

In a similar way, Sodom and Gomorrah and the surrounding towns gave themselves up to sexual immorality and perversion. They serve as an example of those who suffer the punishment of eternal fire.

Dr. Bruce Metzger of Princeton Theological Seminary mentions other references to Sodom's sexual immorality in 3 Maccabees 2:5: "the people of Sodom who acted arrogantly, who were notorious for their vices." And again in Jubilees 16:6: "the uncleanness of the Sodomites."[79]

The pro-gay interpretation of Sodom's destruction has some merit: homosexual rape was attempted, and the Sodomites were certainly guilty of sins other than homosexuality. But in light of the number of men willing to join in the rape, and the many other references, both Biblical and extra-Biblical, to Sodom's sexual sins, it is likely homosexuality was widely practiced among the Sodomites. It is also likely that the sin for which they are named was one of many reasons judgment finally fell on them.

THE LEVITICAL LAW
(Leviticus 18:22; 20:13)

Do not lie with a man as one lies with a woman; that is *detestable* [or, 'an abomination'].

If a man lies with a man as one lies with a woman, both of them have done what is *detestable* [or, 'an abomination']. They must be put to death; their blood will be on their own heads.

Traditional Position:

Under Levitical Law, homosexuality was one of many abominable practices punishable by death.

Pro-Gay Argument:

The practices mentioned in these chapters of Leviticus have to do with idolatry, not homosexuality.

The Hebrew word for "abomination," according to Boswell, has less to do with something intrinsically evil and more to do with ritual uncleanness.[80] The Metropolitan Community Church's pamphlet, "Homosexuality: Not A Sin, Not A Sickness," makes the same point:

The (Hebrew word for abomination) found in Leviticus is usually associated with idolatry.[81]

Gay author Roger Biery agrees, associating the type of homosexuality forbidden in Leviticus with idolatrous practices. Pro-gay authors refer to the heathen rituals of the Canaanites—rituals including both homosexual and heterosexual prostitution—as reasons God prohibited homosexuality among His people. They contend homosexuality itself was not the problem, but it is association with idolatry and, at times, the way it was practiced as a part of idol worship. In other words, God was not prohibiting the kind of homosexuality we see today; He forbade the sort which incorporated idolatry.

Response #1:

The prohibitions against homosexuality in Leviticus 18 and 20 appear alongside other sexual sins—adultery and incest, for example—which are forbidden in both Old and New Testaments, completely apart from the Levitical codes. Scriptural references to these sexual practices, both before and after Leviticus, show God's displeasure with them whether or not any ceremony or idolatry is involved.

Response #2:

Despite the UFMCC's contention that the word for abomination *(toevah)* is usually associated with idolatry, it in fact appears in Proverbs 6:16-19 in connection with sins having nothing to do with idolatry or pagan ceremony:

There are six things the LORD hates, seven that are *detestable* [an abomination or *toevah*] to him: haughty eyes, a lying tongue, hands that shed innocent blood, a heart that devises wicked schemes, feet that are quick to rush into evil, a false witness who pours out lies and a man who stirs up dissension among brothers.

Idolatry plays no part in these scriptures; clearly, then, *toevah* is not limited to idolatrous practices.

Response #3:

If the practices in Leviticus 18 and 20 are condemned only because of their association with idolatry, then it logically follows they would be permissible if they were committed apart from idolatry. That would mean incest, adultery, bestiality and child sacrifice (all of which are listed in these chapters) are only condemned when associated with idolatry; otherwise, they are allowable. No serious reader of these passages could accept such a premise.

PAUL ON "NATURAL" AND "UNNATURAL"
Romans 1:26-27

Because of this, God gave them over to shameful lusts. Even their women exchanged natural relations for unnatural ones. In the same way the men also abandoned natural relations with women and were inflamed with lust for one another. Men committed indecent acts with other men, and received in themselves the due penalty for their perversion.

Traditional Position:

Paul views homosexuality as a symptom of fallen humanity, describing it as unnatural and unseemly.

Pro-Gay Argument #1:

Paul is not describing true homosexuals; rather, he is referring to heterosexuals who, as he says "exchanged natural relations." The real sin here is in changing what is natural to the individual. Boswell takes this argument up when he states:

The persons Paul condemns are manifestly not homosexual: what he derogates are homosexual acts committed by apparently heterosexual persons. The whole point of Romans 1, in fact, is to stigmatize persons who have rejected their calling, gotten off the true path they were once on.[82]

Mollenkott agrees, saying, "What Paul seems to be emphasizing here is that persons who are heterosexual by nature have not only exchanged the true God for a false one but have also exchanged their ability to relate to the opposite sex by indulging in homosexual behavior that is not natural to them."[83]

In short, Paul in Romans 1 describes heterosexuals who have deliberately committed homosexual acts, thus violating their true nature. Homosexuality, if committed by true homosexuals, is not a sin.

Response:

Paul is not speaking nearly so subjectively in this pas-

sage. There is nothing in his wording to suggest he even recognized such a thing as a "true" homosexual versus a "false" one. He simply describes homosexual behavior as unnatural, no matter who it is committed by.

His wording, in fact, is unusually specific. When he refers to "men" and "women" in these verses, he chooses the Greek words that most emphasize biology: *arsenes* and *theleias*. Both words are rarely used in the New Testament. When they do appear, they appear in verses meant to emphasize the gender of the subject, as in a *male* child (arsenes). In this context, Paul is very pointedly saying the homosexual behavior committed by these people was unnatural to them as males and females (*arsenes and theleias*). He is not considering any such thing as sexual orientation. He is saying, in other words, that homosexuality is *biologically* unnatural—not just unnatural to *heterosexuals*, but unnatural to *anyone*.

Additionally, the fact these men were "burning in lust" for each other makes it highly unlikely they were heterosexuals experimenting with homosexuality. Their behavior was born of an intense inner desire. Suggesting, as Boswell and Mollenkott do, that they were heterosexuals indulging in homosexual behavior requires unreasonable mental gymnastics.

Besides which, if verses 26-27 condemn homosexual actions committed by people to whom they did *not* come naturally, but do not apply to people to whom those actions *do* come naturally, then does not consistency compel us to also allow the practices mentioned in verses 29-30—fornication, backbiting, deceit, etc.—so long as the people who commit them are people to whom they *do* come naturally?

Pro-Gay Argument #2:

This scripture describes people given over to idolatry, not gay Christians who worship the true God.

Perry states:

The homosexual practices cited in Romans 1: 24-27 were believed to result from idolatry and are associated with some very serious offenses as noted in Romans 1. Taken in this larger context, it should be obvious that such acts are significantly different than loving, responsible lesbian and gay relationships seen today.[84]

Response

Idolatry certainly plays a major role in Romans Chapter One. Paul begins his writing by describing humanity's rebellion and decision to worship creation rather than the Creator. The pro-gay theorist seizes on this concept to prove that Paul's condemnation of homosexuality does not apply to *him*—he does not worship idols, he is a Christian.

"But," Schmidt cautions, "Paul is not suggesting that

a person worships an idol and decides therefore to engage in same-sex relations. Rather, he is suggesting that the general rebellion created the environment for the specific rebellion. A person need not bow before a golden calf to participate in the general human denial of God or to express that denial through specific behaviors."[85]

A common sense look at the entire chapter bears this out. Several sins other than homosexuality are mentioned in the same passage:

> Fornication, wickedness, covetousness, maliciousness; full of envy, murder, debate, deceit, malignity, whisperers; backbiters, haters of God, disobedient to parents.... (vv 29-30)

Will the interpretation applied to the verse 26-27 also apply to verses 29-30? Any sort of intellectual integrity demands it. If verses 26-27 apply to people who commit homosexual acts in connection with idolatry, and thus homosexuals acts are not sinful if *not* committed in connection with idolatry, then the same must apply to verses 29-30 as well.

Therefore, we must assume that fornication, wickedness, covetousness, maliciousness et al are also condemned by Paul *only* because they were committed by people involved in idolatry; they *are* permissible otherwise.

Which is, of course, ridiculous. Like homosexuality, these sins are not just born of idol worship; they are symptomatic of a fallen state. If we are to say homosexuality is legitimate, so long as it's not a result of idol worship, then we also have to say these other sins are legitimate as well, so long as they, too, are not practiced as a result of idolatry.

PAUL AND 'ARSENOKOITE'
1 Corinthians 6:9-10; 1 Timothy 1:9-10

Do you not know that the wicked will not inherit the kingdom of God? Do not be deceived: Neither the sexually immoral nor idolaters nor adulterers nor male prostitutes nor *homosexual offenders* ['abusers of themselves with mankind']...will inherit the kingdom of God.

We also know that law is made not for the righteous but for lawbreakers and rebels...for adulterers and *perverts* ['them that defile themselves with mankind']...

Traditional Position:
"Them that defile themselves with mankind" comes from the word Greek word *arsenokoite*, meaning "homosexual." Paul is saying homosexuality is a vice excluding its practitioners from the kingdom of God.

Pro-Gay Argument:
'Arsenokoite' is a word coined by Paul. It never appeared in Greek literature before he used it in these scriptures. There were, at the time, other words for "homosexual." Had he meant to refer to homosexuality, he would have used one of the words already in existence. Most likely, he was referring to male prostitution, which was common at the time.

Boswell points out, accurately, that the word is peculiar to Paul, suggesting he did not have homosexuality in mind when he used it.[86] Prostitution is Boswell's first choice. If not that, he suggests Paul was condemning general immorality. At any rate, the term, according to this argument, means some sort of immoral man but not a homosexual.

Response:
Paul coined 179 terms in the New Testament. The terms do not, because they are original, significantly change the context of the verses they appear in.

Nor is it remarkable he would have coined this one, considering he derived it directly from the Greek translation of the Old Testament (the Septuagint):

> meta arsenos ou koimethese koiten gyniakos (Lev 18:22)

> hos an koimethe meta arsenos koiten gynaikos (Lev 20:13)

In other words, when Paul adopted the term *arsenokoite*, he took it directly from the Levitical passages—in the Greek translation—forbidding homosexual behavior. The meaning, then, could not be clearer: Though the term is unique to Paul, it refers specifically to homosexual behavior.

As for the inference that it applies to male prostitution, a breakdown of the word shows it implies nothing of the sort. 'Arsene,' as mentioned earlier, appears few times in the New Testament, always referring to "male." 'Koite' appears only twice in the New Testament, and means "bed," used in a sexual connotation:

> Let us behave decently, as in the daytime, not in orgies and drunkenness, not in *sexual immorality* [koite] and debauchery... (Rom 13:13)

> Marriage should be honored by all, and the marriage *bed* [koite] kept pure, for God will judge the adulterer and all the sexually immoral. (Heb 13:4)

The two words combined, as Paul used them, put "male" and "bed" together in a sexual sense. There is no hint of prostitution in the meaning of either of the words combined to make *arsenokoite*.

I remember clearly, and with inexpressible regret, the day I convinced myself it was acceptable for me to be both gay and Christian. Not only did I embrace the pro-gay theology—I promoted it as well, serving on the staff of the local Metropolitan Community Church and presenting the arguments cited in this series. Twelve years have passed since I realized my error, and during those years the pro-gay theology has enjoyed unprecedented exposure and acceptance, both in mainline denominations and among sincere (albeit sincerely deceived) believers.

Many Christians are unaware that there is such a thing as pro-gay theology, much less a movement built around it. And many who are aware of it have no idea how to answer its claims. Yet an answer is required; the pro-gay theology, like the gay rights movement it represents, grows daily in scope and influence. With the love Christ showed while weeping over Jerusalem, and the anger He displayed when clearing the Temple, the Church must respond.

[This article was revised and abridged from the book, *A Strong Delusion: Confronting the "Gay Christian" Movement*, by Joe Dallas (Harvest House 1996).]

Joe Dallas, founder of Genesis Counseling, is the author of three books on homosexuality: *Desires in Conflict, Unforgiven Sins,* and *A Strong Delusion: Confronting the "Gay Christian" Movement.* A former gay rights activist and staff member of a Metropolitan Community Church, he has worked with hundreds of men and women struggling with homosexuality and related problems. Mr. Dallas is available for conferences and seminars, and can be reached at Genesis Counseling, 307 E. Chapman Ave., Orange, CA 92666, (714) 744-3326.

Endnotes:

[1] Praeger in Broward Jewish World, October 16, 1990, cited in Grant and Horne, *Legislating Immorality* (Chicago: Moody Press,1993), p. 24-25.

[2] See Boswell, John. *Christianity, Social Tolerance and Homosexuality* (Chicago: University of Chicago Press, 1980), p. 61-87, Grant and Horne, p. 21-38, and Churchill, Wainwright, *Homosexual Behavior Among Males* (New York: Hawthorne Books, 1967), p. 121-141.

[3] Bayer, Ronald. *Homosexuality and American Psychiatry* (New York: Basic Books, 1981), p. 15.

[4] Praeger, Dennis. "Why Judaism Rejected Homosexuality" *Mission and Ministry: The Quarterly Magazine of Trinity Episcopal School for Ministry,* Summer Edition, 1995, Vol. 10, No. 3, p.13.

[5] From Jeff Levi's speech to the National Press Club during the 1987 Washington Rally, cited in *Shadow in the Land* Dannemeyer, William (San Francisco: Ignatious Press, 1989), p. 86.

[6] White, Mel. *Stranger at the Gate* (New York: Simon and Schuster, 1994), p. 311.

[7] From television special "Gays and the Church" ABC World News Tonight, February 28, 1996.

[8] See Hanegraff, Hank. *Christianity in Crises* (Eugene: Harvest House, 1993), p. 317 for the roles both creeds play in the essentials of Christianity.

[9] Perry, Troy. *Don't Be Afraid Anymore* (New York: St. Martin's Press, 1990), p. 342.

[10] Frame, Randy. "Seeking a Right to the Rite," *Christianity Today,* March 4, 1996, Vol 40, No. 3, p. 66.

[11] Perry, p. 39.

[12] White, p. 295, 300, 309, 315.

[13] Scroogs, Robin. *The New Testament and Homosexuality* (Philadelphia: Fortress Press, 1983), p. 127.

[14] Morris, Paul. *Shadow of Sodom* (Wheaton: Tyndale Press, 1978), p. 89.

[15] Perry, p. 39.

[16] White, p. 36-39.

[17] Ibid., p. 156.

[18] Pennington, Sylvia. *Ex-Gays? There Are None!* (Hawthorne: Lambda Christian Fellowship, 1989), p. 388.

[19] LeVay, Simon. "A Difference in Hypothalamic Structure Between Heterosexual and Homosexual Men," *Science,* August 30, 1991, p. 1034-1037.

[20] Ankerberg, John. "The Myth That Homosexuality Is Due to Biological or Genetic Causes" (Research Paper), PO Box 8977, Chattanooga, TN 37411.

[21] "Is This Child Gay?" *Newsweek,* September 9, 1991, p. 52.

[22] Ibid.

[23] *Los Angeles Times,* September 16, 1992, p. 1, as cited in NARTH Newsletter, December 1992, p. 1.

[24] "Sexual Disorientation: Faulty Research in the Homosexual Debate," *Family* (a publication of the Family Research Council), October 28, 1992, p. 4.

[25] "Is This Child Gay?", p. 52.

[26] *Los Angeles Times,* August 30, 1991, Section A, Page 1.

[26] *Time,* September 9, 1991, Vol. 138, #10, p. 61.

[27] *Newsweek,* September 9, 1991, p. 52.

[28] Chronicle of Higher Education, February 5, 1992, p. A7.

[29] "Gay Genes Revisited," *Scientific American,* Nov. 1995, p. 26.

[30] Bailey and Pillard. "A Genetic Study of Male Sexual Orientation," *Archives of General Psychiatry* #48, 1991, p. 1089-1096.

[31] Gelman, David. "Born or Bred?" *Newsweek,* February 24, 1992, p. 46

[32] Ibid.

[33] Ibid.

[34] King and McDonald. "Homosexuals Who Are Twins," *The British Journal of Psychiatry* March 1992, Vol. 160, p. 409

[35] Hamer, Dean. "A Linkage Between DNA Markers on the X Chromosome and Male Sexual Orientation," *Science,* 261, July 16, 1993, p. 321-327.

[36] "Gay Genes Revisited: Doubts Arise over Research on the Biology of Homosexuality" *Scientific American,* November 1995, p. 26.

[37] Ibid.

[38] Frank Siexas, former Director of the National Council on Alcoholism, quoted in the *Boston Globe,* August 8, 1983.

[39] Dallas, Joe. "Born Gay?" *Christianity Today,* June 22, 1992 p. 22.

[40] "Rethinking the Origins of Sin," *Los Angeles Times,* May 15, 1993 Section A, p. 31.

[41] Wright, Robert. "Our Cheating Hearts," *Time,* August 15, 1994, Vol. 144, No 7, p. 44-52.

[42] *Chronicle of Higher Education,* February 5, 1992, p. A7.

[43] Ibid.

[44] Ibid.

[45] Ibid.

[46] Richard Isay, PhD. "Gays and the Church," ABC World News Tonight, February 28, 1996.

[47] Isay, Richard. *Being Homosexual* (New York: Farrar, Straus,

Giroux, 1989), p. 112.

[48] Wood and Dietrich. *The AIDS Epidemic* (Portland: Multnomah, 1990), p. 238.

[49] Fine, Ruben. *Psychoanalytic Theory, Male and Female Homosexuality: Psychological Approaches* (New York: Hemisphere, 1987), p. 84-86.

[50] Bieber, Irving. *Homosexuality: A Psychoanalytic Study* (NewYork: Basic Books, 1962), p. 318-319.

[51] Masters and Johnson. *Homosexuality in Perspective* (Boston: Little Brown and Company, 1979), p. 402.

[52] Wood and Dietrich. *The AIDS Epidemic* (Portland: Multnomah, 1990), p. 238.

[53] Reinisch, June. *The New Kinsey Report* (New York: St Martin's Press, 1990), p. 138, 143.

[54] Jones, Stanton. "The Loving Opposition," *Christianity Today,* July 19, 1993, Vol 37, No. 8.

[55] Kinsey, Pomeroy and Martin. *Sexual Behavior in the Human Male* (Philadelphia: Saunders Press, 1948), p. 625.

[56] Ibid., p. 638.

[57] Reinisch, p. 138.

[58] Reisman, Judith. *Kinsey, Sex and Fraud* (Layfayette: Huntington, 1990), p. 9.

[59] Lesbian activist with ACT-UP, interviewed in "Gay Rights-Special Rights" video.

[60] Jones.

[61] Barna, George. *What Americans Believe* (Ventura: Regal Books, 1991), p. 36, cited in Rhodes.

[62] Lang, Stephen. "Is Ignorance Bliss?", *Moody Magazine,* January/February 1996, Vol. 96, No. 5, p. 13.

[63] Colson, Charles. Excerpt from *The Body,* reprinted in *Christianity Today,* November 23, 1992 p. 29.

[64] Miller, Elliot. *A Crash Course on the New Age Movement* (Grand Rapids: Baker Book House, 1993), p. 16, cited in Rhodes.

[65] Plantinga, Cornelius. "Natural Born Sinners," *Christianity Today,* November 14, 1994, Vol. 38, No. 13, p. 25.

[66] Lang, p. 13.

[67] Perry, p. 40.

[68] White, p. 268.

[69] Biery, Roger. *Understanding Homosexuality: The Pride and the Prejudice* (Austin: Edward Williams Publishing, 1990), p. 138

[70] "Gays and the Church," ABC World News Tonight, February 28, 1996.

[71] Biery, p. 176.

[72] Laurie, Greg. *The Great Compromise* (Dallas: Word Publishing, 1994), p. 8.

[73] Schmidt, Thomas. *Straight & Narrow?* (Downers Grove: InterVarsity Press, 1995), p. 41.

[74] Jones.

[75] See Boswell, John. *Christianity, Social Tolerance and Homosexuality* (Chicago: University of Chicago Press, 1980), p. 93-94.

[76] Mollenkott and Scanzoni. *Is the Homosexual My Neighbor?* (San Francisco: Harper Collins, 1978), p. 57-58.

[77] Ibid.

[78] Schmidt, p. 88-89.

[79] Metzger, Bruce. "What Does the Bible Have to Say About Homosexuality?" *Presbyterians for Renewal,* May 1993, p. 7.

[80] Boswell, p. 100.

[81] Perry, p. 341.

[82] Boswell, p. 109.

[83] Ramey and Mollenkott, p. 65-66.

[84] Perry, p. 342.

[85] Schmidt, p. 78-79.

[86] Boswell, p. 344-345.

The Other Way Out

The Stories Of John And Anne Paulk

Homosexuality is one of the most controversial topics of our day. Its causes have been debated and people wonder, "Can the homosexual be changed?" According to many, the answer is no; however, it is possible to change one's sexual orientation. This article gives the true stories of a man and woman whose lives speak to this intensely important yet highly delicate subject.

Anne:
Secure in My Feminine Identity

I grew up as a classic tomboy, mostly playing cowboys and Indians or cops and robbers. When I was about four years old, an event happened which profoundly shook my inner security. A teenage boy approached me sexually, then warned me not to tell my parents. I never said a word, fearful that we would both get into big trouble. This silence left me to reap a lot of self-inflicted pain, and the whole incident only reinforced my tomboy image. I did not feel protected or valued as a girl.

I also craved special affirmation as a girl from my dad, but could not tell him why. For years I believed lies about myself, God and men. And the sexual experience (when I was four) kept me from embracing femininity which, to me, meant being weak and vulnerable.

Then I found myself having crushes on some of my girlfriends. I was talented in athletics, so I joined the softball team in high school, but continued to avoid most feminine activities. I didn't feel pretty or lovable.

At church, the youth group seemed shallow. I felt disappointed that everyone behaved just like the non-Christian kids at school, and I became disillusioned. Soon I discarded church altogether, and began getting into wild behavior: drinking, dating three boys at one time, and eventually exploring homosexual relationships.

Then I went to college and met Sara. She seemed so confident and strong as a woman. Men adored her, but they only seemed to ridicule and use me. It was then, in early 1982, I realized my feelings for Sara were sexual. So I decided to look up an old boyfriend to "test" my orientation. Although he was a nice guy, I felt no attraction to him. After that, I decided to pursue my attractions for women. At the suggestion of a gay counselor, I joined the college gay/lesbian group.

But during one of those meetings, I had a piercing thought: *There really is something wrong with this lifestyle.* I was heartbroken by the words that shattered my dreams of finding happiness with a female life-partner. After the meeting, I went home and cried. "God," I prayed, "please show me who you are, and fill the void in my heart."

After that prayer, I began experiencing a new hunger to know Jesus Christ. Within six months, I made a firm decision to forsake homosexuality and follow him. But, unfortunately, none of the leaders on campus or at church knew how to give me hope that my sexual attraction for women would change. My commitment to Christ, however, enabled me to persevere in the face of this discouragement. I immersed myself in Christian activity, although the homosexual attractions never went away.

Eventually I fell into a sexual relationship with Laura, a Christian girlfriend who, like me, struggled with lesbianism. Laura and I looked to each other for emotional fulfillment. At first, it seemed like many of my childhood dreams were being fulfilled through our relationship. But along with some satisfaction came conviction, deception and emotional instability. Laura became my top priority over work, family and friends. Many areas in our lives suffered as a result. Laura even battled with suicidal thoughts. Then Laura and I tried to remain friends, but stop the sexual part of our relationship. But it never worked, because we never addressed the underlying issues.

Finally, after three months of resisting God, I said a

very honest prayer: "Lord, you know that I really enjoy this lifestyle, but I want you to be my first love. I need your help. I need you to change my heart." This prayer marked a major turning point in my life.

Shortly after my prayer, Laura and I had dinner with a Christian woman who was a former lesbian. She listened to our story and our questions, and through her we made contact with a Christian ministry solely devoted to helping people overcome homosexuality. The people loved us and cared for us, and eventually Laura and I agreed to give our relationship to God and avoid all contact with each other.

Though angry and frustrated over the break-up with Laura, I continued going to the ministry's meetings for the next 18 months. The insights I gained there were incredibly valuable. I learned how to look for patterns in my same-sex attractions, so I could understand the underlying needs which sparked the temptations in the first place.

I continued to grow in my relationship with God, and eventually I realized that something had changed deep inside of me. God changed my sexual identity from ex-gay to godly woman. I was learning that God loved me with a gentle delight, especially when I relied on his strength.

During this time, I found myself having a new interest in men, and began spending time with them in group situations. Then, in mid-1991, I began dating John Paulk, a man in my church who like me had come out of homosexuality. On December 31, 1991, he presented me with a ring and asked me to marry him. We were married the following July. I kept looking happily at the ring, thinking, "Wow! Me married!" I was filled with joy as God established something so beautiful and holy in our lives.

Since then, God has used John to comfort me and to confront areas of distrust in my life. This has been difficult, but the Lord has been faithful to fulfill his promise to heal, even when the process is uncomfortable. I am so glad that my Father took the time to unearth the hurts that held me back from growing into godly femininity. Now I don't need to compare myself to other women and don't seek to gain femininity from them through emotional dependency or homosexual relationships. My identity is secure as a woman because I know Christ.

John:
Taking Off the Mask

My parents divorced when I was five. My dad took my sister and me to a park, knelt down beside us, and told us good-bye. For the rest of my childhood, I lived with a continuous insecurity that the people I loved would always walk out of my life.

Around other boys, I felt terribly insecure and different. And because I wasn't good in sports and was effemi-nate, they called me names like *fag*, *queer* and *sissy*.

I started drinking alcohol when I was 14. I drank to numb the pain inside and to escape from my feelings of self-hatred and inadequacy. Then, when I was 15, a girl from school told me about Jesus Christ while we were talking on the phone one day. I believed everything she said about the Bible, and, after hanging up the phone, I knelt down and asked Jesus to come into my life. I sought him fervently after that, but since no one else in my family was a Christian, I fell away after six months.

When I was a senior in high school, a friend took me to a gay bar for the first time. A whole new world opened up to me. All the attention I got from other men was overwhelming. I soon fell in love with a guy named Curt. Our sexual relationship seemed so natural, and I slipped into the gay lifestyle and let go of my childhood dream of having a wife and family. But my relationship with Curt began to deteriorate and we split up after a year. Once again I lost someone who I thought would stay with me forever. Our break-up was so hard on me that I dropped out of college and moved back home with my mother.

My drinking increased, and I became so miserable that I tried to take my life. Then, due to my poor self-image and lack of money, I started working as a male prostitute. I'd be dropped off at a hotel room and sell my body for $80 an hour. By the end of that summer, I was emotionally burned out. I remember crying myself to sleep after I came home from allowing myself to be sexually used all night.

Another significant event happened that summer. At a gay bar, I saw a male friend dressed like a woman. His feminine appearance looked so real. I was fascinated and one night he put makeup and a wig on me. I was astonished to see a beautiful "woman" looking back at me.

Over the next three years I threw everything into being the best woman I could. I was proud to be a drag queen and even adopted the name "Candi." Soon I became popular as a female impersonator, not just locally but in neighboring states as well. But inside I still hated myself. One night on the dance floor I said to God, "I know you can help me—someday I'll come back to you."

In October 1985, my psychologist confronted me about my heavy drinking. I began attending AA meetings. After six months of sobriety, my head began to clear. One day I put all of my dresses, high heels, wigs, jewelry and makeup into a cardboard box and threw it into a dumpster. "Candi, I don't need you anymore. I'm saying good-bye" I said. My drag friends tried to convince me that I'd be back.

Very shortly after that, a college pastor from a nearby church asked if he could talk to me. He came to my apartment and told me about Jesus Christ. I stopped him after twenty minutes and said, "I know all about the Gospel. I used to be a Christian when I was 15. But I was born gay, so forget it!"

"No, you weren't," he answered. Then he read from Genesis 2: "And God created man...male and female... And God saw all that he had made, and behold, it was very good." The truth came shining through. I was convinced that homosexuality was not something I was born with or something I had to stay in. That week I dug out my Bible and started to read it again. After wrestling with the decision for days, I knelt down beside my bed. "Lord, I don't know how to get out of homosexuality, but I will follow you. No matter how difficult it gets, I'll never turn away from you again." It was February 10, 1987. I had finally found someone who would never leave me.

Something inside me was different now. At a gay AA meeting, the topic of whether homosexuals go to heaven came up. "It doesn't matter if you're gay or straight," I told them, "If we believe in Jesus Christ we'll go to heaven." My friends were shocked. They'd never heard me say such a thing before. Most of them I never heard from again.

Over the next year, I struggled quite a bit. I had gotten rid of all my homosexual paraphernalia and pornography, but I was terribly afraid of rejection by straight men, even at my church. During that time I found the name of a Christian ministry that reached out to homosexuals. I contacted the ministry and eventually moved to the town where it was located. As I was leaving, my mother said, "John, you've worked hard to change your life this past year. I'm so proud of you."

"I only had Christ to lean on," I told her. "He did the changing—not me."

With that Christian ministry's help, I discovered that my concept of God was distorted. I had a difficult time accepting the reality of his total love and acceptance. The concept of being loved for just being me was totally incomprehensible. But God wanted to change my identity as a man. He did, and over time I no longer doubted his acceptance of me. I was also finally able to forgive my parents for their emotional neglect and the ways I felt they had rejected me.

My process out of homosexuality has been slow, but solid. My male friendships have eventually grown to a place where I feel secure in my masculinity and know who I am among other men. And at some point, even though Christ had filled the empty places of my heart, he also gave me the desire to have someone else there. In 1991 I fell in love with a beautiful, godly woman who had also come from a homosexual background. We were married in 1992. I cried all the way through our wedding vows, knowing Christ was fulfilling my dream. God's transforming power was so evident during our wedding that my mother and stepfather prayed to receive Jesus Christ that night.

In the past, I could never say, "I'm a man." But now I'm a different person, a "new creature in Christ." I can be loved just because I'm his. In the past, there were many masks I hid behind to protect myself from being hurt again. But now I see that they only stood in the way of God's love reaching through to me. In Jesus Christ I've found the love and acceptance I was looking for all along.

No Easy Way

If you're someone whose emotional and sexual attractions are clearly towards people of the same sex, life is going to be tough, no matter what. Consider the options:

You can pursue *the gay lifestyle*. For most people, this means pursuing that person who will satisfy those deep inner longings—a pursuit that never seems to end. For others, the pursuit turns very sexual, and the other person becomes merely a warm body, a sexual object who can ease the pain and longing temporarily, but who meets no lasting need.

There is a second difficult road you can take: *withdrawal*. Knowing that the gay life will not satisfy, or perhaps sensing that it is somehow wrong, but believing that you have no other option, you can withdraw. At best, you can deny your emotional and sexual feelings, stay away from relationships that could cause you pain.

There is a third way, also difficult, that many have found—*the way of freedom and real change*. Right now this might seem like the most difficult option, even an impossible one. However, through a relationship with God it is possible to experience a new life...a genuinely changed life. God can free us from things in our lives that we have absolutely no power to change on our own. He has changed the lives of many homosexuals. Usually, it's not instantly, not overnight, but steadily.

The Way Out of Homosexuality

Homosexuality is overcome by building a relationship with Jesus Christ and letting him heal the underlying root issues. Our deliverance comes from a person, rather than from a method. Therefore, it is important that we build a relationship with God, our Deliverer. We must know him better than we know those around us. And in fact, for true deliverance, Christ must become the most important person in our lives. How can we come to know Jesus Christ?

Agreement with God

To begin with, if you are seeking the truth, you have already been touched by the Holy Spirit. One of the purposes of the Holy Spirit is to bring conviction of sin.

The first message Christ gave was one of repentance. Through the Holy Spirit, we have been given an awareness that homosexuality is not pleasing to God (Leviticus

18:22; Romans 1:26; 1 Corinthians 6:9-11). So the first step is to agree with God that homosexual activities are sin.

Receiving Jesus Christ

John 1:12 gives us the next step: "To all who received him [Jesus Christ], to those who believed in his name, he gave the right to become children of God." In order for Jesus to work in our lives, we must not only agree with him that homosexuality is sin, but we must *trust* in *him* for the *forgiveness* of *all* of our sins, including homosexuality.

The Bible says that, "God so loved the world that he gave his one and only Son, that whoever believes in him shall not perish but have eternal life" (John 3:16). Jesus Christ was crucified—nailed to a cross until death—for our sins. He died in our place: "God made him who had no sin to be sin for us, so that in him we might become the righteousness of God" (2 Corinthians 5:21). When we trust in Christ for the forgiveness of our sins, God looks upon us as if we'd lived the same perfect life that Jesus lived. That's God's grace. No matter what activities you've been involved in, God offers you his forgiveness.

After receiving Christ, we enter into a love relationship with him...the God of the universe. This is an eternal relationship and we no longer have to worry and wonder how we are going to know him—he will reveal himself to us daily in many ways. We are now his child.

A New Life

Upon receiving Christ, God says that we become a new creation (2 Corinthians 5:17). He changes us on the inside and gives us new desires. We find ourselves making decisions to live a more upright life. We experience a new freedom to say "no," with a motivation to please God. Satisfying our sexual urges becomes secondary. God brings new priorities into our life—living according to the truth, living with self-respect, living with greater concern for others' welfare, living a less self-centered life.

Also, God gives us a peace we never had before. This doesn't mean a "rose garden" from God or from the world. We will pass through many struggles and the change may come painfully at times and may be very gradual. However, we are not struggling alone. In the midst of our troubles, we have the peace of Christ in our hearts.

This peace is something the world knows nothing about—only someone who belongs to Christ can know the comfort of his peace. Through Christ living within us, we become adequate for any trial. He asks that we give all of our anxiety over to him, because he cares for us (1 Peter 5:7).

Submission to Christ

In spite of the change God will bring in our life, we still have a will that often will want to slip back into our "pre-Christ" ways. Therefore, the height of victory over homosexuality is directly related to our willingness to submit ourselves completely to God.

To experience the most abundant life, we must relinquish all control of our life to God's love and power. Our own plans and desires must come second to God's plans and desires for us. To come out of homosexuality, we must be submitted to Jesus Christ as our Lord, and we must do this on a daily basis.

Many people, after a length of time, believe that they are sufficiently out of homosexuality to once again take control of their life. This is a serious error—the commitment we make to Christ is for life. When we take back control of our life, we ask for trouble. The results can often be disastrous.

Role of the Church

Once we enter into a relationship with Christ, we become part of his body, the church. As part of a body of many members, we are interdependent with others. That means attending a church. Admittedly, many people have had painful experiences with the church, yet we must be involved in the lives of others, and allow others to be involved in our life, in order to grow.

No body of believers will be perfect and there will be things that we don't like. Still, we must join a church and become a productive part of that body of people. Therefore, contact an ex-gay ministry who can suggest a good church in your area.

Christ speaks to us in many ways, including through his Word (the Bible) and through others who know him. If we are not involved in a church, we will be missing many messages that he has for us, as well as the privilege and joy of being a blessing to someone else.

Talking with God

If you don't know how to talk with God, follow the example set forth in the Disciples' Prayer (often called the Lord's Prayer; Matthew 6:9ff), which the context shows to be a *daily* prayer.

Thank God for his goodness, for his mercy, for him being your Father. Understand that he is worthy of your complete trust. Ask that his will would be done in your life. Ask him for your needs. Ask him for forgiveness for your going astray and not listening to him. Ask forgiveness for your treatment of others.

Ask for his protection against temptations and whatever strong feelings come your way. Close your prayer again with praise and thankfulness. Whatever you ask of God the Father, ask in the name of Jesus Christ (John 15:16).

The Word of God

Experience the benefits of obedience to Christ. To do this, we must be familiar with his Word. Start by reading the book of John in the New Testament. Then try reading one of Paul's letters, such as the book of Ephesians. As you begin to study God's Word, start by asking him to reveal to you what you need to hear from it.

The Bible will be your road map to a new life. Use it and study it. Set aside time every day for prayer and Bible study. God is faithful. Do your part, and he will do his. Reading his Word will allow you to grow closer to him day by day.

There Is Hope

God created you for a purpose, and is able to bring wholeness, a sense of rightness, and fulfillment to your life. And he is the only one who can accomplish that full depth of transformation. Allow God the opportunity to enter your life. Receive his forgiveness. Know his love.

The following is a suggested prayer (the words aren't as important as is the attitude of your heart):

God, I confess my sin to you. Thank you Jesus, for taking all of my sin upon yourself on the cross. I want to receive your forgiveness. I want to enter into a relationship with you. I ask you to come into my life right now. I want you to make me into the person you created me to be.

If anyone is in Christ, he is a new creation;
the old has gone, the new has come!
(2 Corinthians 5:17)

[Special thanks to the following persons and ministries who contributed to this article: Anne Paulk, John Paulk, Bob Davies, Exodus International, Love in Action, Regeneration, and Frank Worthen.]

When a Friend Says, "I'm Gay"

by Anita Worthen and Bob Davies

Todd can vividly remember the night he met Sue. He was attending a new church, and it was his first time at the College and Career group which met Friday nights. "I walked into the fellowship hall. Sue was talking with several of her girlfriends. I noticed her immediately. She had long auburn hair, a sparkling laugh and she was attractively dressed. I was smitten with her right away." Over the next three months, Todd saw Sue weekly at College and Career. She was always warm and friendly toward him. Then one night after the meeting, he asked if she would be interested in going out for coffee. To Todd's amazement, they ended up talking for over two hours. Todd was aware of an emotional intensity and a growing mutual attraction. The next week, they went out on Saturday evening for their first official date. After the movie, they went for a drive.

"Todd, there's something important that I want you to know about me," Sue said as they drove down the highway, then she described how, as a child, she had always felt "different." When puberty hit, she had felt confused about her lack of interest in boys. Then, in high school, Sue met two senior students who were known lesbians. She found herself wondering if perhaps she was gay. After several months, Sue got to know these women better and they introduced her to other students who were experimenting with lesbianism. During the rest of high school, Sue had become sexually involved with three different women. Then, through a man at work, Sue was challenged to consider Christianity. By the end of that summer, she had prayed to commit her life to Christ. She had now been a Christian about two years. "I've never been in a serious dating relationship with a guy," Sue concluded. "And I've never felt such strong feelings for a man."

During the coming months, Todd and Sue became an established "pair" at church. Others began affirming their relationship, especially Sue's close friends who knew of her past involvement in lesbianism. Todd was thrilled at this development in his life, even as further details unfolded about Sue's troubled childhood. Her parents had divorced when she was seven after her father committed adultery. Sue was deeply wounded by her parents' break-up and remembered vowing never to trust a man again. She had built up thick walls around her heart to keep from being hurt again—until Todd came along, that is.

Todd remembers some warning signs of trouble ahead in their relationship, but he ignored them. Sue was struggling with a strong emotional attachment to another woman at church. Todd knew that she had not been out of lesbianism for very long, but the excitement of their relationship erased his slight misgivings. "I had never been happier, especially when Sue told me she was willing to take the risk of loving me."

After nine months of dating, Todd took Sue to a well-known exclusive restaurant with a view overlooking the city. It was a perfect summer evening. A thousand lights sparkled below them as the sky darkened. After their dinner, Todd presented Sue with a small gift-wrapped box. Inside was an engagement ring. He held his breath as Sue read the accompanying note: "I have sought the Lord and believe he wants us to be always together. I love you. Will you marry me?"

Sue looked up, her eyes misty. "Yes, I will," she said softly. Todd could feel his own eyes flooding with tears. "I was never more happy," Todd said later, "and I assumed that she was feeling the same way." But over the next two months, Todd sensed some unsettling changes within Sue. He especially remembers the weekend that they went to visit Sue's mom and stepfather, and how cool her stepfather acted toward him. Sue cried most of the two-hour drive home, confessing to Todd that her stepfather was not a Christian and was strongly opposed to their relationship.

During the next week, Sue totally withdrew emotionally and Todd felt hurt and confused. Here's how he explained it later: "That weekend was a turning point in our relationship. Due to her stepfather's rejection, all her unresolved feelings toward her real father came rushing to the surface. Our relationship began to crumble from that day on."

Then Todd phoned Sue. During their conversation, Sue started weeping and it was several minutes before she could speak. "I have these feelings of aggression toward men. I don't want to be around you right now." Several days later, Todd answered the doorbell. To his surprise, Sue stood on the doorstep, holding out a small box. "This is never going to work," she blurted out. "I've been thinking about this for days and I have to tell you the truth. I'm not in love with you and I can't marry you." She handed him the box and ran back to her car while Todd stood in his doorway, frozen with shock.

He stood in place while Sue drove off, then finally closed the door. A flood of emotions erupted inside him. "I sank down on the couch and started screaming and sobbing. It sounded like I was dying—and that's the way I felt. All I could do was pray, *Lord, help me. I can't deal with this. Help me make sense of what is happening right now.*"

Later Todd phoned Sue and tried to reason with her. "I think you do love me deep down inside but your issues with men have come up and you can't deal with the pain. So you've shut off your heart to me."

She denied it. "You're wrong. This has nothing to do with any of those issues."

Todd tried to convince her that she was overreacting by giving up on their relationship. "If you will only face your issues with men and with your father, I'm willing to wait. I don't care how long this takes. I want to support you and see our relationship grow again in the future." But Sue refused and soon their conversation ended.

Todd knew that he was working to revive something that was already dead. "I needed to let her go. It was killing me inside but I had to do it." He cried himself to sleep that night.

That was three years ago. Since then, Sue has moved to another part of the country. Todd is now dating another young woman from work. Periodically he hears news of Sue through mutual friends at church. She is doing well, although he does not know if she has been able to process further the issues which were raised in their relationship. "I knew after that last conversation that it was time to really let her go and move on with my life," he says today. "I wish her God's very best. And, despite the outcome, I have no regrets that I pursued that relationship. I learned a lot, especially the fact that I am capable of loving someone very deeply. In fact, some of the lessons I learned are playing out in my current relationship. I'm a better person for knowing Sue."

Many of you reading this article have a friend or acquaintance whom you suspect or know is gay. Maybe the person is a relative, someone you see occasionally at family gatherings. For others, the person is a neighbor, fellow student or co-worker. Whatever the situation, in this article we will examine specific strategies on how to effectively reach out to them.

When You Don't Really Know

If you have a strong suspicion that friends are lesbian or gay but the subject has never come up, it is important that you do not label them by asking if they are homosexual. They may never have thought about it, and raising the question can make them begin to question their identity. Or it may strengthen a latent fear they already have within themselves.

The belief, "Once gay, always gay," is very strong in our culture. We have seen many men go into a gay lifestyle because of something as simple as a same-sex dream that went unchecked. They gave into fear and then became curious about homosexuality. "I tried it once just to prove that I wasn't gay," explained one man who was subsequently drawn into many same-sex encounters.

World-renowned sex researchers Masters and Johnson found that the fourth most prevalent fantasy of "straight" men was homosexual encounters. And, in our society, those who have a gay thought or desire are urged to accept their homosexuality. But this reasoning runs exactly opposite to the Bible. All of us have fleshly desires which war against the soul (Rom 7:23). Taking on the gay identity is a major step into spiritual deception. All of us have areas of temptation, but our identity as Christians is centered in Christ, not in our fleshly struggles.

How Can We Help a Friend If We Suspect That He or She Has This Problem?

Work on deepening your friendship.

Become a "safe" person with whom that man or woman can be honest. Sexuality is an intimate area of life, and it takes time to deepen a friendship to the level where such private subjects can be discussed openly. Make an effort to become a reliable, consistent friend.

Pray for your friendship. Even if the other person's problem is not homosexuality, you may be discerning a struggle which needs prayer. Ask the Lord to show you how to be a better friend and find specific ways to support this person.

Be open about your own struggles.

Be willing to risk your own reputation. If you are hoping that your friend will open up at a deep level, you can reach that level of communication by opening up first.

Often as Christians we feel that people expect us to be perfect and we try hard to live up to that false image. What a mistake! We end up erecting false barriers because others with deep life struggles feel that we could never understand them. But our honesty opens the door for others to share openly with us. We begin to connect with each other in a way that is genuine and life-changing.

Mention homosexuality in a neutral context.

Those who struggle with this issue constantly have their "radar" on full alert, picking up the attitudes of those around them in regard to this subject. They remember unkind remarks and cutting jokes about gays for months or even years.

A married pastor who struggles with homosexual temptation relates, "Recently the music minister at my church made some comment to another man and held out his hand in the stereotypical limp-wristed fashion. They both laughed and I hurt inside. I consider myself a fairly masculine male. I play sports, work on cars and do house repairs. Yet I would never feel comfortable going to these two men in a time of need. They wouldn't understand me." Be careful not to offend those who may secretly struggle in this area. As Christians we are called to love others, not condemn them.

People who profess Christianity but who hold up signs at the gay parades like "AIDS is the cure for homosexuality" are not responding in true Christ-like love. Sometimes our judgmental attitude is less obvious. We know better than making a remark such as, "Get a load of those two faggots across the street!" But we may still project an attitude of hostility when we meet someone who has outward signs of being gay.

If you struggle with being judgmental (and all of us do at times), be honest with God. Become educated on the subject of homosexuality. As you gain understanding of the early life traumas which often lead to homosexual behavior, you will gain compassion for those caught in its trap.

Non-Christian Friends

Many of you have no doubt: Your friend *is* gay or lesbian. This person has talked about it with you or others. Now what?

The authors of this article are often asked, "How do you share Christ with a homosexual?" Our response: "The same way you share him with anyone else!" We make a mistake when we imagine that the person dealing with homosexuality needs to be approached with the claims of the Gospel in some totally unique way.

When we become aware of something "different" about other people, we can become uncomfortable and overly focused on that one area of their life. It's like talking to a man with a crooked nose—as much as we try, we cannot keep from looking at his nose! The same principle tends to operate when we are talking to homosexuals: We become consumed with their sexuality, forgetting that there are many other aspects of their lives which have nothing to do with same-sex inclinations.

Ideally, sharing the claims of the Gospel occurs in the context of an ongoing friendship. John Paulk likes to tell the story of his conversion. John was heavily involved in "drag" culture, performing on-stage and entering numerous beauty contests as a female impersonator. In the natural, he seemed an unlikely candidate for becoming a conservative Christian!

John worked as manager of an instant copy center on his college campus. On a regular basis, the man who led one of the campus Christian fellowships would bring in small copying jobs. John can remember what an impression this man made on him: "Tom always seemed so interested in *me* as an individual. He treated me differently from any of my other customers. I found myself looking forward to talking with him when he came in, even though I knew he led a Christian group on campus."

After several months of building a friendship, Tom asked if he could visit John at home. *Uh oh, he's going to talk to me about God,* John thought—but he was so curious that he agreed. Later, Tom visited his apartment and began talking about Jesus Christ.

After about twenty minutes, John stopped him. "I know all about the Gospel," he said. "I used to go to church when I was fifteen. But I was born gay, so forget it!"

"No, you weren't," Tom answered and read from the first chapter of Genesis: "And God created man ... male and female ... God saw all that he had made, and it was very good." That afternoon, after Tom showed him additional Bible passages, John became convinced that homosexuality was not something he was born with--or something that he had to stay in. That week he dug out his Bible and started to read it again. After wrestling with the decision for days, he knelt down beside his bed.

"God," he prayed, "I don't know how to get out of homosexuality, but I will follow you. No matter how difficult it gets, I'll never turn away from you again." Since that day in February 1987, John's life has changed dramatically. After several years of involvement in an ex-gay ministry in California, he fell in love with a woman in his church. He and his wife, a former lesbian, were married in July 1992 and now are involved in an ex-gay ministry in Portland, Oregon. John has had numerous opportunities to share his story with radio and television audiences across the country, giving hope about the reality of change that is possible through Jesus Christ.

Don't make homosexuality the primary point of your evangelistic conversations, but don't avoid the subject if it comes up. Most non-Christians know that the traditional biblical viewpoint condemns homosexual behavior. Gently explain that the Bible condemns *all* sexual behavior outside of heterosexual marriage, so the same standard applies to all single people, no matter to whom they are sexually attracted. If you're single, it can be helpful to share how God is helping you live up to this standard. If you are married, talk about the inappropriate attractions you have had to deal with—before and after your wedding day. Emphasize that God empowers us to obey him; we don't attain sexual purity on our own strength. If we desire to please the Lord, he will help us in our weakness (2 Cor 12:9,10).

Be very clear that God condemns homosexual behavior—but not homosexuals as people. A homosexual may wonder, "Does God hate me?" The answer is: "No. The Bible is clear that God has a deep love for everyone, including you [Jn 3:16, Rom 5:8, etc.]. It's because of his love that he prohibits sexual behavior which he knows will harm us."

If the subject of homosexuality does keep coming up, however, a helpful book to give your friend is *You Don't Have to be Gay* by Jeff Konrad. This book consists of a series of letters between a former homosexual and his gay friend who is seeking the truth. They discuss roots and causes of homosexuality, loneliness, the dynamics of gay relationships, and a multitude of other issues that your friend will probably be wondering about. The book is also excellent study material for you. Seeing how Jeff handled these topics will give you lots of ideas on how to discuss them with your friend. About halfway through the book, Jeff's friend becomes a Christian and the remainder shows how you can encourage a new believer who is dealing with homosexual issues.

Christian Friends Involved in Homosexuality

What about friends who profess to be Christian but who are actively involved in lesbianism or homosexuality—and defending their moral choices? Some of them may have once been part of your church, attempting to walk away from illicit same-sex relationships. But they grew tired of resisting the pull toward homosexual or lesbian behavior and now they have adopted a pro-gay theology. How should we respond?

Treat them as you would a heterosexual friend who is pursuing sex outside of marriage. You may know other friends from church who have discarded conservative moral values and now are pursuing sinful behaviors. If so, how do you relate to them? If not, picture yourself in this situation. What is an appropriate response?

In determining how to react, we have to take several factors into consideration. As believers, we want our relationship with Jesus Christ to impact others who have not yet discovered his reality in their lives. Yet we worry about being too lenient of sinful behavior in others. There are several possible responses. Some people totally ignore another person's morality. *Their private behavior is none of my business,* they reason. On the surface, this may seem like the most "loving" approach—but is it biblical? We think not. The Bible discusses our private behavior and even our thoughts at great length. It doesn't hesitate to give moral standards that we are commanded to obey. For example, the Apostle Paul commands Christians to "flee from sexual immorality" (1 Cor 6:18). The writers of the Scriptures did not hesitate to detail the moral failures of biblical figures and discuss how their behavior brought grief to God's heart. God loves us—but he does not overlook our moral choices.

Another possible reaction is shunning a Christian involved in homosexuality or lesbianism. Those who act this way usually quote such scriptures as "Therefore come out from them and be separate, says the Lord" (2 Cor 6:17) and Paul's instruction, "You must not associate with anyone who calls himself a brother but is sexually immoral" (1 Cor 5:11). Paul adds, "With such a man do not even eat." How do these verses apply to this situation?

Some Christians take these passages at face value—and avoid even speaking to a person who professes Christianity yet indulges in homosexual acts. To have an ongoing relationship of any kind, they reason, would imply approval of the friend's immorality. And other weaker Christians who see our friendship may wrongly think that homosexuality must be OK. Will our actions "stumble" or confuse others in the church?

Social isolation seems to contradict Jesus' behavior, however. He didn't shun people around him who lived contrary to his standards. He reached out to them—but confronted them about their behavior. "Neither do I condemn you," he told one adulterous woman. "Go now and leave your life of sin" (Jn 8:11). He attended social events with "sinners," much to the disdain of the Pharisees (Mt 9:11).

Other Christians interpret Paul's instructions to mean, "Do not have *ongoing* fellowship with someone who is sexually immoral." In the light of this interpretation, a periodic phone call is different from ongoing, regular communication. The main motive of the relationship is to be a redemptive influence, reminding that person of the truth and attempting to lead them to a place of repentance regarding their immoral behavior.

Here is how one man, Rob, found himself working through this situation: "James and I were close friends at one time. He had been in the church for several years when I first came, and he reached out to me with genuine friendship that was really encouraging. Soon we were getting together for hiking or other activities several times a month." When James disclosed his ongoing homosexual struggles, Rob found the fact surprising—but it didn't his interest in their friendship.

Then, about two years later, James decided to get an HIV test. He had fallen periodically into homosexual behavior and knew that he was at risk. Unfortunately his AIDS test came back positive. Over the next few months, he struggled with deep anger and disappointment. Why had God allowed him to get infected? He was making concerted efforts to stop his immoral behavior and was eagerly pursuing a closer relationship with the Lord. He had even served overseas for a one-year short-term missions project. And now this!

Soon afterward, James left the church and began spending time on weekends at gay bars in a nearby city. Months later, he called Rob and announced that he had "married" his male roommate in a gay church ceremony.

Rob was in a quandary. He had enjoyed a close friendship with James, but didn't agree with his homosexual involvement. Should he continue to see James or cut off the relationship? "I decided to back away somewhat," he explained. "If James would call, I'd certainly talk with him. However, I tried to focus our conversation on the positive things that God was doing in my life—the same kinds of discussions that we had enjoyed in the past."

Rob found that the "glue" of their relationship—their mutual faith—had been disrupted. Suddenly a major disagreement hung over the relationship and the dynamic of their friendship changed. "I know we both felt it," Rob observed. "He knew I strongly disagreed with his active homosexual involvement. And I noticed that, as he got pulled more and more into friendships with gay men, he lost interest in the spiritual things that our friendship had focused on in the past."

As James began exploring various New Age religions, their friendship became more distant. However, Rob always tried to leave the door open for future communication. "I never wanted to close the door totally on the relationship. I kept praying that, one day, James would become dissatisfied with the gay life and would turn back to the common faith we had previously shared." James waited until the final weeks of his life to abandon his New Age beliefs and reclaim Christianity. However, he never did renounce his homosexuality.

Even so, Rob was able to see James several times just prior to his death. They talked about eternity and James said he was ready to meet the Lord. They prayed together and James expressed deep appreciation for Rob's visits. "When the big crisis came," Rob said, "most of James' gay friends disappeared. It's almost like they couldn't face this last chapter of death and dying in his life. But I had the Lord to help me. I could 'be there' for James. I had earned the right to speak into his life at the end because I

had maintained the relationship." When Rob saw James for the final time, he was slipping into unconsciousness. Within several days, James was dead.

Rob says that seeking to maintain balance in such a relationship is difficult, and something that should be prayed about regularly. "I think there is a fine line between staying in touch for the sake of being a witness, and compromising by maintaining the friendship as if you're in agreement with that person's behavior. I'm glad that several of us from church stayed in periodic contact with James, as I believe it paved the way for him to return to Christ in his final days. But, at the same time, I couldn't remain in a close friendship with him and pretend that nothing was wrong with his homosexual relationships. It wasn't easy or always clear to me, but I tried to maintain a balance. I think God honored my efforts."

Rob says that one important question helped him evaluate his relationship with James: *What is the spiritual impact of this relationship?* Rob tried to discern the results of their times together. Was their interaction pushing him away from Christ—or pulling James toward Christ? Quite frankly, sometimes it wasn't easy to tell. One night James wanted to talk about how wonderful it was to finally engage in gay sex after repressing his feelings for many years. He wasn't open to considering what the Bible had to say about sex before marriage—whether with a same-sex or opposite-sex partner. Rob went home feeling like the evening had been a waste of time.

Another night, James seemed more reflective than usual. He had "married" his lover and they had entered into a lifelong relationship--only to find themselves splitting up seven months later because they couldn't agree which part of the city to live in. Rob found that James was much more open to talking about spiritual things that night, including an evaluation of whether homosexual relationships were really God's best for us.

Rob did not hesitate to seek input from his other friends and church leaders on how to best spend his time with James. Although he probably made some mistakes, Rob felt satisfied that he had played a significant role in James's life—with eternal consequences. There are no hard-and-fast rules for this type of situation. Pray for God's guidance, as Rob did. And pray that you will have positive spiritual input into your friend's life.

Another woman observes, "When I run into someone who has been part of our church and I know they have left the Lord, we usually have a warm interchange. These men and women are dear to me. Several of them are involved in immoral relationships, but usually I don't say anything about their lifestyle choices. I just pray that seeing me and sensing my love will be a reminder of good things they have left behind."

If your friend is open to discussing the biblical perspective on homosexuality, we recommend that you become acquainted with the principles behind the pro-gay theology. For a quick "crash course" on the basics, we recommend appendix A in the back of *Coming Out of Homosexuality* by Bob Davies and Lori Rentzel (InterVarsity Press, 1993). For a more in-depth treatment—and a book which would be excellent to share with any active gay or lesbian friend who claims to be a Christian—we recommend *Straight and Narrow?* by Thomas Schmidt (InterVarsity Press, 1995).

As your friendship progresses, you may be faced with many of the same questions that parents ask about their gay children: What about inviting your friend's lover to dinner? What boundaries should you place on seeing them together? and so on. For further guidance on these types of situations, see the relevant sections of Chapter 8 in our book, *Someone I Love Is Gay: How Family & Friends Can Respond* (InterVarsity Press, 1996).

Supporting Ex-Gay Friends

Now let's discuss the situation where your friend is seeking help in dealing with his or her homosexuality. Do you have anything to offer, even though you have never struggled with this issue? Yes, you do! But, depending on the genders of you and your friend, your friendship has special opportunities and also potential problems. First, we will examine the dynamics of same-sex supportive friendships.

Female Friend Helping a Female Struggler

Being accepted by a female straight friend is very healing for an ex-gay woman. Many lesbians are struggling with rejection issues at the deep level of their sexual identity or sense of womanhood. You can show God's love through your actions and words. Typically, these women feel an intense need for same-sex approval and emotional bonding with other women. You can provide a godly example of a non-sexual friendship.

Many years ago while my husband was out of town, I (Anita) spent a Saturday night at Patty's house so we could attend her church together the next morning. I was a little uncomfortable because Patty was fairly new out of the lesbian life, but soon we were chatting together and having a great time.

As we were getting ready for church the next morning, I noticed that, although Patty was very attractive, she could benefit from a little blush and lipstick. But did I dare suggest it? Would she think I was being critical of her looks, or trying to change her in an outward, artificial way? After a minute's thought, I realized that I would share make-up tips with any other friend, so why not Patty too? "Do you want to try this light lipstick?" I asked, and she was eager to try it. She liked the result and we went off to church. The next time I saw her, she couldn't wait to show me her "new" look. Patty had visited a make-up counter at a department store and looked great—except for the bulging pockets of her blazer. She saw me looking at her pockets and explained, "These are the things that lady at the store said I have to carry with me." A frown crossed her face as she thought for a moment. "I guess I will have to start carrying a purse!" Just a little encouragement at the right time can have quite an impact in your friend's life. (Today, many years later, Patty and I have a great friendship; I rarely think about her lesbian background.)

You can help your friend break old patterns of relating, such as manipulation, self-pity and selfish emotional demands, by remaining constant and faithful. You can also hold her accountable for her end of the relationship, challenging her to develop mutuality rather than dependency.

But there are special cautions for this situation. Some "straight" women fall into a lesbian relationship with another woman seeking help. Even women with no previous history of lesbianism—but who are emotionally needy—have experienced strong lesbian feelings in the midst of these types of friendships.

We cannot be naive in this regard. Same-sex attraction between women is based on a genuine God-given need for intimacy that has been twisted. We all have a need for love. God made us social beings and it is common for women to find a deep satisfaction in forming significant friendships with other women. If these same-sex needs are currently unmet, even "straight" women can find themselves drawn into inappropriate relationships.

The fall into lesbianism can be *very* subtle, starting with an exaggerated emotional need to be with the other person. One of the major danger signs that this relationship has taken a bad turn is the presence of jealousy and possessiveness. Your lesbian friend feels insecure and you need to increasingly reassure her of your commitment to the friendship. Some feelings of jealousy are common. But when they begin to control the relationship, it's time for an evaluation, perhaps with the help of a counselor or spiritual advisor.

Another danger sign is feeling overly responsible for your friend's feelings. You may begin to be consumed with making your friend happy, taking on a responsibility that God never gave you. Overall, this relationship becomes hard work as you do more and more to assure your friend of your unconditional love. Beware of the "just us" mentality. A healthy friendship is not exclusive. It welcomes others into its company. And a healthy relationship is flexible. If a luncheon date or night out together is canceled now and then, it's disappointing but not crushing. The person who cancels should not be made to feel guilty. Emotionally dependent relationships are marked by a clinging possessiveness, not wanting to let go at any time, even though the reasons for being apart are fully understandable.

Make sure that you maintain other close friendships. They are an important safeguard to keep your relationships in balance. Encourage your friend to pursue other friendships, too. Do not believe for one moment that you are the only one who can *really* help her! It will help to spend time with your friend in a group setting. Invite others out to lunch with the two of you. Get involved in church groups where you interact with others. These safeguards will help avoid the exclusivity which can lead to an emotional dependency.

Women coming from a lesbian background may have fallen into overly-dependent relationships because they don't know proper boundaries in a healthy friendship. I was counseling Martha one day on this subject. She had phoned me and asked me out to lunch. Soon we were sitting at an outside restaurant on a beautiful sunny day.

Martha seemed somewhat preoccupied as we started our meal. I asked her what was wrong, and she looked up at me. "Anita," she asked, "do you think two greeting cards and a phone call are too much in one week?" I started laughing—realizing that I tended to have the same problem in my relationships—and she joined in. Then her face grew sober again. "You know...with Sarah. I value our relationship, but I don't know what is normal."

Martha and Sarah were both coming out of a lesbian past, and they had become emotionally dependent on each other during the past year. Now they were trying to find a balance in their relationship. I was encouraged that Martha could be so vulnerable with me, and I weighed my words carefully. "Yes, I think that two cards and a phone call are a little excessive in one week, unless there is a special reason for it." She didn't look too pleased at my response. I continued, "Think about your relationship with Betty from church. You two are close, aren't you?" When she quickly agreed, I asked, "How much contact do you have with her in a week?"

Martha thought a moment before answering. "I guess we talk about once a week and I send her a card on special occasions or if she needs a little extra encouragement." She couldn't hide her disappointment as she asked, "I guess that's what is normal for friends?" I nodded, and then we both smiled. Even though it was hard, Martha was learning healthy patterns in relating to other women. She persevered in the following months, continuing to interact in a healthy way with Sarah. Today, over five years later, they live in different parts of the country but have a good friendship and still keep in touch periodically.

Male Friend Helping a Male Struggler

Most male homosexuals have suffered a deprivation of same-sex bonding in their early lives. They are eager to have approval from other men. So you have a special opportunity to build confidence in your friend's life through your acceptance of him as another man. You can help him by being vulnerable about your own life, discussing your weaknesses and fears as well as your strengths. This openness helps him realize that many of his problems are the same as any man's. Not all his struggles are "gay" issues.

Become a prayer partner and invite mutual accountability. Your friend needs someone to offer support during times of sexual temptation. If you have had problems with heterosexual immorality in the past, you have much to offer your friend in terms of practical insights into the battle against lust. Most men struggle with visual temptation. Whatever spiritual strategies have worked for you will also be effective against your friend's homosexual lust. Enlist his prayer support in your areas of weakness, too.

Be willing to hear some of the nitty-gritty details of your friend's struggles (he shouldn't have to be afraid to say the word "masturbation" in your presence, for example), but there is a difference between being honest and being graphic. Details of his past sexual exploits are unnecessary. He can be informative without burdening you with inappropriate details of specific people, places and sexual acts.

You will also have to be honest in letting him know how much specific detail you can handle about his current struggles. For example, if knowing his attraction to a mutual friend is too burdensome for you, he needs to know that. He can keep you abreast of his struggles without giving specific names. He needs to know your limits in other areas too, so that he does not cause you to sin by stirring up sexual fantasies in your own mind.

You may be surprised to discover how many current or past struggles in your life match those of your friend. His homosexuality is not really a sexual problem—it is merely the surface symptom of deeper root issues which need healing. The roots of homosexuality are mainly emotional, and center on issues like envy (I'm not as masculine/secure/aggressive as other men), rejection (I've never felt really loved), loneliness (nobody would love me if they knew the real me), and deception (I'll never amount to anything). Do any of these sound familiar? Of course they do—many of these feelings and thoughts plague all of us to varying degrees. So you can share with your friend that these issues are not "gay," they are universal. And you can share how God has helped you deal with comparable struggles in your own life.

Your friend may become too dependent upon you. He may become too demanding of your time. In a few cases, he may even confess sexual attraction toward you or feelings of "falling in love" with you. Lots of straight men run for the hills at this point, which confirms to your friend that he's a complete failure and will never form a healthy friendship.

Running away is not God's best solution to this awkward situation. This is an important time in your relationship and an opportunity for you to make right decisions which will impact your friend's life in a major way. The answer is not to flee but to establish appropriate boundaries. Let's look at some specific guidelines.

First of all, if a dependency develops, do not ignore the signals that he is becoming demanding of you. You need to stand firm and gently confront him. You might say something like this: "Chuck, I can't be there for you all the time. Only God can. I am still your friend but I feel that you are becoming too dependent on our friendship." So be honest in your communication with him; don't dodge the issue in the hope that the emotional dependency will somehow resolve itself on its own.

Second, your friend may need some basic education about the dynamics of male relationships in our culture. In a nutshell, men tend to bond in groups while doing activities together. Your friend may have unrealistic expectations about an intense one-on-one friendship with you. Perhaps this is the pattern he experienced in gay relationships, but that is atypical in heterosexual culture. He needs to understand that reality so he will not feel rejected when you begin inviting him along on group activities, rather than just spending time alone with him.

The safety of a group dynamic is especially important if he is being pulled sexually or emotionally toward you in wrong ways. He needs to be drawn into other male-male relationships and you might have to set some clear boundaries on the time you spend with him. Don't retreat entirely, but seek balance in your friendship by limiting your time alone with him. Welcome him into group activities by inviting him along when you and your buddies attend a ball game or church retreat. You can become his "bridge" to forming significant relationships with other straight men.

Finally, do not push your friend into premature dating. This may seem like a logical answer to his friendship needs, but this is the last thing he needs if he is just beginning the process of emotional healing. Until he becomes secure in his masculinity through forming right relationships with other men, he is not ready to tackle an opposite-sex romance. Now we will look at the situation where you are helping a gay friend of the opposite sex.

Male Friend Helping a Female Struggler

Women who struggle with same-sex attractions often have a distorted view of men. Your friendship can be very healing in this regard. Show her respect and let her get to know you as a brother. She needs to know that you are not expecting anything romantic or sexual from this relationship.

In our experience, the vast majority of women dealing with lesbianism have been sexually abused. Often they have a fear and even hatred of men because of deep emotional wounding. Your friend may have many fears lurking behind her friendly facade.

Give her time to establish trust in your relationship. For example, one woman declined a ride home after Bible study because she would be alone with a man she didn't know well. Unknown to him, she had been raped as an older teen. Respect her boundaries and don't get offended if she says "no" to what you consider a kind offer.

Similarly, because many ex-gay women are dealing with abuse issues, be sensitive to her body cues regarding affection. Even if you are in a church where hugging is common, your friend may not appreciate you taking the initiative in expressing such familiarity with her. Watch how she interacts with other men in the church for guidance on how to relate with her.

Lesbians often struggle with control. They tend to dominate in order to avoid "losing control" and therefore risk being victimized again. Equality is the key to a comfortable relationship in this situation.

Be careful to avoid a "buddy" relationship. Lesbians are often comfortable relating to men in this fashion but your friend is seeking to overcome past patterns. Remind yourself that she is a female and needs to be treated with appropriate respect.

Beware of premature romantic involvement if your friend is just beginning the process of overcoming her lesbian background. Sometimes a woman will become emotionally entangled with a male friend who seems "safe." If you see this occurring, don't pull away totally but seek to establish healthy boundaries in the relationship. You may want to become accountable to a mature Christian friend.

It is possible that you will feel romantically or sexually attracted to your friend. If she is just beginning her healing process, assume that she is *not* at all interested. In fact, your attractions could be her greatest nightmare come true. It is nothing personal, just that you are male. If she has been abused by men, she has struggled for years with thoughts like *I'll never trust a man again* and *Men are only interested in one thing.* Don't confirm those messages. She may have her guard down. You are a Christian and a "safe" friend. If you begin to pursue a premature romance, the relationship will quickly crumble when she realizes what is occurring. And her healing process will be badly derailed. Your friend can never enter into a successful heterosexual romance until she has resolved her lesbian issues. Both of you will be badly wounded if you enter into a premature emotional involvement.

Female Friend Helping a Male Struggler

It is common for men struggling with homosexual issues to confess their secret to a woman. Often these men have had a closer relationship with their mother than with Dad, so they find it easy to confide in a female friend.

Seek to maintain the relationship as equals; resist the tendency to become a rescuer or substitute parent figure.

Your friend needs to grow up. Many male homosexuals resist facing the realities of adult manhood. Don't keep him in a "little boy" syndrome by taking responsibility for his life.

Don't shield him from the consequences of his bad choices. Many gay men are masters at blame-shifting; their problems are the fault of everyone else but themselves. Don't allow your friend to manipulate you into thinking that he is always the victim and you need to rescue him.

Encourage his friendships with other men. This is one of the most important things you can do. Often, gay men have felt separated from other men as they grow up; they fear other men and feel insecure around them. They have attempted to bond with men through sexual relationships. Now they must learn to bond emotionally through appropriate activities which may seem foreign to them. Typically, gay men feel very comfortable around women and may even enter into "woman talk" about make-up and current female fashions. Affirm his masculinity by resisting this kind of interaction.

If you are a sports enthusiast or enjoy other activities which attract male participation in our culture, so much the better. Engage in these activities with your friend, so he can move a step closer to enjoying them with his male friends as well. For example, if your friend is a novice at tennis but you are accomplished, offer to give him a few lessons. He will find it much less threatening to learn from you than another man (vast numbers of gays have been ridiculed in their youth by male peers for being athletically-challenged!). Perhaps you and your friend can invite along other people from church to enjoy a hike or ball game with you. Including others in your activities can be a good safeguard for you, too.

Too often, women in these types of relationships begin to become romantically inclined toward the man. They begin to hope that this platonic relationship could develop into a romance. Unless the man has had considerable time to move forward in his healing process, such a hope will only lead to hurt and disappointment. Typically, the ex-gay man will "turn tail and run" when he senses even a hint of romantic interest on your part. The relationship will quickly become strained and probably break apart.

So enjoy your friendship but realize your limitations. You are a woman and your friend will find his primary source of healing through appropriate emotional intimacy with other men. Keep your relationship with him in balance by spending quality time with other men and women, and you will be an important part of his support system in finding emotional wholeness and spiritual maturity.

[Reprinted from *Someone I Love Is Gay: How Family & Friends Can Respond* by Anita Worthen and Bob Davies © 1996 by Anita Worthen and Bob Davies. Used by permission of InterVarsity Press, P.O. Box 1400, Downers Grove, IL 60515.]

Anita Worthen has been involved with ministry to family members and friends for over 12 years. She and her husband, Frank, one of the founders of the ex-gay movement, have spoken about homosexual ministry on four continents. They work together at New Hope Ministries in San Rafael, California.

Bob Davies is executive director of Exodus International North America, a network of agencies for men and women seeking freedom from homosexuality. He is also the coauthor of *Coming Out of Homosexuality* (InterVarsity Press, 1993). He and his wife, Pam, live in Seattle, Washington.

Exodus International Referral Ministry List

September 1996

This referral list is updated regularly. Applications for referral status in Exodus are available from our headquarters office. *Qualifications for Referral Ministries:* Agreement with Exodus doctrine and policy; in existence at least two years; has a policy-making board or governing body with the power to remove or change leadership. The ministry director has been free from immoral sexual behavior for at least two years; attends a national Exodus conference at least once every three years; and is active in a local church and has spiritual accountability there.

Each entry gives the ministry name, address, phone, and director. It lists people the ministry is equipped to help, which may include any of the following (abbreviations listed in parentheses after group name) men overcoming homosexuality ["men"], women overcoming homosexuality ["women"], family/friends, spouses, adolescent ["adol."] females and males, children of gay parents, clergy with sexual issues ["clergy"], hearing impaired persons ["hearing impaired"], HIV+ persons ["HIV+"], pedophiles, female and male survivors of sexual abuse, heterosexual and homosexual sexual addicts, transsexuals, and transvestites. Each entry also lists services available in four categories: support, resources, other (e.g., Bible studies, live-in programs, speaking engagements), and foreign language ministry. Contact ministries directly for further details on services they offer. Branch offices and out-of-state groups of a referral list only the phone of the headquarter ministry; call them for details of services available.

Other abbreviations and terms: "lay consult." = individual consultation with a lay minister; "library" = a lending and/or reference library is available; "lic./prof." = licensed/professional counseling. Letter support is general–unless specifies willing to correspond with prisoners/sex offenders–and may be for a limited only. "Living Waters" is a structured, small group program for addressing issues surrounding sexual brokenness.

Miscellaneous: If a ministry is listed as offering several kinds of groups in several locations, not necessarily each type of group is offered in each location. Most ministries have phone message machines, and some ministries will *only* return long-distance phone calls if you specify they may call you back collect. Ministries may not answer their phones during lunch hour. Also, phone support may require your making an appointment, and letter support may be for a limited time only. Ministry fax number, if any, is listed at the end of the entry.

NORTH AMERICA

ALABAMA

Nikon Counseling, PO Box 19631, Birmingham, AL 35219. 205/978-5355 (M-F/10-5). Tom Nelson. Serves: men, women, family/friends, spouses, adol. (men), clergy, sexual abuse surv. (men, women), sexual addicts (heterosexual, homosexual). Support: lay consult. Other: seminars, speaking engagements.

ARIZONA

His Image, PO Box 642, Peoria, AZ 85380. 602/259–7226 (8 AM-8 PM/voice mail). John Butler. Serves: men, family/friends, spouses, HIV+. Support: groups—Phoenix (men, wives), lay consult., letter (general), Living Waters (men), phone (spontaneously 8 AM-8 PM daily—we return voice mail calls as soon as possible). Resources: audiotapes, newsletter. Other: semi-nars, speaking engagements.

ARKANSAS

Sanctuary, c/o Christian Life Cathedral, 1285 Millsap Rd., Fayetteville, AR 72703. 501/521–5683 (M-F/8–5 church office). Johnny Moore. Serves: men, sexual abuse surv. (men), sexual addicts (heterosexual, homosexual). Support: lay consult., letter (general), Living Waters (men), other (pastoral counseling and professional referrals available). Other: Bible studies. Fax: 501/521-8198.

CALIFORNIA
Southern California
Desert Stream, PO Box 17635, Anaheim, CA 92817-7635.

Phone: 714/779-6899 (M-F/1-5). Andrew Comiskey. Serves: men, women, adol. (men, women), clergy, HIV+, pedophiles, sexual abuse surv. (men, women), sexual addicts (heterosexual, homosexual), others (heterosexual sexual/relational brokenness). Support: groups (soaking prayer for ministry leaders; HIV/AIDS), lay consult., Living Waters (men, women), letter (general), phone (M-F/1-5). Resources: audiotapes, literature, newsletter, videotapes. Other: HIV/AIDS ministry, Living Waters Leadership Training, Pursuing Relational Wholeness conferences, seminars, speaking engagements. Fax: 714/701-1880.

Journey Christian Ministries, 30713 Riverside Dr. Ste. 203, Lake Elsinore, CA 92530. 310/798-8284 or 909/245-2402 (M-Sat). Pastor Andria Sigler. *Contact for details of services available.*

Thomas Aquinas Psychological Clinic, 16542 Ventura Blvd. #416, Encino, CA 91436. 818/789-4440. Joseph Nicolosi, Ph.D. Serves: men, family/friends, spouses, adol. (men), children of gay parents, clergy, HIV+, pedophiles, sexual abuse surv. (men), sexual addicts (heterosexual, homosexual). Support: group (men), lay consult., lic./prof. Resources: literature. Other: seminars, speaking engagements. Fax: 805/373-5084.

Sacramento Area
HIS Ministry, c/o Sunrise Baptist Church, 8321 Greenback Ln., Fair Oaks, CA 95628-2699 (Sacramento area). 916/969-3929 (M-F/8-5). Carl Conli. Serves: men, family/friends, spouses, adol. (men). Support: groups (men, wives, parents/family), lay consult. Fax: 916/726-7580.

San Francisco Bay Area
Apokata Psychological Services, 220 Montgomery St. Ste. 1098, San Francisco, CA 94104; 1357 Mowry Ave., Fremont, CA 94538-1701. 415/421-6848 (San Francisco: M, Tu); 510/475-1475 (Fremont: W, F). Melvin W. Wong, Ph.D. Serves: men, women, family/friends, spouses, adol. (men, women), children of gay parents, clergy, HIV+, pedophiles, sexual abuse surv. (men, women), sexual addicts (heterosexual, homosexual), transsexuals, transvestites, other (forensic evaluations and testimonies; expert witness; neuropsychology). Support: lic./prof. Other: seminars, speaking engagements, cultural competency in counseling African Americans, developing ministry in Hong Kong. Languages: Chinese (Cantonese, Mandarin). Fax: 510/475-1473.

Love In Action. *This ministry has relocated; see entry under Tennessee.*

New Hope Charitable Foundation, PO Box 10246, San Rafael, CA 94912-0246. 415/453-6475 (M-F/9-5). W. Frank Worthen. Serves: men, women, family/friends, spouses, children of gay parents, clergy, HIV+, sexual abuse surv. (men, women), sexual addicts (homosexual). Support: groups (men), lay consult., letter (general), lic./prof., phone. Resources: literature, newsletter. Other: live-in program (men), seminars, speaking engagements. Fax: 415/455-9758.

NEW [Nurturing and Encouraging to Wholeness] Ministries, PO Box 3288, San Leandro, CA 94578. 510/728-9300 (voice mail). Mark Gebhardt. Serves: men, women, family/friends. Support: groups (men, women, parents/family), letter (general, prisoners/sex offenders). Other: speaking engagements.

Transformed Image, PO Box 18055, San Jose, CA 95118. 408/496-9888 (M-F/9-4). Pastor Michael Dismore. Serves: men, women, family/friends, spouses, hearing impaired individuals, HIV+, sexual addicts (heterosexual, homosexual). Support: groups (men, women), lay consult., letter (general), phone (by appointment). Resources: audiotapes, literature, videotapes. Other: evangelism, seminars, speaking engagements.
Other Areas

New Creation Ministries, 2513 W. Shaw Ave. #102–A, Fresno, CA 93711. 209/227-1066 (M-F/9-4). Bud Searcy. Serves: men, women, family/friends, spouses, adol. (men, women), clergy (including seminarians/ministry candidates with sexual issues), sexual addicts (heterosexual, homosexual). Support: groups (men, women, wives, other—clergy), lay consult., letter (general), phone. Resources: literature, newsletter. Other: seminars, speaking engagements, other (consultations with pastors/leaders on Transforming Congregations). Fax: 209/227-4182.

COLORADO
Janelle M. Hallman. M.A., 6475 Wadsworth Blvd. #104, Arvada, CO 80003. 303/273-2877 (voice mail). Serves: men, women, family/friends, spouses, adol. (men, women), children of gay parents, sexual abuse surv. (women), sexual addicts (heterosexual, homosexual). Support: lic./prof. Other: seminars, speaking engagements.

His Heart, 12162 E. Mississippi Ave., Box 12321, Aurora, CO 80012. 303/369-2961. Rev. Shaun McDonald. Serves: men, family/friends, spouses, adol. (men), clergy, HIV+, sexual addicts (homosexual). Support: group—Aurora (men), lay consult., letter (general), lic./prof. Resources: audiotapes, literature. Other: HIV/AIDS ministry, speaking engagements.

Where Grace Abounds, PO Box 18871, Denver, CO 80218-0871. 303/863-7757 (Tu-F/10-5). Mary Heathman. Serves: men, women, family/friends, spouses, clergy, HIV+, sexual abuse surv. (men, women), sexual addicts (heterosexual, homosexual), transsexuals, transvestites. Support: groups (men, women, parents/family, other [growth group; survivors of abuse for men and women]); lay consult., letter (general, prisoners/sex offenders), lic./prof., phone (by appointment only). Resources: audiotapes, literature, newsletter. Other: seminars, speaking engagements. Fax: call first.

CONNECTICUT
HOPE Ministries of Connecticut, Box 604, 60 Skiff St., Hamden, CT 06517. 203/248-5274. Dr. Bill Consiglio. Serves: men, family/friends, spouses, adol. (men), clergy, sexual abuse surv. (men), sexual addicts (heterosexual, homosexual), transvestites. Support: groups (men), lay consult., lic./prof., phone. Other: seminars, speaking engagements. Branches: Springfield, MA. Fax: 203/287-1562.

Shoreline Christian Counseling, 45 Durham Rd. Ste. 10, Madison, CT 06443. 203/318-0700 (M-Th/10:30-5). Tom Ruotolo. Serves: men, women, family/friends, spouses, adol. (men, women), clergy, hearing impaired individuals, sexual abuse surv. (men, women), sexual addicts (heterosexual, homosexual). Support: lic./prof. Resources: newsletter. Other: seminars, speaking engagements. Fax: 203/318-0701.

FLORIDA

Betach Ministries, Inc., PO Box 6455, Callaway, FL 32404 (Panama City area). 904/271-4069 (24 hours). Bob and Kathy Fisher. Serves: men, women, family/friends, spouses, clergy, HIV+, sexual abuse surv. (men, women), sexual addicts (heterosexual, homosexual), transsexuals, transvestites. Support: groups—Panama City (men, parents/family, HIV/AIDS), lay consult., letter (general), phone. Resources: books, literature, newsletter. Other: Bible studies, HIV/AIDS ministry, seminars, speaking engagements.

Eleutheros, Inc., 1298 Minnesota Ave. Ste. D, Winter Park, FL 32789-7114 (Orlando area). 407/629-5770 (M-F/8-5). Michael H. Barber. Serves: men, women, family/friends, spouses, adol. (men, women), children of gay parents, clergy, hearing impaired, pedophiles, sexual abuse surv. (men, women), sexual addicts (heterosexual, homosexual), transsexuals, transvestites. Support: groups (men, women, parents/family, wives, HIV/AIDS, other [sexually addicted men; Search for Significance; leadership]), lay consult., letter (general, prisoners/sex offenders), lic./prof., Living Waters (men, women). Resources: audiotapes, literature, newsletter, videotapes. Other: HIV/AIDS ministry, seminars, speaking engagements.

Straight Ahead Ministries, PO Box 16889, Temple Terrace, FL 33687 (Tampa area). 813/985-8891 (M-F/10-4). Greg Lewis. Serves: men, women, family/friends, spouses. Support: groups—Clearwater, Tampa (men, women, wives, parents/family), Living Waters (men). Other: seminars, speaking engagements.

Worthy Creations, 3601 Davie Blvd., Ft. Lauderdale, FL 33312. 954/680-3538 (M-F/10-4). Richard Culbertson. Serves: men, women, family/friends, spouses, children of gay parents, clergy, HIV+, pedophiles, sexual abuse surv. (men, women), sexual addicts (homosexual). Support: groups—Ft. Lauderdale, Miami, West Palm Beach (men, women, parents/family, HIV/AIDS), lay consult., letter (prisoners/sex offenders), lic./prof., Living Waters (men). Resources: audiotapes, literature. Other: HIV/AIDS ministry, seminars, speaking engagements. Fax: 305/791-8226.

GEORGIA

Living Stones Fellowship, c/o Mt. Paran Church of God, 2055 Mt. Paran Rd. NW, Atlanta, GA 30327. 404/261–0720, extension 280 (M-F/8-5). John A. Barber and Wynema B. Barber. Serves: men, women, family/friends, spouses, adol. (men), clergy, sexual addicts (heterosexual, homosexual). Support: groups (men, wives), lay consult., phone (by appointment after initial screening).

Pneumatikos, PO Box 6808, Macon, GA 31208. 912/825–0102 (M-Th/7 PM-9 PM; F-Sun/all day). Randy L. Hortman.

Serves: men, women, family/friends, spouses, HIV+. Support: group (men), lay consult., letter (general, prisoners/sex offenders), lic./prof. (referrals), phone. Resources: newsletter. Other: speaking engagements, other (prison support groups).

Resurrection Life Ministries, PO Box 95205, Atlanta, GA 30347. 404/636-5924 (M-F/9-5). Mike Caven. Serves: men, women, family/friends, spouses, adol. (men, women), children of gay parents, clergy, HIV+, sexual abuse surv. (men, women), sexual addicts (heterosexual, homosexual), transsexuals, transvestites. Support: groups (men, parents/family, HIV/AIDS), lay consult., letter (general, prisoners/sex offenders), Living Waters (men, women), phone. Resources: newsletter. Other: Bible studies, evangelism, HIV/AIDS ministry, seminars, speaking engagements. Fax: 404/636-1211.

HAWAII

New Creation Ministries/He Kanaka Hou, PO Box 61337, Honolulu, HI 96839-1337. 808/261-7008. Jonathan Cuneo. Serves: men, women, family/friends, clergy, HIV+. Support: groups (men), lay consult., letter (general, prisoners/sex offenders), Living Waters (men), phone (by appointment). Other: Bible studies, seminars, speaking engagements. Languages: Chinese (Cantonese, Mandarin). Fax: 808/262-8724.

IDAHO

Bellwether Ministries, PO Box 15766, Boise, ID 83715-5766. 208/345-7994 (M-F/6 PM-10 PM; Sat. 10-6). Sharon Slocum. Serves: men, women, clergy, HIV+, sexual addicts (homosexual). Support: groups (men), lay consult., Living Waters (men, women), phone. Resources: audiotapes, newsletter. Other: seminars, speaking engagements. Fax: 208/343-4993.

ILLINOIS

Transformed By Grace, PO Box 6237, Evanston, IL 60204-6237. 847/733-0511 (8-3). Douglas and Melanie Geyer. Serves: men, women, family/friends, sexual addicts (heterosexual, homosexual). Support: groups—Evanston, Oakbrook, Wheaton (combined men and women overcoming homosexuality, parents/family, other—sexual addiction), lay consult.; letter (general). Resources: audiotapes, literature, newsletter. Other: seminars, speaking engagements.

For details on a Peoria, IL, branch office, contact Broken Yoke Ministries in Pewaukee, WI (414/896-0841).

IOWA

Freedom Ministries, PO Box 12189, Des Moines, IA 50312-9404. 515/244-8073 (M, W/9-3). Jack Morlan. Serves: men, women, clergy, sexual addicts (heterosexual, homosexual). Support: groups (men, women, wives), Living Waters (men, women). Resources: literature. Other: speaking engagements. Fax: 515/243-2958.

KANSAS

Freedom At Last, PO Box 13314, Wichita, KS 67213. 316/945-7050 (M-F/8-5). Michael S. Babb. Serves: men, women, family/friends, spouses, adol. (men, women), children of gay parents, clergy, hearing impaired individuals, HIV+, pedophiles, sexual abuse surv. (men, women), sexual addicts (heterosexual, homosexual), transsexuals, transvestites. Support: groups (men, women, parents/family, wives), lay consult., letter (general, prisoners/sex offenders), Living Waters (men, women), phone. Resources: literature, newsletter. Other: Bible studies, evangelism, HIV/AIDS ministry, live-in programs (men, women), seminars, speaking engagements. Fax: 316/946-9966.

Second Chance Ministry, Inc., PO Box 12265, Overland Park, KS 66282–2265 (Kansas City area). 913/381-4253 (M-F/12-5). Pat Smith. Serves: men, women, family/friends, spouses, sexual abuse surv. (men, women), sexual addicts (homosexual). Support: groups (men, women), lay consult., Living Waters (men, women). Resources: audiotapes. Other: Bible studies, seminars, speaking engagements.

KENTUCKY
CrossOver, Inc., PO Box 23744, Lexington, KY 40523. 606/277-4941 (M-F/8 AM-10 PM). Rev. Jerry Leach. Serves: men, women, family/friends, spouses, adol. (men, women), clergy, hearing impaired individuals, sexual abuse surv. (men, women), sexual addicts (heterosexual, homosexual), transsexuals, transvestites, other (addiction to pornography). Support: groups (men, women, parents/family, wives, transsexuals and transvestites), lay consult., letter (general), lic./prof., phone. Resources: audiotapes, literature, newsletter. (Reality is a monthly newsletter for those with transgender issues.) Other: Bible studies, live-in programs (men, women; homosexuality and/or transgender issues), seminars, speaking engagements. Languages: German. Fax: 606/278-9721.

Pathway Ministries, PO Box 9404, Louisville, KY 40209–0404. Martin K. Ward. Serves: men, family/friends, spouses, adol. (men), clergy, sexual abuse surv. (men), sexual addicts (heterosexual, homosexual). Support: groups (men, parents/family), lay consult., letter, phone (appointment only). Resources: literature, newsletter. Other: seminars, speaking engagements.

MAINE
Amazing Grace, PO Box 8234, Portland, ME 04104. 207/879-2554. Jane Boyer. Serves: men, women, clergy, HIV+, pedophiles, sexual addicts (heterosexual, homosexual), transsexuals, transvestites. Support: lay consult., letter (general, prisoners/sex offenders), lic./prof. (referrals), Living Waters (men, women), phone. Resources: newsletter. Other: seminars, speaking engagements, other (media interviews).

Crown of Life Ministry, PO Box 11404, Portland, ME 04104. 207/772-7626. Rev. Edgar M. Bailey. Serves: men, family/friends, spouses, sexual abuse surv. (men), sexual addicts (homosexual), transsexuals, transvestites. Support: group—South Portland (men), lay consult., lic./prof., phone. Resources: audiotapes, literature. Other: seminars, speaking engagements.

MARYLAND
Regeneration, PO Box 9830, Baltimore, MD 21284. 410/661-0284 (M-F/9:30-noon; 1-5). Regeneration Books information line: 410/661-4337. Alan Medinger. Serves: men, women, family/friends, spouses, children of gay parents, clergy, pedophiles,

sexual addicts (heterosexual, homosexual), transsexuals, transvestites. Support: groups—Baltimore, MD; Silver Spring, MD; Charlottesville, VA (men, women, parents/family, wives, other [New Directions 21-week program for men and women overcoming homosexuality; New Beginnings for men with heterosexual compulsion problems]), lay consult., letter (general). Resources: catalog of books for sale, literature, newsletter, New Directions program is available to other ministries. Other: seminars, speaking engagements. Fax: 410/882-6312.

MASSACHUSETTS
Transformation Ministries, PO Box 1313 Back Bay Annex, Boston, MA 02117. 617/445-1787. Peter Robicheau. Serves: men, women, family/friends, spouses, adol. (men), clergy, sexual abuse surv. (men), sexual addicts (heterosexual, homosexual). Support: group (men, women), lay consult., letter (general, prisoners/sex offenders), phone. Resources: literature, newsletter. Other: evangelism, seminars, speaking engagements.

For details on a Springfield, MA, branch office, contact HOPE Ministries in Hamden, CT (203/248-5274).

MICHIGAN
Jericho Ministries, PO Box 224, Oshtemo, MI 49077-0224. 616/375-7354 (answering machine). Rev. Regina Carl, S.W. Serves: men, women, family/friends, spouses, clergy, sexual abuse surv. (men, women). Support: groups—Kalamazoo (women, sexual abuse, codependency), lay consult., lic./prof., Living Waters (men, women). Other: Bible studies, seminars, speaking engagements.

Reconciliation Ministries, c/o Restoration Christian Fellowship, 22575 W. Eight Mile Rd., Detroit, MI 48219. 313/255-0212 (M-F/9-5). Tom Cole. Serves: men, women, family/friends, clergy, sexual abuse surv. (men, women), sexual addicts (homosexual). Support: groups—Detroit, Waterford (parents/family), lay consult., letter (general, prisoners/sex offenders, Living Waters (men, women), phone. Resources: audiotapes, newsletter. Other: seminars, speaking engagements. Fax: 313/255-1865.

WellSpring Ministries of West Michigan, 1460 Buttrick SE, Ada, MI 49301–9600. 616/676-8777. Noel G. Christoff. Serves: men, family/friends, spouses, clergy, sexual addicts (homosexual). Support: group—Grand Rapids (men), lay consult., Living Waters (men). Other: speaking engagements.

MINNESOTA
Eagles' Wings, PO Box 11246, Minneapolis, MN 55411. 612/522-2782 (M-Th/1-5). Nancy L. Anderson. Serves: men, women, family/friends, spouses. Support: groups (men, women, parents/family, wives), lay consult., letter (general), phone. Resources: audiotapes, literature, newsletter, videotapes. Other: live-in program (women; under development), seminars, speaking engagements. Fax: 612/522-1757.

KEYS Ministries, Box 97, Wykoff, MN 55990. 507/352-4110 (answering machine). Rev. Rodel Eberle. Serves: men, women, family/friends, spouses, adol. (men, women), clergy, HIV+, sexual abuse surv. (men, women), sexual addicts (heterosexual, homosexual), transsexuals, transvestites. Support: groups—Rochester, MN; LaCrosse, WI (combined men and women), letter (prisoners/sex offenders), phone. Resources: audiotapes, literature, newsletter. Other: seminars, speaking engagements.

Outpost, Inc., PO Box 49278, Minneapolis, MN 55449-0278. 612/754-5687 (M-F/8:30-4:30). Gary Bawden, Managing Director, and Dan Puumala, Associate Director. Serves: men, family/friends, spouses, clergy. Support: groups—Crystal, Minneapolis (men, other—general open meeting), lay consult., letter (general, prisoners/sex offenders), lic./prof., Living Waters (men), phone. Resources: audiotapes, literature, newsletter, videotapes. Other: seminars, speaking engagements. Fax: 612/754-5730.

MISSOURI
Jubilee, 4650 Highway A, Washington, MO 63090. 314/239-9080. George Stricker. Serves: men, spouses. Support: groups—St. Louis (men), lay consult.

New Dawn West, 444 W. Grand, Springfield, MO 65807. 417/866-2361 (M-F/9-5). Wayne and Joan Doyle. Serves: men, women, family/friends, spouses, clergy, sexual abuse surv. (men, women). Support: groups (we combine men, women, and parents/family; it has worked well since 1981), lic./prof. (starting May 1996), phone. Other: seminars, speaking engagements.

NEBRASKA
Father-Heart Ministries, Trinity Church Interdenominational, 15555 W. Dodge Rd., Omaha, NE 68154-2099. 402/330-5724 ext. 3346 (M-F/8-5). Kevin D. Hutchison. Serves: men, women, family/friends, spouses, sexual abuse surv. (men, women), sexual addicts (heterosexual, homosexual). Support: group (men, women), lay consult., letter (general, prisoners/sex offenders), phone (M-Th/9-4 by appointment). Resources: audiotapes, videotapes. Other: Bible studies, evangelism, seminars, speaking engagements. Fax: 402/330-2084.

NEW HAMPSHIRE
ReCreation, Inc., PO Box 788, Manchester, NH 03105-0788. 603/485-2199 (answering service). Warren A. Aldrich. Serves: men, women, family/friends, spouses, clergy, HIV+, sexual abuse surv. (men, women), sexual addicts (heterosexual, homosexual). Support: groups—Concord (men, women, wives, other—HA 14-step program), lay consult., phone. Resources: audiotapes, literature, videotapes. Other: seminars, speaking engagements.

NEW JERSEY
New Dawn Ministries East, PO Box 3689, Wayne, NJ 07474-3689. 201/694-2938 (This is our church office number. Please ask for New Dawn Ministries, leave a message/number, and we will phone back.) Sal and Carol Latella. Serves: men, women, family/friends, spouses, adol. (men, women), children of gay parents, clergy, hearing impaired individuals, pedophiles, sexual abuse surv. (men, women), sexual addicts (heterosexual, homosexual). Support: group (combined men's/women's group; parents/family; wives), lay consult., letter (general), lic./prof. (referrals), phone (evenings and weekends by appointment only). Resources: audiotapes, videotapes. Other: seminars, speaking engagements.

NEW MEXICO
Free Indeed Ministries, c/o God's People of Praise/Glory Hall, 2417 Wyoming NE, Albuquerque, NM 87112. 505/275-9623 (M, Tu, Th, F/9-noon). Ronald and Barbara Swallow. Serves: men, women, family/friends, spouses, adol. (men, women), children of gay parents, clergy, pedophiles, sexual abuse surv. (men, women), sexual addicts (homosexual), transsexuals, transvestites Support: groups (men, other: prayer counseling and discussion on Exodus reading material), lay consult., letter, Living Waters (men, women), phone 505/831-5528 (9 AM-10 PM). Other: seminars, speaking engagements.

New Mercy Outreach, PO Box 90, Cloudcrost, NM 88317. 505/682-1406. W. F. (Fred) Griffin. *Group meetings in El Paso, Texas. See entry under Texas.*

NEW YORK
All In His Name Ministries, c/o New Life Assembly of God Church, 14 North St., Buffalo, NY 14202. 716/884-3227. Terry Cowles. Serves: men, women, family/friends, spouses, adol. (men, women), children of gay parents, clergy, pedophiles, sexual abuse surv. (men, women), sexual addicts (heterosexual, homosexual). Support: groups (men, parents/family, wives), letter (general), phone (by appointment only). Resources: audiotapes, literature, newsletter, videotapes. Other: Bible studies, evangelism, speaking engagements.

Whosoever Will Ministry, PO Box 277, Middletown, NY 10940. 914/374-8128 (M-F/1-5; answers with just "hello"). Penny Dalton. Serves: men, women, family/friends, spouses, sexual abuse surv. (men, women). Support: groups (combined men and women; married couples), lay consult., letter (general), phone (M-F/1-5; ask for Elaine Sinnard). Resources: audiotapes, literature. Other: Bible studies, speaking engagements.

NORTH CAROLINA
Breaking Free, PO Box 225 DTS, Boone, NC 28607. 704/297-2277 (M-F/8-noon). John Benson. Serves: men, women, family/friends, spouses, clergy, sexual abuse surv. (men, women), sexual addicts (heterosexual, homosexual), other (codependency, self-worth). Support: groups (men; other: overcoming codependency, Search for Significance), lay consult., letter (general, prisoners/sex offenders), phone. Resources: audiotapes, literature, videotapes. Other: seminars, speaking engagements.

New Life Ministries, c/o Liberty Church, PO Box 2014, Burlington, NC 27216-2014. 910/226-5277 (M, Tu, Th/10-3). Bob Foote. Serves: men, family/friends, spouses, sexual abuse surv. (men), sexual addicts (heterosexual, homosexual). Support: groups (men, wives), lay consult., phone. Resources: audiotapes, literature. Other: speaking engagements.

OHIO
Healing Touch Ministry, PO Box 750282, Dayton, OH 45475-0282. 513/885-1051 or 513/433-0332 (M-F/8-5). Charles Voelker. Serves: men, women, family/friends, spouses, adol. (men, women), children of gay parents, clergy, HIV+,

pedophiles, sexual abuse surv. (men, women), sexual addicts (heterosexual, homosexual), transsexuals, transvestites. Support: groups (men, women, parents/family), lay consult., letter (general, prisoners/sex offenders), Living Waters (men, women), phone. Resources: literature, newsletter. Other: seminars, speaking engagements. Fax: 513/433-6076.

In His Image, PO Box 174, Willoughby, OH 44094. 216/953-1536. [East of Cleveland.] Brenda and Paul Barbarino. Serves: men, women, family/friends, spouses, adol. (men, women), children of gay parents, clergy, HIV+, pedophiles, sexual addicts (heterosexual, homosexual), transsexuals, transvestites. Support: groups—Eastlake, Willoughby, Willowick (men, women, parents/family), lay consult., letter (general), phone. Resources: audiotapes, literature, newsletter, videotapes. Other: HIV/AIDS ministry, seminars, speaking engagements.

Prodigal Ministries, PO Box 19949, Cincinnati, OH 45219-0949. 513/861-0011 (Tu-F/9-5). Jerry Armelli and Kathy Fisher. Serves: men, women, family/friends, spouses, adol. (men, women), clergy, HIV+, pedophiles, sexual abuse surv. (men, women), sexual addicts (homosexual), transvestites. Support: groups (men, women, HIV/AIDS, parents/family), lay consult., letter (general, prisoners/sex offenders), phone. Resources: audiotapes, literature, ministry newsletter, women's newsletter. Other: Christian AIDS Network 513/861-0409 (Tu-F/9-5), seminars, speaking engagements. Fax: 513/861-0011.

Pure Life Ministries, PO Box 770232, Lakewood, OH 44107-0232. 216/228-4149. Jim Suchenski. Serves: men, women, spouses, adol. (men), clergy, sexual addicts (heterosexual, homosexual). Support: groups (men, women, wives), lay consult. Resources: audiotapes, literature, newsletter. Other: Bible studies, speaking engagements.

OKLAHOMA
First Stone Ministries, 1330 N. Classen Blvd. #G–80, Oklahoma City, OK 73106-6619. 405/236-4673 (M-F/9-5). Jeff and Lezlie Janes. Serves: men, women, family/friends, spouses, clergy, HIV+, pedophiles, sexual abuse surv. (men, women), sexual addicts (heterosexual, homosexual), transsexuals, transvestites. Support: groups—Oklahoma City, Lawton (HIV/AIDS, parents/family, wives), lay consult., letter (prisoners/sex offenders), Living Waters (men, women), phone. Resources: literature, newsletter, videotapes. Other: HIV/AIDS ministry, speaking engagements. Branches: Lawton, OK.

Restoration Outreach, PO Box 55236, Tulsa, OK 74155-1236. 918/254-1175 (Tu-F/8-4; Sat/9-1). Jerry and Wanda Harris. Serves: men, women, family/friends, spouses, adol. (men, women), children of gay parents, clergy, HIV+, pedophiles, sexual abuse surv. (men, women), sexual addicts (heterosexual, homosexual), transsexuals, transvestites. Support: groups (men, women, parents/family, wives), lay consult., letter, lic./prof., phone. Other: seminars, speaking engagements, other (ministerial/medical student practicums).

For details on a Lawton, OK, branch office, contact First Stone Ministries in Oklahoma City, OK (405/236-4673).

OREGON
The Portland Fellowship, PO Box 9205, Portland, OR 97207. 503/235-6364 (M-F/9-4). Phil Hobizal. Serves: men, women, family/friends, spouses, adol. (men), HIV+, sexual addicts (homosexual), transsexuals. Support: groups (men, women, HIV/AIDS, parents/family, wives), lay consult. Resources: newsletter. Other: HIV/AIDS ministry, speaking engagements. Fax: 503/235-3896.

PENNSYLVANIA
Day Seven Ministries, PO Box 575, Elizabethtown, PA 17022. 717/367-7117. Peter Lines. Serves: men, women, family/friends, spouses, pedophiles, sexual addicts (heterosexual, homosexual), transsexuals, transvestites. Support: groups (men, women, wives), lay consult., letter (general, prisoners/sex offenders), lic./prof., phone. Resources: newsletter, videotapes. Other: Bible studies, evangelism, seminars, speaking engagements. Languages: Spanish. Fax: 717/531-6491.

Free!, 105 S. Market St., Mechanicsburg, PA 17055-6328. 717/766-7904. Gene Chase. Serves: men, women, family/friends, spouses, children of gay parents, clergy, pedophiles, sexual abuse surv. (men, women), sexual addicts (heterosexual, homosexual). Support: groups (men, wives), lay consult., letter (general, prisoners/sex offenders), phone (M-Su/9 PM-10PM; other times by appointment). Resources: audiotapes, literature, newsletter, videotapes. Other: speaking engagements, tape lending library. Fax: 717/697-0271.

Harvest USA, PO Box 11469, Philadelphia, PA 19111. 215/342-7114 (M-F/9-4:30). John B. Freeman. Serves: men, women, family/friends, spouses, adol. (men, women), clergy, pedophiles, sexual abuse surv. (men, women), sexual addicts (heterosexual, homosexual), transsexuals, transvestites. Support: groups (men, women, parents/family, other [sexual addiction group for heterosexual men; teens]), lay consult., Living Waters (men), lic./prof. (referrals). Resources: audiotapes, literature, newsletter, videotapes. Other: seminars, speaking engagements. Fax: 215/342-3585.

TENNESSEE
Living Hope, P.O. Box 52883, Knoxville, TN 37950. 423/470-9800. Jay Henderson. Serves: men, women, family/friends, spouses, adol. (men), children of gay parents, clergy, pedophiles, sexual abuse surv. (men), sexual addicts (homosexual), transsexuals. Support: groups (parents/family, wives), lay consult. Resources: audiotapes, literature. Other: seminars, speaking engagements. Fax: 423/470-2820.

Love In Action International, Inc., PO Box 753307, Memphis, TN 38175-3307. 901/542-0250 (M-F/9-5). John J. Smid. Serves: men, women, family/friends, spouses, adol. men, children of gay parents, clergy, sexual abuse surv. (men), sexual addicts (homosexual). Support: lay consult., letter (general), phone. Resources: audiotapes, literature, newsletter. Other: live-in program (men), seminars, speaking engagements. Fax: 901/542-9742

Mastering Life Ministries, PO Box 54, Hermitage, TN 37076-0054. 615/885-9098 (M-F/10-5). David Kyle Foster. Book/

Tape Orders Only: 1-800-705-0020. <u>Serves</u>: men, women, family/friends, spouses, adol. (men, women), children of gay parents, clergy, pedophiles, sexual abuse surv. (men, women), sexual addicts (heterosexual, homosexual), transsexuals, transvestites. <u>Support</u>: lay consult., letter (general, prisoners/sex offenders), phone. <u>Resources</u>: audiotapes, literature, newsletter, videotapes. <u>Other</u>: weekly radio program on Focus on the Family Satellite Network (call for details), and daily TV program on WHTN-TV 39 (cable 21) in Nashville. <u>Fax</u>: 615/885-9098.

Promise, c/o Christian Counseling Services, PO Box 60383, Nashville, TN 37206. 615/254-8342 (M-F/8-6). <u>Serves</u>: men, women, family/friends, spouses, adol. (men, women), children of gay parents, clergy, HIV+, sexual abuse surv. (men, women), sexual addicts (heterosexual, homosexual). <u>Support</u>: groups (men, women, parents/family), lic./prof. <u>Resources</u>: newsletter. <u>Other</u>: seminars, speaking engagements. <u>Fax</u>: 615/254-8336.

Restoration in Him, c/o Central Church, 6655 Winchester, Memphis, TN 38115. 901/375-8111 (M-F/9-5). Gerald and Sharis Blackburn. <u>Serves</u>: men, women, family/friends, spouses. <u>Support</u>: groups (men, women, parents/family, wives), lay consult. <u>Other</u>: all programs of church.

TRUEHOPE ... for the Best Alternative, PO Box 3574, Brentwood, TN 37024-3574. 615/221-8946 (M-F). Michael Malloy, LCSW. <u>Serves</u>: men, women, family/friends, spouses, adol. (men, women), children of gay parents, clergy, HIV+, sexual abuse surv. (men), sexual addicts (heterosexual, homosexual). <u>Support</u>: groups (men, women, parents/family, other—monthly support/accountability group meeting for men and women), lic./prof. <u>Other</u>: speaking engagements. <u>Fax</u>: 615/298-3351 c/o Daystar.

TEXAS

Awakening–Christian Prayer and Support Group, Inc., PO Box 201004, San Antonio, TX 78220. 210/633-2235 (all days/all hours). Gloria J. Zwinggi. <u>Serves</u>: family/friends, spouses, children of gay parents. <u>Support</u>: groups (parents/family, wives), lay consult., leter, lic./prof. (referrals), phone (all days/all hours). <u>Resources</u>: newsletter. <u>Other</u>: speaking. <u>Fax</u>: 210/633-2235.

Christian Coalition for Reconciliation, PO Box 420437, Houston, TX 77242-0437. 713/465-7045 (M-F/12-5). Michael R. Newman. <u>Serves</u>: men, women, family/friends, spouses, adol. (men, women), HIV+, pedophiles, sexual abuse surv. (men, women), sexual addicts (homosexual). <u>Support</u>: groups (men, women, parents/family), lay consult., Living Waters (men, women). <u>Resources</u>: literature, newsletter. <u>Other</u>: seminars, speaking engagements. <u>Languages</u>: French, Spanish; some materials translated into these languages. <u>Fax</u>: 713/984-2262.

LifeGuard Ministries, 6611 Berrywood Ln., Georgetown, TX 78628. 512/930-3970 (9 AM-10 PM). Don and Nancy Brown. <u>Serves</u>: men, women, family/friends, spouses, adol. (men, women), children of gay parents, clergy, HIV+, sexual abuse surv. (men, women), sexual addicts (homosexual). <u>Support</u>: groups (wives), lay consult., letter, Living Waters (men, women), phone. <u>Resources</u>: literature. <u>Other</u>: speaking engagements.

Living Hope Ministries, PO Box 6595, Arlington, TX 76005-6595. 817/640-4044 (M, W/10:30 AM-1 PM). Eddie Traughber. <u>Serves</u>: men, women, family/friends, spouses, clergy, sexual addicts (homosexual). <u>Support</u>: groups (men, women, parents/family, wives), lay consult., letter (prisoners/sex offenders), lic./prof. <u>Other</u>: speaking engagements, other (newcomer meetings on Sunday nights). <u>Fax</u>: 817/633-5058.

[MEETINGS IN EL PASO, TX] New Mercy Outreach, PO Box 90, Cloudcrost, NM 88317. 505/682-1406. W. F. (Fred) Griffin. <u>Serves</u>: men, women, family/friends, spouses, adol. (men, women), children of gay parents, clergy, sexual abuse surv. (men, women), sexual addicts (heterosexual, homosexual), transsexuals, transvestites. <u>Support</u>: groups–El Paso (men, women, parents/family, wives), lay consult., letter (prisoners/sex offenders), Living Waters (men), phone. <u>Other</u>: seminars, speaking engagements.

Sexual Wholeness Ministries, 10909 Sabao #215, Houston, TX 77089-2520. 713/992-8800 (M-Th/9AM-8PM; F/9-noon). Tim Gould. <u>Serves</u>: men, family/friends, spouses, adol. (men, women), children of gay parents, clergy, sexual abuse surv. (men, women), sexual addicts (heterosexual, homosexual). <u>Support</u>: groups (men, parents/family), lay consult., lic./prof., Living Waters (men). <u>Fax</u>: 713/992-8886.

VIRGINIA

Regeneration—Northern Virginia, PO Box 1034, Fairfax, VA 22030-1034. 703/591-4673 (M-F/11-5). Bob Ragan. <u>Serves</u>: men, women, family/friends, spouses, adol. (men, women), pedophiles, sexual abuse surv. (men, women), sexual addicts (heterosexual, homosexual), transsexuals, transvestites. <u>Support</u>: groups (men, parents/family), lay consult., letter (general), Living Waters (men, women), phone. <u>Resources</u>: literature, newsletter. <u>Other</u>: seminars, speaking engagements.

Set Free, Inc., PO Box 14835, Richmond, VA 23221. 804/358-8150 (M/1:30-8 PM; Tu-F/9-3:30). Barry Anderson. <u>Serves</u>: men, women, family/friends, spouses, adol. (men, women), adult children of gay parents. <u>Support</u>: groups (men, women, parents/family, wives), lay consult., letter (general, prisoners/sex offenders), phone. <u>Resources</u>: audiotapes, literature, newsletter. <u>Other</u>: seminars, speaking engagements. <u>Fax</u>: 804/358-7520.

Sought Out, PO Box 62019, Virginia Beach, VA 23466-2019. 804/631–0099 (M-F/1-5). Katherine M. Allen. <u>Serves</u>: men, women, family/friends, spouses, children of gay parents, clergy, HIV+, sexual abuse surv. (men, women), sexual addicts (heterosexual, homosexual), transsexuals, transvestites. <u>Support</u>: lay consult., Living Waters (men, women). <u>Resources</u>: newsletter. <u>Other</u>: seminars, speaking engagements.

For details on a Charlottesville, VA, group, contact Regeneration in Baltimore, MD (410/661-0284).

WASHINGTON

Metanoia Ministries, PO Box 33039, Seattle, WA 98133-0039. 206/783-3500 (M-F/9-5). Robert K. Brown. <u>Serves</u>: men, women, family/friends, spouses, adol. (men, women), children of gay parents, clergy, sexual addicts (heterosexual, homosexual). Support: groups—Everett, Seattle, Tacoma (men, women, parents/family, wives), lay consult., letter (general; prisoners/sex offenders in our local area), lic./prof., Living Waters (men, women), phone (by appointment only). Resources: literature, newsletter. Other: evangelism, seminars, speaking engagements, other (intercessory prayer ministry). Languages: Spanish. Fax: 206/783-0080.

WASHINGTON, D.C.
Transformation Ex-Gay Christian Ministries, 1017 12th St. NW, Washington, DC 20005. 202/371-0800 (M-F/9-5:30). Anthony A. Falzarano. Serves: men, women, family/friends, spouses, clergy, HIV+, pedophiles, sexual abuse surv. (men, women), sexual addicts (heterosexual, homosexual), transsexuals, transvestites. Support: groups (men, women, parents/family, wives), lay consult., letter (general, prisoners/sex offenders), phone. Resources: literature, newsletter, videotapes. Other: evangelism, seminars, speaking engagements. Fax: 202/371-0378.

WISCONSIN
Broken Yoke Ministries, 25050 Bluemound Rd., Pewaukee, WI 53072 (Milwaukee area). 414/896-0841 (routine calls: business hours; emergency: anytime). Robert J. Van Domelen. Serves: men, women, family/friends, spouses, clergy, pedophiles, sexual abuse surv. (men). Support: groups (men, women, parents/family), lay consult., letter (general, prisoners/sex offenders), lic./prof. (on call), phone (seven days a week). Resources: audiotapes, newsletter. Other: seminars, speaking engagements. Fax: 414/896-0841 (call first). Branches: Peoria, IL; Madison, WI; Neenah, WI.

For details on a Madison, WI, branch office, contact Broken Yoke Ministries in Pewaukee, WI (414/896-0841).

For details on a Neenah, WI, branch office, contact Broken Yoke Ministries in Pewaukee, WI (414/896-0841).

CANADA

ALBERTA
Flight Ministries, 208–11125–107 Ave., Edmonton, AB T5H 0X9. 403/421-8283 (M-F/10-4). Rev. Daneen Burk. Serves: men, women, family/friends, spouses, adol. (men, women), children of gay parents, clergy, pedophiles, sexual abuse surv. (men, women), sexual addicts (heterosexual, homosexual), transsexuals, transvestites. Support: groups (parents/family, wives), lay consult., letter (general), Living Waters (men, women), phone. Resources: audiotapes, literature, newsletter, videotapes. Other: evangelism, live-in program (men, women), seminars, speaking engagements. Languages: French. Fax: 403/421-8283.

BRITISH COLUMBIA
Another Chance Ministries, Burnaby Christian Fellowship, 7325 MacPherson Ave., Burnaby, BC, V5J 4N8. 604/430-4154 (M-F/9-5). Marjorie Hopper. Serves: men, women, family/friends, spouses, children of gay parents, clergy, pedophiles, sexual abuse surv. (men, women), sexual addicts (heterosexual,

homosexual), transsexuals, transvestites. Support: groups—Abbotsford, Burnaby, Surrey (men, women, parents/family), lay consult., letter (general), Living Waters (men, women), phone. Resources: audiotapes, literature, newsletter, videotapes. Other: seminars, speaking engagements. Fax: 604/430-6843.

MANITOBA
New Direction for Life Ministries, PO Box 1493, Winnipeg, MB, R3C 2Z4. 204/452-1826 (M-F/9:30-3:30). Tye Gamey. Serves: men, women, family/friends, spouses, adol. (men, women), HIV+, pedophiles, sexual abuse surv. (men, women), sexual addicts (homosexual), transsexuals, transvestites. Support: groups (men, women, parents/family, wives), lay consult., letter (general), lic./prof., Living Waters (men, women), phone. Resources: audiotapes, literature, newsletter, videotapes. Other: seminars, speaking engagements. Fax: 204/452-1799.

ONTARIO
New Direction for Life Ministries, PO Box 1078 Stn. F., Toronto, ON, M4Y 2T7. 416/921-6557 (M-F/9-5). Barry S. Lee. Serves: men, women, family/friends, spouses, adol. (men, women), HIV+, pedophiles, sexual abuse surv. (men, women), sexual addicts (homosexual), transsexuals, transvestites. Support: groups—Kitchener-Waterloo, London, St. Catharines, Toronto (men, women, parents/family, wives), lay consult., letter (general), phone. Resources: newsletter. Other: seminars, speaking engagements. Languages: Cantonese. Fax: phone first.

INTERNATIONAL CONNECTIONS

EXODUS INTERNATIONAL BRAZIL, Caixa Postal 222, 36571-000 Viçosa, MG, Brasil.

EXODUS INTERNATIONAL EUROPE, PO Box 407, Watford WD1 5DU, United Kingdom. Phone from USA/Canada: 011-44-181-420-1066. Fax: 011-44-181-421-1692.

EXODUS INTERNACIONAL LATINOAMERICA: Esly Regina Carvalho, EIRENE International/Exodus Internacional Latinoamérica, Box 26202, Colorado Springs, CO 80936, USA/EUA. Fax: 719/637-3481.

EXODUS INTERNATIONAL SOUTH PACIFIC: Liberty, PO Box 308, Fortitude Valley, Queensland 4006, Australia. (07) 3371-4705. Phone from USA/Canada: 011-61-7-3371-4705. Fax: 011-61-7-3368-3505. Peter Lane.

PHILIPPINES: Bagong Pag-asa, PO Box 9139, MCS Mailing Center, 1200 Makati, MM, PHILIPPINES. Phone/Fax from USA/Canada: 011-632-631-9160.

SINGAPORE: CHOICES, Blk 203B, #09-13, Henderson Road, SINGAPORE 159546. Phone from USA/Canada: 011-65-278-2210. Fax: 011-65-278-0130.